Chilton's
AUTO TROUBLESHOOTING GUIDE

Second Edition

Kerry A. Freeman, Assistant Managing Editor

Robert F. King, Editor

CHILTON BOOK COMPANY   Radnor, Pennsylvania

Manufactured in the United States of America

123456789   654321098

Library of Congress Cataloging in Publication Data

Chilton Book Company. Automotive Editorial Dept.
  Chilton's auto troubleshooting guide, 2nd edition.

    1. Automobiles—Maintenance and repair.   I. Title.
TL152.C5226   629.28′8   77-167726
ISBN 0-8019-6702-3, trade hc.
ISBN 0-8019-6703-1, trade pbk.
ISBN 0-8019-6748-1, auto pbk.
ISBN 0-8019-6749-X, institutional hc.

Contents

Purpose of this Book

This book is designed to aid both the amateur and the professional mechanic in troubleshooting all automotive systems, from the engine to the rear axle. While this book is intentionally general in scope, theories of operation are covered in each chapter, and, where necessary, troubleshooting becomes specific instead of general (as in the case of electronic ignition systems). Before going on to any troubleshooting, it might be wise to review several things.

Know Your Car

Since this book is designed to be general in scope, it will be necessary for you to have all the specific information you will need about your car. If, for instance, you are working on the engine, you will obviously need all the engine specifications. While some things (such as drum brakes) are fairly standard across all car lines, other systems are not.

Necessary Tools

You probably have a fairly complete collection of hand tools already. Most of the tools we will be concerned with in this book are diagnostic tools such as ohmmeters, voltmeters, etc. It is assumed that you have such things as a dwell-tach and a timing light. In the event specific tools are necessary, it will be noted in the text.

Using The Book

Before attempting any job, read the section of the book which pertains to it first. The sections on basic operating principles are particularly important. It is quite difficult to repair a system if you don't understand it, even if you have a procedure to follow in front of you. Remember, the most important key to effective diagnosis is complete understanding.

Troubleshooting As An Exercise In Logic

While adequate automotive repairs can be performed by many people, both professional and amateur, troubleshooting seems to be a very rare skill indeed. The ability to correctly diagnose automotive maladies is viewed by many people as an arcane science, somewhat akin to being able to find water with a stick or summon the dead. Such of course is not the case. Troubleshooting is not an art form. Troubleshooting, in its simplest state, is an exercise in logic. It is essential to realize that an automobile is composed of a series of systems. Some of these systems are interrelated, others are not. The key lies, of course, in having a firm grasp of all automotive systems. Obviously, if you don't know the charging system from the ignition system, you can't be expected to troubleshoot a problem in your electrical system, or even to realize the problem is in your electrical system. A thorough knowledge of all the systems of your car will allow you to pinpoint problem areas and eliminate a lot of unnecessary guesswork. Automobiles operate in accordance with a logical series of rules and physical laws. As long as you keep this in mind and proceed in an orderly manner, troubleshooting will be no trouble at all.

1

Quick Problem Locator

Listed below are 30 common automotive problems. To locate troubleshooting information quickly, find your problem and read across. A primary chapter is listed where information will be found.

Since all automotive systems (and problems) are interrelated, a secondary listing of chapters is given where additional information to solve your problem may be found.

PROBLEM	FIRST CHECK THIS CHAPTER	THEN CHECK THESE CHAPTERS AS WELL
Starter won't crank the engine	3	
Engine won't start, but cranks normally	3	1, 4
Engine cranks slowly	3	
Rough idle	4	2, 3
Engine hesitates (misses on acceleration)	4	1, 2, 3
Engine misses at high speed	3	4
Engine runs-on (diesels)	2	4
Engine lacks power	1	2, 3, 4
Excessive oil consumption	1	
No oil pressure	1	
Engine knocks or pings	2	1, 3, 4
Noisy valves	2	1
Engine overheats	9	
Engine does not reach normal operating temp.	9	
Alternator light stays on or flickers	3	5
Tires wear unevenly	8	
Cupped or scuffed tires	8	
Front end noise	8	
Hard steering	8	
Car pulls to one side	8	10
Front wheels shimmy	8	
Automatic transmission shifts hard	6	
No drive in "D" (automatic transmission)	6	
Manual transmission sticks in gear	6	
Manual transmission will not go into gear	6	
Manual transmission jumps out of gear	6	
Clutch will not release	6	
Low brake pedal	10	
Clunk when you let off the gas	7	6, 8
Whine or hum from the rear of the car	7	

Chapter 1

The Basics of Engine Operation

Theory of Engine Design

The modern automobile engine is certainly the most complex and highly stressed of all household machines. Its parts are subjected to higher temperatures, greater pressures and vibration, and more extreme frictional loads and changes in velocity than those of other common machines. It has also been developed and refined to a greater extent than most machines. As a result, while the basic operating principles are fairly simple, the specifics are quite complex, and even the smallest deviation from the norm in the dimensions or the condition of a part, or in the setting of an individual adjustment can result in an obvious operating defect.

This first section is designed to relate engine operating principles to the most common malfunctions so that the troubleshooter may visualize the physical relationship between the two. While it will be a review for many, it will help to provide the type of understanding that will enable the reader to replace time-consuming guesswork with quick, efficient troubleshooting.

The engine is a metal block containing a series of chambers. The volume of these chambers varies in relation to the position of a rotating shaft. There is a port for each chamber which provides for the admission of combustible material and another port for the expulsion of burned gases. The combustion chambers' volumes must be variable in order for the engine to be able to make use of the expansion of the burning gases. This ability also enables the chamber to compress the gases before combustion, and to purge itself of burned material and refill itself with a combustible charge after combustion has taken place. (A description of how these four functions are accomplished follows the material on basic engine construction.)

The upper engine block is usually an iron or aluminum alloy casting, consisting of outer walls which form hollow water jackets around the four, six, or eight cylinder walls. The lower block provides an appropriate number of rigid mounting points for the bearings which hold the crankshaft in place, and is known as the crankcase. The hollow jackets of the upper block add to the rigidity of the structure and contain the liquid coolant which carries the heat away from the cylinders and other parts of the block. The block of an air-cooled engine consists of a crankcase which provides for the rigid mounting of the crankshaft and for the studs which hold the cylinders rigidly in place. The cylinders are usually individual, single-wall castings, and are finned for cooling.

The block (both air-cooled and water-cooled) also provides rigid mounts for the engine's camshaft and its drive gears or drive

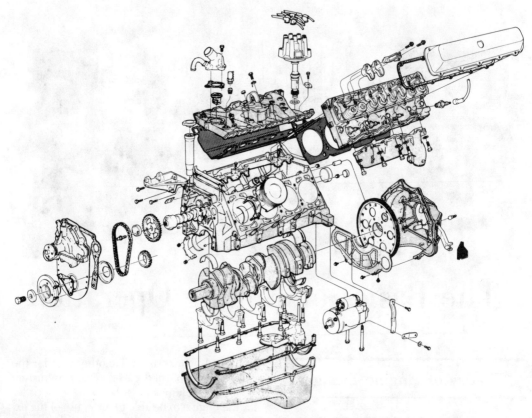

Exploded view of a typical V8 engine

chain. In water-cooled engines, studs are installed in the top of the block to provide for the rigid mounting of the cylinder heads on to the top of the block. The water and oil pumps are usually mounted directly to the block.

The crankshaft is a long iron alloy or steel fabrication which consists of bearing points or journals, which turn on their own axes, and counterweighted crank throws or crankpins which are located several inches from the center of the shaft and turn in a circle. The crankpins are centered under the cylinders which are machined into the upper block. Aluminum pistons with iron sealing rings are located in the cyclinders and are linked to the crankpins via steel connecting rods. The rods connect with the pistons at their upper ends via piston pins and bushings, and at their lower ends fasten to the crankpins around the bearings.

When the crankshaft turns, the pistons move up and down within the cylinders, and the connecting rods convert their reciprocating motion into the rotary motion of the crankshaft. A flywheel at the rear of the crankshaft provides a large, stable mass for smoothing out the rotation.

The cylinder heads form tight covers for the tops of the cylinders, and contain machined chambers into which the contents of the cylinders are forced as the pistons reach the upper limit of their travel. Two poppet valves in each cylinder are opened and closed by the action of the camshaft and valve train. The camshaft is driven at one-half crankshaft speed and

Cutaway view of an overhead cam four cylinder engine

Cutaway view of an overhead valve four cylinder engine

operates the valves remotely through pushrods and rocker levers via its eccentric lobes or cams. Each combustion chamber contains one intake valve and one exhaust valve. The cylinder heads also provide mounting threads for spark plugs which screw right through the heads so their lower tips protrude into the combustion chambers.

Lubricating oil, which is stored in a pan at the bottom of the engine and force-fed to almost all the parts of the engine by a gear type pump, lubricates the entire engine and also seals the piston rings.

THE FOUR-STROKE CYCLE

1. *Intake Stroke:* The intake stroke begins with the piston near the top of its travel, the exhaust valve nearly closed, and the intake valve opening rapidly. As the piston nears the top of its travel and begins its descent, the exhaust valve closes fully, the intake valve reaches a fully open position, and the volume of the combustion chamber begins to increase, creating a vacuum. As the piston descends, an air/fuel mixture is drawn from the carburetor into the cylinder through the intake manifold. (The intake manifold is simply a series of tubes which links each cylinder with the carburetor and the carburetor is a device for using the motion of air moving into the engine to mix just the right amount of fuel into the air stream.) The intake stroke ends with the piston having passed the bottom of its travel. The intake valve reaches a closed position just after

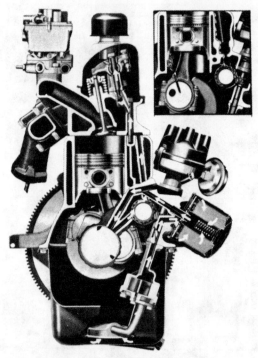

Front sectional view of an inline six-cylinder engine

the piston has begun its upstroke. The cylinder is now filled with the fuel/air mixture.

2. *Compression Stroke:* As the piston ascends, the fuel/air mixture is forced into the small chamber machined into the cylinder head. This compresses the mixture until it occupies ⅛th to ¹⁄₁₁th of the volume that it did at the time the piston began its ascent. This compression raises the temperature of the mixture and increases its pressure, vastly increasing the force generated by the expansion of gases during the power stroke.

3. *Power Stroke:* The fuel/air mixture is ignited by the spark plug just before the piston reaches the top of its stroke so that a very large portion of the fuel will have burned by the time the piston begins descending again. The heat produced by combustion increases the pressure in the cylinder, forcing the piston down with great force.

4. *Exhaust Stroke:* As the piston approaches the bottom of its stroke, the exhaust valve begins opening and the pressure in the cylinder begins to force the gases out around the valve. The ascent of the piston then forces nearly all the rest of the unburned gases from the cylinder. The cycle begins again as the exhaust valve closes, the intake valve opens and the piston begins descending and bringing a fresh charge of fuel and air into the combustion chamber.

VARIATIONS ON A THEME

Previously, we have discussed the operation of a four-stroke, overhead valve, carbureted, spark-ignition engine. While this is certainly the most common type of engine available, there are several other variants which are becoming more and more prevalent.

The Overhead Cam Engine

With the popularity of import economy cars, designs which were once considered exotic are now considered commonplace. Certainly the most common variation of the Overhead Valve (OHV) engine is the overhead cam (OHC) engine. This particular design is very well suited to the small displacement economy engines being produced today. Basically, the difference is that, in the overhead valve (OHV) engine the valves are actuated by lifters and pushrods which operate off the camshaft; in an OHC engine the camshaft actuates the valves in a much more direct manner. The camshaft is located in the cylinder head (hence the name) rather than in the block. Since the cam is located in the head instead of in the engine block, a substantial portion of the valve gear (which is simply the

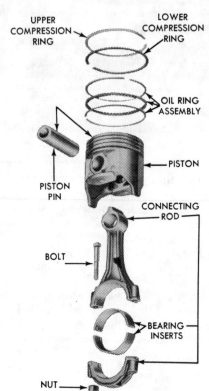

Typical piston and connecting rod

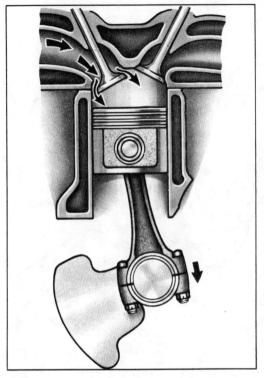

A piston on the intake stroke

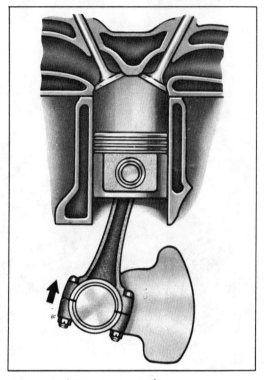

A piston on the compression stroke

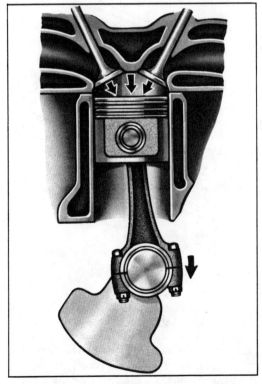

A piston on the power stroke

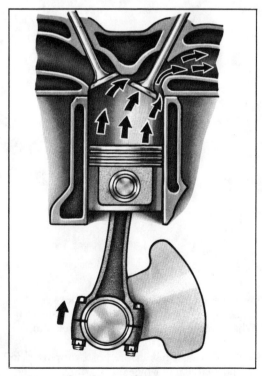

A piston on the exhaust stroke

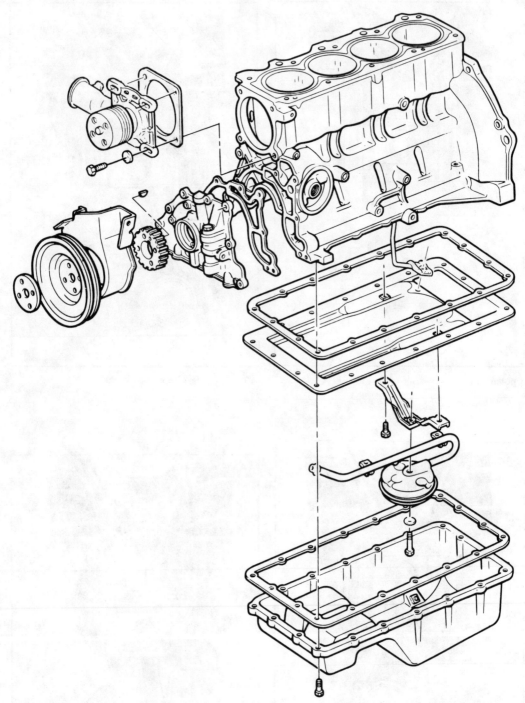

Engine block assembly—four cylinder engine

term used to describe everything between the camshaft and the valves) can be eliminated. When you think about it, it's a much simpler method of valve actuation.

The camshaft lies in the head supported in the normal manner by cam bearings. Beneath the cam are rocker arms or lifters. In some OHC designs, the cam lobes act directly on the valves, but the rocker arm arrangement is the most common. The rocker arms are generally pedestal-mounted with their centers slightly offset from the camshaft. As the cam turns, the camshaft lobes actuate the rockers. The other end of the rocker arm bears on the

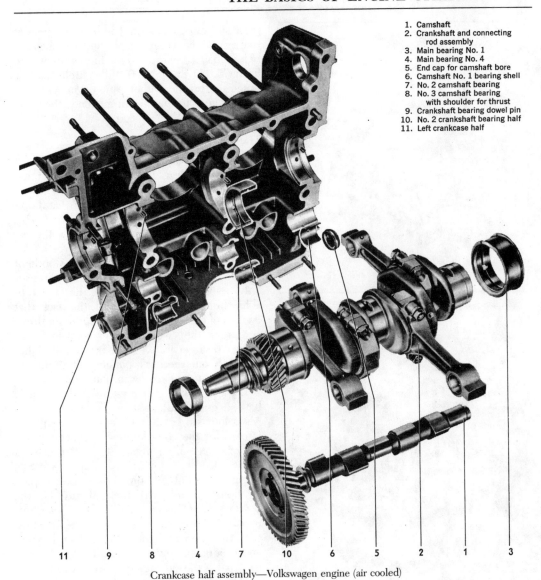

1. Camshaft
2. Crankshaft and connecting rod assembly
3. Main bearing No. 1
4. Main bearing No. 4
5. End cap for camshaft bore
6. Camshaft No. 1 bearing shell
7. No. 2 camshaft bearing
8. No. 3 camshaft bearing with shoulder for thrust
9. Crankshaft bearing dowel pin
10. No. 2 crankshaft bearing half
11. Left crankcase half

Crankcase half assembly—Volkswagen engine (air cooled)

Cylinder head of an overhead cam four cylinder engine

tip of the valve stem, thereby moving the valve on and off its seat. This sort of direct valve actuation allows much lighter valve train reciprocating weight and consequently higher rpm and greater engine efficiency. However, due mainly to reasons of cost, the design is really only practical for mass production use in inline engines, since V-type engines would obviously require a camshaft in each cylinder head. Not only would production costs be high, but valve adjustment would be that much more complex, and there would be twice as many parts to wear out. For inline engines, though, OHC engines are the sim-

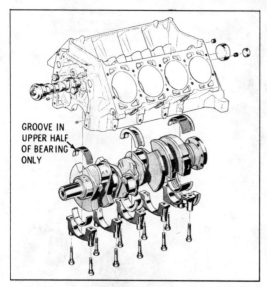

GROOVE IN
UPPER HALF
OF BEARING
ONLY

Crankshaft assembly—V8 engine

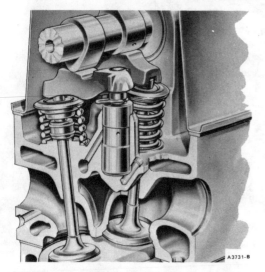

A3731-B

Closeup of overhead cam valve actuation

Cylinder—air-cooled engine

plest and most efficient. The only component that routinely wears out is the cam chain or belt. Chains have a useful life of anywhere from 75,000 to 100,000 miles. Belts have a much shorter life, but are quieter in operation and cheaper to manufacture, hence their use by a number of automakers.

The Diesel Engine

For years, the use of diesel engines was confined to large trucks. Even today, that remains the popular image of the diesel—a smoke belching, rumbling monster that didn't go very fast, but would last forever. This image of the diesel was bolstered by the occasional glimpse of a stately Mercedes or Peugeot diesel laboring away from a stop light or struggling up an incline. These glimpses only reinforced our view of the diesel as reliable, but slow (and ignored the fact that owners of these types of cars *habitually* drove as though they were on a journey to somewhere disagreeable). Today, the diesel has suddenly emerged as a possible alternative to the conventional spark-ignition engine.

Diesels, like gasoline-powered engines, have a crankshaft, pistons, a camshaft, etc. Also, four-stroke diesels require four piston strokes for the complete cycle of actions, exactly like a gasoline engine. The difference lies in how the fuel mixture is ignited. A diesel engine does not rely on a conventional spark ignition to ignite the fuel mixture for the power stroke. Instead, a diesel relies on heat produced by compressing air in the combustion chamber to ignite the fuel/air mixture and produce a power stroke. It is for this reason that a diesel engine is known as a compression-ignition engine. No fuel enters the cylinder on the intake stroke, only air. Since only air is present on the intake stroke, only air is compressed on the compression stroke. At the end of the compression stroke, fuel is sprayed into the combustion chamber, and the mixture ignites. The fuel/air mixture ignites because of the very high combustion chamber temperatures generated by the extraordinarily high compression ratios used in diesel engines. Typically, the compression ratios used in automotive diesels run anywhere from 16:1 to 23:1. A typical spark-ignition engine has a ratio of about 8:1. (This is why a spark-ignition engine which continues to run after you have shut off the engine is said to be "dieseling." It is running on combustion chamber heat alone).

Designing an engine to ignite on its own

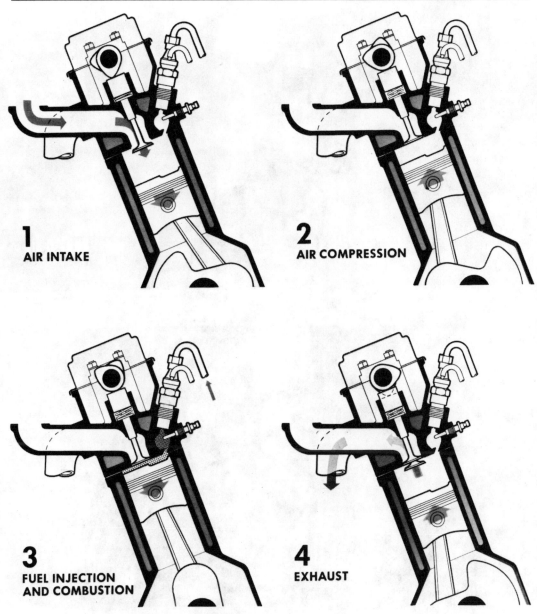

1
AIR INTAKE

2
AIR COMPRESSION

3
**FUEL INJECTION
AND COMBUSTION**

4
EXHAUST

Diesel engine power cycle

combustion chamber heat poses certain problems. For instance, although a diesel engine has no need for a coil, spark plugs, or a distributor, it does need what are known as "glow plugs." These superficially resemble spark plugs, but are only used to warm the combustion chambers when the engine is cold. Without these plugs, cold starting would be impossible, due to the enormously high compression ratios. Also, since fuel timing (rather than spark timing) is critical to a diesel's operation, all diesel engines are fuel-injected rather than carbureted, since the precise fuel metering necessary is not possible with a carburetor.

The Wankel Engine

Like a conventional piston engine, the Wankel engine is an internal combustion engine and operates on the four-stroke cycle. Also, it runs on gasoline and the spark is generated by a conventional distributor-coil ignition system. However, the similarities end there.

In a Wankel engine, the cylinders are replaced by chambers, and the pistons are re-

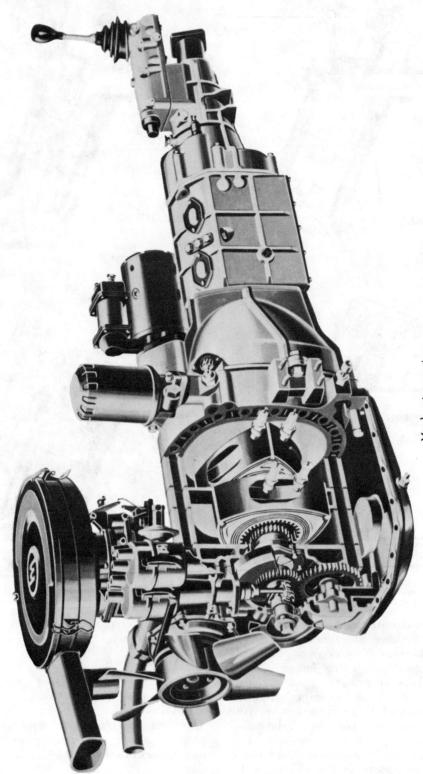

Mazda rotary engine

placed by rotors. The chambers are not circular in section, but have a curved circumference that is identified as an *epitrochoid*. An epitrochoid is the curve described by a given point on a circle as the circle rolls around the periphery of another circle of twice the radius of the generating circle.

The rotor is three-cornered, with curved sides. All three corners are in permanent contact with the epitrochoidal surface as the rotor moves around the chamber. This motion is both orbital and rotational, as the rotor is mounted off center. The crankshaft of a piston engine is replaced by a rotor shaft, and crank throws are replaced by eccentrics. Each rotor is carried on an eccentric. Any number of rotors is possible, but most engines have one or two rotors. The valves of the piston engine are replaced by ports in the Wankel engine housing. They are opened and closed by rotor motion.

One of the key differences between the Wankel rotary engine and the piston engine is in the operational cycle. In the piston engine, all the events take place at the top end of the cylinder (intake, compression, expansion, and exhaust). The events are spaced out in time only. The Wankel engine is the opposite. The events are spaced out geographically, and are taking place concurrently and continuously around the epitrochoidal surface.

The intake phase takes place in the area following the intake port, and overlaps with the area used for compression. Expansion takes place in the area opposite the ports, and the exhaust phase takes place in the area preceding the exhaust port, overlapping with the latter part of the expansion phase. All three rotor faces are engaged in one of the four phases at all times.

In other words, one rotor gives three working spaces, all of which are permanently in action. As one rotor apex sweeps past the intake port, it ends the intake phase in the leading space, and starts it in the trailing space. The third space is then engaged in its expansion phase. As rotor motion continues, the leading space will approach the point of maximum compression and ignition, while the trailing space will enter the compression phase as the following apex closes it off from the intake port.

The trochoidal shape of the chamber, combined with the orbital motion of the rotor, produces large variations in displacement in the three spaces. Displacement is at its minimum on one rotor face when its opposite apex is centered on the minor axis. The minor axis is the line across the chamber where it is narrowest, and the major axis is the line across the chamber where it is widest. The major and minor axes intersect perpendicularly in the center of the chamber. Displacement is at its maximum on one rotor face when its opposite apex is centered on the major axis. These differences in displacement produce the pumping action required for operation as an engine.

How does rotor motion turn the rotor shaft? by exerting pressure on the eccentric. Here is what happens. Gas pressure on the rotor face during the expansion phase produces rotor motion. That means rotation. But the rotor is not free to spin—it is mounted on its eccentric, and has to follow an eccentric path. The rotor transfers the gas pressure to the eccentric. That moves the eccentric, which is part of the rotor shaft, and as the eccentric moves, it causes the shaft to rotate.

The relationship between the eccentric and the position of the rotor apices is quite intricate. Each apex is always in contact with the epitrochoidal surface, and to avoid jamming the rotor at some point, its position relative to the eccentric's position must be closely controlled.

This phasing is controlled by a stationary reaction gear that meshes with an internal ring gear in the rotor. It is important to note that this gearing has nothing to do with power flow or torque transmission. It is simply a phasing gear to assure smooth rotation of the eccentric and its rotor.

The stationary reaction gear is carried by a sleeve fixed to the end cover. The gear ratio is 3:2. If the reaction gear has 36 teeth, the rotor ring gear must have 54 teeth. A corresponding 3:1 ratio exists between the rotor and the rotor shaft (eccentric bearing). When the rotor makes one revolution, the shaft makes three revolutions.

When the rotor advances 30°, the eccentric advances 90°. For each time a rotor apex passes the intake port, the main shaft starts another complete revolution. There is a power impulse for each ⅓ turn of each rotor. That gives one expansion (or power) phase for each main shaft revolution.

In passenger car Wankel engines, the housing is water-cooled and the rotor is oil-cooled. The coolant passages in most engines run axially, and the passages are dimensioned to provide the most cooling in the area around the spark plugs(s).

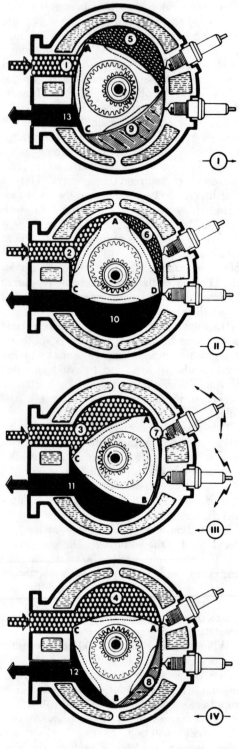

The oil supply can be carried in the sump or in a separate reservoir. It is fed in through the rotor shaft, circulates inside the rotor, and returns to the reservoir (often via a heat exchanger cooled by water). The same oil that cools the rotor also lubricates the eccentric bearing.

It is not exactly true that rotor touches the epitrochoidal surface. The rotor comes close, but is never in direct contact with the surface or the end covers. To seal the spaces for gas leaks, there is a complex seal system. Its duties are similar to those of piston rings in conventional engines.

A radial slot in each apex has a seal strip that rubs against the chamber surface. It is spring-loaded, and designed to make use of gas pressure to increase its sealing effectiveness. The rotor flanks have a seal grid intersecting with the trunnions that provide the mounting base for the apex seals. In order to fulfill their sealing duties, the seals must be lubricated. This oil is, of course, burned. The amounts needed are minute, and oil consumption is on a par with modern V-8 engines. The lube oil for the seals can be mixed with the gasoline (for instance in the carburetor float bowl) or injected separately by a metering pump.

There are two types of intake ports: peripheral ports, and side ports. Examples of both are illustrated. Side ports produce a gas flow that tends to give higher low-range torque, while peripheral ports produce a gas flow that tends to give higher peak power. All Wankel engines have peripheral exhaust ports.

In the air-cooled Fichtel & Sachs and Outboard Marine engines, the rotor is also air-cooled. The incoming charge is led through the rotor, and thereby undergoes a preheating process. This type of engine is not considered suitable for automotive purposes.

THE TWO-STROKE CYCLE

Several cars that have been imported into the United States use two-stroke cycle engines. These operate with only a compression stroke and a power stroke. Intake of fuel and air mixture and purging of exhaust gases takes place between the power and compression strokes while the piston is near the bot-

Here's how the Wankel engine works: As the triangular rotor goes through its mixed sliding/turning motions, a fuel/air mixture is drawn in (1, 2, 3, 4) and then compressed (5, 6) before being ignited by the spark plugs. The high pressure gases created by combustion drive the rotor around (7, 8, 9) and after doing their work are swept out of the exhaust port by the rotor (10, 11, 12, 13).

1-2-3-4   INTAKE   5-6   COMPRESSION

7-8-9   POWER   10-11-12-13   EXHAUST

tom of its travel. Ports in the cylinder walls replace poppet valves located in the cylinder heads on four-stroke cycle engines. The crankcase is kept dry of oil, and the entire engine is lubricated by mixing the oil with the fuel so that a fine mist of oil covers all moving parts. The ports are designed so the fuel and air are trapped in the engine's crankcase during most of the downstroke of the piston, thus making the crankcase a compression chamber that force-feeds the combustion chambers after the ports are uncovered. The pistons serve as the valves, covering the ports whenever they should be closed.

Troubleshooting Gasoline Engines

Problem or Symptom	*Correction*
ENGINE WILL NOT START	
Starter does not crank	Check all connections
	Check battery specific gravity
	Check solenoid or relay (if equipped)
	Check neutral start switch (if equipped)
	Check ignition switch
Starter cranks normally	Check that there is fuel in the carburetor. Check the fuel pump if necessary.
	Check the spark at the plugs. If there is spark at the plugs, check for spark at the coil
	Inspect the points. Clean and regap if necessary
	Check ignition timing. Reset if necessary
	Check the spark plug gap. Clean or replace as necessary
	Check valve timing
Starter cranks slowly	Check to make sure all battery connections are clean and tight
	Check the battery specific gravity
	Check to make sure correct starter is on car
	Check for defective starter. Remove starter and inspect the armature and the brushes
ENGINE RUNS ROUGH	
Ignition timing incorrect	Check timing, reset if necessary
Point dwell incorrect	Check points. Replace or regap as necessary
Defective coil	Check coil on coil tester or by replacement
Defective spark plugs	Check and replace plugs if necessary
	Check spark plug heat range. Evaluate plugs to determine engine condition (see chart in chapter two)
Incorrect valve timing	Check and reset valve timing if necessary
Dirt, moisture, or foreign matter in carburetor, fuel filter or fuel line	Clean lines and carburetor as necessary, replace fuel filter
Incorrect carburetor settings	Check all carburetor specs (see chapter four)
Faulty plug wires	Check for cracked or brittle wires
	Check wires with an ohmmeter. Replace if necessary
Faulty fuel pump	Check fuel pump output

Troubleshooting Gasoline Engines (continued)

Problem or Symptom	*Correction*
LOSS OF POWER—NO POWER ON ACCELERATION	
Incorrect ignition timing	Check and reset timing as necessary
Point dwell incorrect	Check points. Clean or replace points as necessary
Worn-out plugs	Check and replace plugs as necessary. Check for correct heat range (see chapter two)
Faulty distributor or distributor components	Check distributor cap for defects. Check rotor. Check for worn distributor shaft or faulty mechanical advance
Carburetor float setting incorrect	Check and reset float level as necessary
Low engine compression	Check compression
Burned, worn, or sticky valves	Check valves. Do valve job if necessary
Faulty coil	Check coil in tester or by substitution
ENGINE HESITATES ON ACCELERATION	
Defective spark plugs	Check and replace plugs as necessary (see chapter two)
Ignition timing incorrect	Check and reset timing if necessary
Point dwell incorrect—points pitted or burned	Clean or replace the points as necessary. Check the dwell
Faulty fuel pump	Check the pump with a tester
Accelerator pump in the carburetor defective	Check pump. Replace if necessary
ENGINE DIESELS (RUNS-ON)	
Ignition timing incorrect	Check and reset timing as necessary
Throttle linkage sticking	Free up throttle linkage, if necessary
Octane level of gasoline too low	Check to make sure you are using the correct gasoline for your car
ENGINE KNOCKS OR PINGS	
Gasoline octane rating incorrect	Check to make sure you are using the correct grade of gasoline
Ignition timing too far advanced	Check and reset timing as necessary
Fuel mixture too lean	Check carburetor fuel mixture
Excessive carbon on the valves	Check valves for carbon deposits
EXCESSIVE OIL CONSUMPTION	
Oil leaking from engine	Check valve covers, side covers, front and rear main seals for leakage. Repair as necessary
Worn oil control rings	Run a "wet" compression test. See chapter two Replace rings if necessary. Ordinarily, if the oil rings are worn, the rest of the engine is worn out also
Worn valve guides or seals	Perform valve job
Incorrect viscosity oil	Check manufacturer's recommendations. Change to correct oil if necessary. However, on older engines, it is often a good idea to use a heavier oil than that specified

Troubleshooting Gasoline Engines (continued)

Problem or Symptom	Correction
LOW OR NONEXISTENT OIL PRESSURE	
Oil level low	Check oil level
Defective sending unit or gauge	Check gauge and sending unit (see chapter 5)
Excessively thin or diluted oil	Change oil and filter
Excessive bearing clearance	Replace bearings
Faulty oil pump	Replace oil pump
NOISY VALVES	
Incorrect valve lash	Check valve lash. Reset to specifications if necessary
Low oil level	Check oil level
Incorrect oil viscosity or oil thinned out	Change oil
Worn lifters or rocker arms	Check and replace as necessary
Worn valve guides	Install new valve guides
Bent pushrods	Check pushrods, replace if necessary

Troubleshooting Diesel Engines

Problem	Possible Cause
Starter will not crank engine	Battery terminals loose or broken
	Battery discharged
	Starter switch damaged, or wires loose or broken
	Starter clutch or solenoid malfunction
	Starter drive locked
	Hydraulic lock, water or oil in combustion chamber
Failure to start or hard starting	Correct starting procedures not being followed
	Cold start aid inoperative
	Battery low, slow cranking speed
	Starter equipment malfunctioning
	Engine oil too heavy
	Blocked exhaust system
	Air filter dirty
	Low engine compression due to defective valves or piston rings
	Insufficient fuel in tank
	Water or ice in fuel tank
	Excessive fuel device inoperative
	Fuel injection parts scored, poor delivery
	Advance mechanism in advance position. It should be in retarded position when engine is to be started

Troubleshooting Diesel Engines (continued)

Problem	Possible Cause
	Fuel injection pump not timed properly
	Air in the fuel system
	Fuel oil filter plugged or restricted
	Fuel lift pump not operating
	Leak in high pressure delivery lines
Engine runs, but misses	Restricted fuel lines
	Water in fuel or poor quality fuel
	Air leaks in fuel suction line
	Injectors improperly adjusted or plugged
	Low compression, intake or exhaust valves leaking
	Leaking supercharger air connection
	Restricted drain line
Excessive vibration	Engine bearings worn
	Engine supports broken or loose
	Difference in compression pressures between cylinders
	Injector setting pressures unequal
	Unequal fuel delivery, line resistance
	Air in fuel system
Low Engine Torque	Excessive exhaust back pressure
	Engine valve timing not correct
	Fuel filters dirty
	High pressure fuel line leaks
	Poor atomization of fuel
	Dirty or cracked injectors
	Fuel injection pump to engine timing wrong
	Throttle stop set too low
	Inferior quality fuel
	Advance device not working
	Brakes binding
Engine Knocks	Low coolant level
	Engine overloaded
	Crankshaft vibration damper malfunction
	Excessive crankshaft end clearance
	Flywheel loose or unbalanced
	Broken or worn piston rings
	Incorrect bearing clearances
	Damaged or worn main or connecting rod bearings
	Broken tooth in engine gear train
	Worn or scored cylinder liners or pistons
	Broken valve springs
	Fuel injection pump timing too early

Troubleshooting Diesel Engines (continued)

Problem	Possible Cause
	Poor atomization of fuel
	Octane value of fuel low
Excessive Smoke *BLACK SMOKE* consists of a large number of particles of carbon; this carbon forms when the fuel is heated in oxygen-lean regions in the combustion chamber. *BLUE SMOKE* consists of a large number of particles of fuel oil of about 0.5 microns diameter or less; these particles are recondensed droplets of unburned fuel or incompletely burned fuel. These small particles cause blue light to be scattered. When an engine is running fast but under light load, regions of the combustion chamber may be at too low a temperature to permit ignition and blue smoke would appear. When viewed in transmitted light, the blue smoke appears brown. *WHITE SMOKE* consists of a large number of particles of fuel oil larger than about 1.0 micron diameter. To produce white smoke, the fuel must have time to condense into larger droplets than for blue smoke. A cold engine running at light load and low speed could produce white smoke.	Restricted air intake High exhaust back pressure Intake manifold or cylinder head gasket leakage Cracked cylinder head or block Broken or worn piston rings Engine in need of overhaul Incorrect valve timing Worn or scored cylinder liners or pistons Engine overload Low compression Inferior quality fuel Restricted fuel lines Plugged injector spray holes Incorrect injector timing Injectors improperly adjusted Fuel injection pump to engine timing retarded Injector pump improperly adjusted Broken fuel delivery valve or valve sticking
Engine gradually loses power; then stops	Low compression Engine valve clearance too small Air leak at suction side of fuel lines Choked fuel filter Damaged control linkage Fuel tank vent clogged Leak off line blocked Nozzle and delivery valve stuck open
Engine cannot reach maximum speed	Poor condition of engine Throttle stop improperly adjusted Maximum speed setting too low Broken or wrong type governor springs Dirty air filter
Excessive fuel consumption	Restricted air intake High exhaust back pressure Engine overloaded Engine in need of overhaul Inferior quality fuel Restricted fuel lines or filter Fuel leaks external or internal Plugged injector spray holes

Troubleshooting Diesel Engines (continued)

Problem	Possible Cause
	Injectors not adjusted properly
	Cracked injector body or cap
Excessive oil consumption	Broken or worn piston rings
	Worn or scored cylinder liners or pistons
	Externnal or internal oil leaks
	Faulty cylinder oil control
	Wrong grade oil for conditions
	Engine in need of overhaul
	Loose crankcase breather vent
Low oil pressure	Incorrect bearing clearances
	Engine overloaded
	Insufficient coolant
	Worn water pump
	Coolant thermostat not working
	Loose fan belts
	Clogged coolant passages
	Clogged oil cooler
	Radiator core openings restricted
	Air in cooling system
	Leaking coolant hoses, connections or gaskets
	Insufficient radiator capacity
	Oil suction line restricted or cracked
	Oil pickup screen blocked
	Crankcase oil level too low
	Wrong grade of oil for conditions
	Engine in need of overhaul
Overheating (high coolant temperature)	Low coolant level
	Air leaks in suction line
	Low coolant level
	Engine overloaded
	Injectors not properly adjusted
	Injector pipe partially clogged
	Faulty injectors
	Injector timing too early
	Worn or scored cylinder liners or pistons
	Broken valve springs
	Crankshaft vibration damper faulty
	Excessive crankshaft end clearance
	Flywheel loose or unbalanced
	Broken or worn piston rings
	Incorrect bearing clearances
	Engine in need of overhaul
	Broken tooth in engine gear train

Chapter 2

The Tune-Up

The dictionary defines a tune-up as a procedure used to bring a group of things into a harmonious working order, as in tuning an orchestra. An automotive tune-up is an orderly process of inspection, diagnosis, testing, and adjustment that is periodically necessary to maintain peak engine performance or restore the engine to original operating efficiency.

Tests by the Champion Spark Plug Company showed that an average 11.36% improvement in gas economy could be expected after a tune-up. A change to new spark plugs alone provided a 3.44% decrease in fuel use. As for emissions, significantly lower emissions were recorded at idle after a complete tune-up on a car needing service. An average 45.37% reduction of CO (carbon monoxide) emissions was recorded at idle after a complete tune-up. HC (hydrocarbon) emissions were cut 55.5%

The tune-up is also a good opportunity to perform a general preventive maintenance checkout on everything in the engine compartment. Look for failed or about to fail components such as loose or damaged wiring, leaking fuel lines, cracked coolant hoses, and frayed fan belts.

Necessary Tools

In order to perform a proper tune-up, several specific tools are needed; a dwell-tach, a timing light, a spark plug socket, feeler gauges (both the flat type and the round wire type for gapping plugs), and a compression tester. If you have a late-model car with electronic ignition, you won't need a dwell-meter since dwell is nonadjustable on these cars. Also keep in mind that some tachometers will not

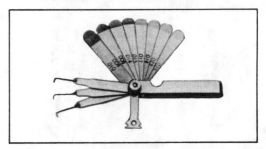

Combination feeler gauge set

Compression gauge—push-in type. There are also screw-in types which provide a more accurate reading.

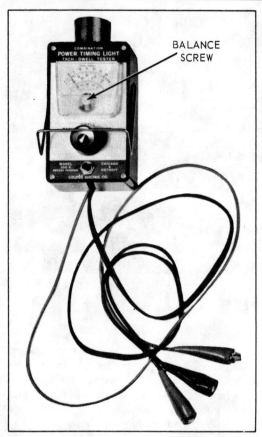

BALANCE
SCREW

This is a combination timing light and dwell-tach. These are generally purchased as separate instruments.

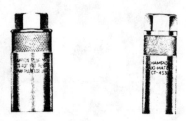

13/16 in. spark plug socket   5/8 in. spark plug socket

operate on cars equipped with electronic ignition, and neither will some timing lights. So before you buy anything, check to make sure it will work on your particular car.

Tune-Up Procedures

COMPRESSION

Along with vacuum gauge readings and spark plug condition, cylinder compression test results are extremely valuable indicators of internal engine condition. Most professional

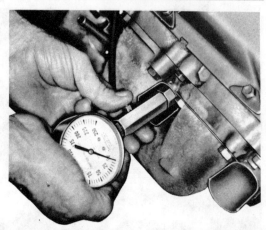

Checking compression

mechanics automatically check an engine's compression as the first step in a comprehensive tune-up. Obviously, it is useless to try and tune an engine with extremely low or erratic compression readings, since a simple tune-up will not cure the problem. However, before we go any further, it might be wise to review just exactly what compression is.

In the description of engine operation, it was mentioned that, after the closing of the intake valve, the air/fuel mixture is trapped in the cylinder as the piston rises. The volume of the combustion chamber after the piston reaches TDC is about 1/8th to 1/11th of the volume of the whole cylinder. Compressing the mixture in this manner raises the pressures and temperatures in the combustion chambers during the power stroke, thus improving combustion and increasing the amount of power delivered to the piston on the downstroke.

Any leakage in the combustion chamber will reduce the pressure created during the compression stroke. The pressure created in the combustion chamber may be measured with a gauge that remains at the highest reading it measures, through the action of a one-way valve. This gauge is inserted into the spark plug hole. A compression test will uncover many mechanical problems that can cause rough running or poor performance.

Compression Testing and Troubleshooting

A. Prepare the engine for the test as follows:

1. Operate the engine until it reaches operating temperature. The engine is at operating temperature a few minutes after hot water begins circulating through both radiator hoses.

2. Remove the primary lead from the positive terminal on the coil. Remove all high-tension wires from the spark plugs.

3. Clean all dirt and foreign material from around the spark plugs (compressed air works well) and remove all spark plugs.

4. If a remote starter switch is available, hook it up according to its manufacturer's instructions.

5. Remove the air cleaner and block or wire the throttle and choke in the wide open position. The secondary bores may be ignored on four-barrel carburetors.

B. Zero the gauge, place it firmly in one of the spark plug holes, and crank the engine for about five compression strokes. Record the reading and the number or position of the cylinder tested. *Release pressure from the gauge.*

C. Repeat the test for all the other cylinders.

D. Evaluate the results. Consult a manual for the compression pressure rating of the engine. Engines with compression ratios of 8:1–8.5:1 usually produce 140–150 lbs pressure. Higher compression ratios produce up to 175 lbs. The readings should be within 25 percent of each other. (See chart.)

If the test had to be performed on a cold engine because it could not be started, the readings will be considerably lower than normal, even if the engine is in perfect mechanical condition. A substantial pressure should still be produced, and variations in the readings are still indicative of the condition of the engine. If all readings are acceptable, see F.

E. Perform a "wet" compression test if any or all of the cylinders read low. Pour about one teaspoon of engine oil in each of the cylinders with low compression and repeat the test for each cylinder in turn.

F. Further evaluate the results. One or more of the symptoms below should apply:

1. All cylinders fall within the specified range of pressures. The engine internal parts are in generally good condition.

2. One or more cylinders produced a low reading in D which was substantially improved by the "wet" compression test. Those cylinders have worn pistons, piston rings, and/or cylinder bores.

3. Two adjacent cylinders (or several pairs whose cylinders are adjacent) have nearly identical low readings, and did not respond to the "wet" compression test. These cylinders share leaks in the head gasket. This may be cross-checked by performing the cooling sys-

Minimum and Maximum Compression Readings

Max Pressure Lbs Sq In.	Min Pressure Lbs Sq In.	Max Pressure Lbs Sq In.	Min Pressure Lbs Sq In.
134	101	188	141
136	102	190	142
138	104	192	144
140	105	194	145
142	107	196	147
146	110	198	148
148	111	200	150
150	113	202	151
152	114	204	153
154	115	206	154
156	117	208	156
158	118	210	157
160	120	212	158
162	121	214	160
164	123	216	162
166	124	218	163
168	126	220	165
170	127	222	166
172	129	224	168
174	131	226	169
176	132	228	171
178	133	230	172
180	135	232	174
182	136	234	175
184	138	236	177
186	140	238	178

tem pressure tests in the cooling system section, and by looking at the oil on the dipstick to see if coolant bubbles are present.

4. Compression buildup in one or more cylinders is erratic—it climbs less on some strokes than on others. Normally, the pressure rises steadily and then levels off. This indicates sticking valves. This problem may be cross-checked with a timing light. Remove the valve covers. Since this test is run with the engine operating and the valve covers removed, it would be wise to purchase and install special clips that are designed to stop oil flow to the valve train. Connect a timing light to the spark plug lead of the cylinder suspected of having sticky valves. Aim the timing light at the valves of the cylinder in question. Loosen the distributor and then start the engine and watch the valves. Vary the timing slightly, smoothly, and gradually in order to observe the position of the valve at slightly different points in the rotation of the engine. If there is an erratic motion of either valve, that valve is sticking. Remember to retime the ignition system and remove the oil clips.

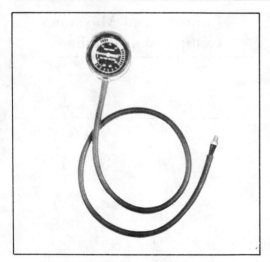

Vacuum gauge

Vacuum gauge hookup. Attachment points vary from car to car.

VACUUM GAUGE READINGS

Strictly speaking, vacuum gauge readings are not a necessary part of the everyday tune-up, which is why a vacuum gauge was not included in the list of necessary tools. Properly used, however, a vacuum gauge is an entremely useful diagnostic tool. Gauge readings and their meanings are given here.

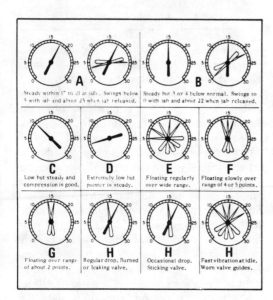

A. Normal Engine

The needle should be steady between 17 and 21 while idling. Then, when the throttle is suddenly opened, it should drop to below 5 and then bounce up to around 25 when it is closed.

B. Leaking Piston Rings

The gauge behavior will be very much like a normal engine (above), except that all readings are down about 3 or 4 divisions. Thus, the reading when idling will be about 13 to 17 and when the throttle is suddenly opened and closed, the needle may drop to zero and then bounce back to around 22.

C. Late Timing

If the engine compression is known to be good and yet the needle reads lower than it should, the ignition timing may be late. A considerable lower than normal reading can be due to late valve timing.

D. Leaking Intake

A steady needle but extremely low reading indicates a probable air leak in the carburetor, intake manifold or gaskets.

E. Leaking Head Gasket

If the needle fluctuates regularly between a high and a low reading, the cylinder head gasket has probably blown between two adjacent cylinders.

F. Carburetor Out of Adjustment

If the needle fluctuates very slowly over a range of 4 or 5 points, the carburetor probably requires adjustment.

G. Incorrect Spark Plug Gap

When the needle fluctuates very slowly over a range perhaps about 2 points, indicates that the spark plug gaps may be spaced too close.

H. Defective Valve Action

If the needle vibrates rapidly at idle speed, the intake valve guides are probably worn. If the needle vibrates rapidly when the engine is accelerated, there is probably one or more weak valve springs. An intermittent drop of 3 or 4 points indicates sticking valves, whereas a regular drop indicates a burned or leaking valve.

SPARK PLUGS

A typical spark plug consists of a metal shell surrounding a ceramic insulator. A metal electrode extends downward through the center of the insulator and protrudes a small distance. Located at the end of the plug and attached to the side of the outer metal shell is the side electrode. The side electrode bends in at a 90 degree angle so that its tip is even with, and parallel to, the tip of the center electrode. The distance between these two electrodes (measured in thousandths of an inch) is called the spark plug gap. The spark plug in no way produces a spark but merely provides a gap across which the current can arc. The coil produces anywhere from 20,000 to 40,000 volts, which travels to the distributor where it is distributed through the spark plug wires to the spark plugs. The current passes along the center electrode and jumps the gap to the side electrode, and, in so doing, ignites the air/fuel mixture in the combustion chamber.

Spark plug life and efficiency depend upon the condition of the engine and the temperatures to which the plug is exposed. Combustion chamber temperatures are affected by many factors such as compression ratio of the engine, air/fuel mixtures, exhaust emission equipment, and the type of driving you do.

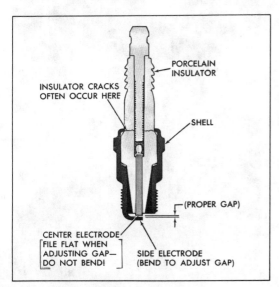

Spark plug cutaway view

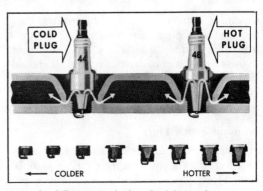

Note the difference in the length of the insulators

Spark plugs are designed and classified by number according to the heat range at which they will operate most efficiently.

Spark Plug Heat Range

While spark plug heat range has always seemed to be somewhat of a mystical subject for many people, in reality the entire subject is quite simple. Basically, it boils down to this: the amount of heat the plug absorbs is determined by the length of the lower insulator. The longer the insulator (or the farther it extends into the engine), the hotter the plug will operate; the shorter the insulator the cooler it will operate. A plug that absorbs little heat and remains too cool will quickly accumulate deposits of oil and carbon since it is not hot enough to burn them off. This leads to plug fouling and consequently to misfiring. A plug that absorbs too much heat will have no deposits, but, due to the excessive heat, the electrodes will burn away quickly and in some instances, preignition may result. Preignition takes place when plug tips get so hot that they glow sufficiently to ignite the fuel/air mixture before the actual spark occurs. This early ignition will usually cause a pinging during low speeds and heavy loads. In severe cases, the heat may become high enough to start the fuel/air mixture burning throughout the combustion chamber rather than just to the front of the plug as in normal operation. At this time, the piston is rising in the cylinder making its compression stroke. The burning mass is compressed and an explosion results, forcing the piston back down in the cylinder while it is still trying to go up. Obviously, something must go, and it does—pistons are often damaged.

The general rule of thumb for choosing the correct heat range when picking a spark plug is: if most of your driving is long distance, high speed travel, use a colder plug; if most of your driving is stop and go, use a hotter plug. Factory-installed plugs are, of course, compromise plugs, since the factory has no way of knowing what sort of driving you do. It should be noted that most people never have occasion to change their plugs from the factory-recommended heat range.

Reading Spark Plugs

Your spark plugs are the single most valuable indicator of your engine's internal condition. Study your spark plugs carefully every time you remove them. Compare them to the following chart which illustrates the most common plug conditions.

Replacing Spark Plugs

A set of spark plugs usually requires replacement after about 10,000 miles on cars with conventional ignition systems and after about 20,000 to 30,000 miles on cars with electronic ignition. These figures are dependent on your particular style of driving, however. The electrode on a new spark plug has a sharp edge, but with use, this edge becomes rounded by erosion causing the plug gap to increase. In normal operation, plug gap increases about 0.001 in. for every 1,000–2,500 miles. As the gap increases, the plug's voltage requirement also increases. It requires a greater voltage to jump the wider gap and about two to three times as much voltage to fire a plug at high speeds than at idle.

Tools needed for spark plug replacement include a ratchet handle, short extension, spark plug socket (there are two types; either $^{13}/_{16}$ in. or $\frac{5}{8}$ in. depending upon the type of plug), a combination spark plug gauge and gapping tool, and a can of penetrating oil. When you're removing spark plugs, you should work on one at a time. Don't start by removing the plug wires all at once, because unless you number them, they may become mixed up. Take a minute before you begin and number the wires with tape. The best location for numbering is near where the wires come out of the cap.

1. Twist the spark plug boot and remove the boot and wire from the plug. Do not pull on the wire itself as this will ruin the wire.

2. Once the wire is removed, use a brush or rag to clean the area around the spark plug. Make sure that all the dirt is removed so that none will enter the cylinder after the plug is removed.

3. Remove the spark plug using the proper size deep socket. Turn the socket coun-

terclockwise to remove the plug. Be sure to hold the socket straight on the plug to avoid breaking the plug, or rounding off the hex on the plug.

4. Once the plug is out, check it against the plugs shown in this section to determine engine condition. This is a crucial operation, as plug readings are vital signs of engine condition.

5. Most new spark plugs come pre-gapped, but the factory setting should be checked anyway. Use a round wire feeler gauge. Flat feeler gauges are not really accurate when used on plugs. The correct size gauge should pass through the electrode gap with a slight drag. If you're in doubt, try one size smaller and one larger. The smaller gauge should go through easily while the larger one shouldn't go through at all. If the gap is incorrect, use the electrode bending tool on the end of the gauge to adjust the gap. When adjusting the gap, always bend the side electrode. The center electrode is non-adjustable.

6. Squirt a drop of penetrating oil on the

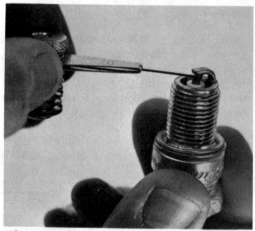

When you're checking the gap, make sure the gauge isn't on an angle.

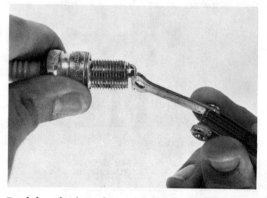

Bend the side electrode carefully to adjust the gap.

Reading Spark Plugs

A close examination of spark plugs will provide many clues to the condition of an engine. Keeping the plugs in order according to cylinder location will make the diagnosis even more effective and accurate. The following diagrams illustrate some of the conditions that spark plugs will reveal.

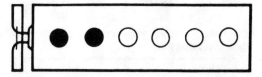

Two adjacent plugs are fouled in a 6-cylinder engine, 4-cylinder engine or either bank of a V-8. This is probably due to a blown head gasket between the two cylinders.

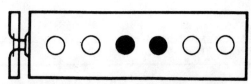

The two center plugs in a 6-cylinder engine are fouled. Raw fuel may be "boiled" out of the carburetor into the intake manifold after the engine is shut-off. Stop-start driving can also foul the center plugs, due to overly rich mixture. Proper float level, a good needle and seat or use of an insulating spacer may help this problem.

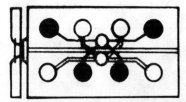

An unbalanced carburetor is indicated. Following the fuel flow on this particular design shows that the cylinders fed by the right-hand barrel are fouled from overly rich mixture, while the cylinders fed by the left-hand barrel are normal.

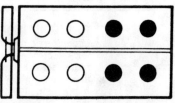

If the four rear plugs are overheated, a cooling system problem is suggested. A thorough cleaning of the cooling system may restore coolant circulation and cure the problem.

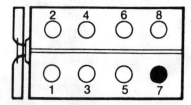

Finding one plug overheated may indicate an intake manifold leak near the affected cylinder. If the overheated plug is the second of two adjacent, consecutively firing plugs, it could be the result of ignition cross-firing. Separating the leads to these 2 plugs will eliminate cross-fire.

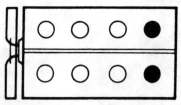

Occasionally, the 2 rear plugs in large, lightly used V-8's will become oil fouled. High oil consumption and smoky exhaust may also be noticed. It is probably due to plugged oil drain holes in the rear of the cylinder head, causing oil to be sucked in around the valve stems. This usually occurs in the rear cylinders first, because the engine slants that way.

NORMAL
Brown to grayish tan color and slight electrode wear. Correct heat range for engine and operating conditions.

RECOMMENDATION. Service and reinstall. Replace if over 10,000 miles of service.

MODIFIER DEPOSITS
Powdery white or yellow deposits that build up on shell, insulator and electrodes. This is a normal appearance with certain branded fuels. These materials are used to modify the chemical nature of the deposits to lessen misfire tendencies.

RECOMMENDATION. Plugs can be cleaned. If replaced, use same heat range.

OIL DEPOSITS
Oily coating.

RECOMMENDATION. Caused by poor oil control. Oil is leaking past worn valve guides or piston rings into the combustion chamber. Hotter spark plug may temporarily relieve problem, but positive cure is to correct the condition with necessary engine repairs.

CARBON DEPOSITS
Dry soot.

RECOMMENDATION. Dry deposits indicate rich mixture or weak ignition. Check for clogged air cleaner, high float level, sticky choke or worn breaker contacts. Hotter plugs will temporarily provide additional fouling protection.

PREIGNITION
Melted electrodes. Center electrode generally melts first and ground electrode follows. Normally, insulators are white, but may be dirty due to misfiring or flying debris in combustion chamber.

RECOMMENDATION. Check for correct plug heat range, overadvanced ignition timing, lean fuel mixtures, clogged cooling system, leaking intake manifold, and lack of lubrication.

TOO HOT
Blistered, white insulator, eroded electrodes and absence of deposits.

RECOMMENDATION. Check for correct plug heat range, overadvanced ignition timing, cooling system level and/or stoppages, lean fuel/air mixtures, leaking intake manifold, sticking valves, and if car is driven at high speeds most of the time.

HIGH SPEED GLAZING
Insulator has yellowish, varnish-like color. Indicates combustion chamber temperatures have risen suddenly during hard, fast acceleration. Normal deposits do not get a chance to blow off, instead they melt to form a conductive coating.

RECOMMENDATION. If condition recurs, use plug type one step colder.

SPLASHED DEPOSITS
Spotted deposits. Occurs shortly after long delayed tune-up. After a long period of misfiring, deposits may be loosened when normal combustion temperatures are restored by tune-up. During a high-speed run, these materials shed off the piston and head and are thrown against the hot insulator.

RECOMMENDATION. Clean and service the plugs properly and reinstall.

Photos courtesy of Champion Spark Plug Co.

threads of the new plug and install it. Don't oil the threads too heavily. Turn the plug in clockwise by hand until it is snug.

7. When the plug is finger tight, tighten it with a wrench. If a torque wrench is available, tighten the plug to specs. If you don't have a torque wrench, give the plug about ⅛th of a turn with the wrench after it's finger tight. Don't overtighten it.

8. Install the plug boot firmly over the plug. Proceed to the next plug.

Checking and Replacing Spark Plug Cables

Visually inspect the spark plug cables for burns, cuts, or breaks in the insulation. Check the spark plug boots and the nipples on the distributor cap and coil. Replace any damaged wiring. If no physical damage is obvious, the wires can be checked with an ohmmeter for excessive resistance. Remove the distributor cap and leave the wires connected to the cap. Connect one lead of the ohmmeter to the corresponding electrode inside the cap and the other lead to the spark plug terminal (remove it from the spark plug for the test). Replace any wire which shows over 50,000 ohms. Generally speaking, however, resistance should not run over 35,000 ohms and 50,000 ohms should be considered the outer limits of acceptability. Test the coil wire by connecting the ohmmeter between the center contact in the cap and either of the primary terminals at the coil. If the total resistance of the coil and cable is more than 25,000 ohms, remove the cable from the coil and check the resistance of the cable alone. If the resistance is higher than 15,000 ohms, replace the cable. It should be remembered that wire resistance is a function of length, and that the longer the cable, the greater the resistance. Thus, if the cables on your car are longer than the factory originals, resistance will be higher and quite possibly outside of these limits.

When installing a new set of spark plug cables, replace the cables one at a time so there will be no mixup. Start by replacing the longest cable first. Install the boot firmly over the spark plug. Route the wire exactly the same as the original. Insert the nipple firmly into the tower on the distributor cap. Repeat the process for each cable.

DISTRIBUTOR SERVICE

Essentially, a distributor performs two functions: It switches primary current on and off at the coil;

It distributes secondary current to the spark plugs through the distributor cap. To do this (in a conventional ignition system), it relies on breaker points and a condenser.

Breaker Points and Condenser

The points and condenser function as a circuit breaker for the primary circuit of the ignition system. The ignition coil must boost the 12 volts (V) of electrical pressure supplied to it by the battery to about 20,000 V in order to fire the spark plugs. To do this, the coil depends on the points and condenser for assistance.

The coil has a primary and a secondary circuit. When the ignition key is turned to the "on" position, the battery supplies voltage to the primary side of the coil which passes the voltage on to the points. The points are connected to ground to complete the primary circuit. As the cam in the distributor turns, the points open and the primary circuit collapses.

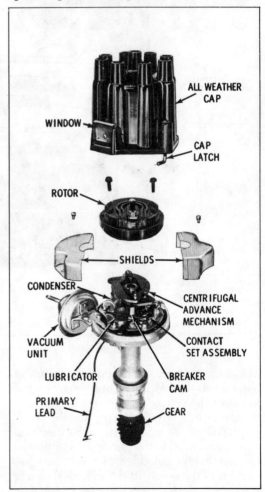

Typical conventional distributor disassembled

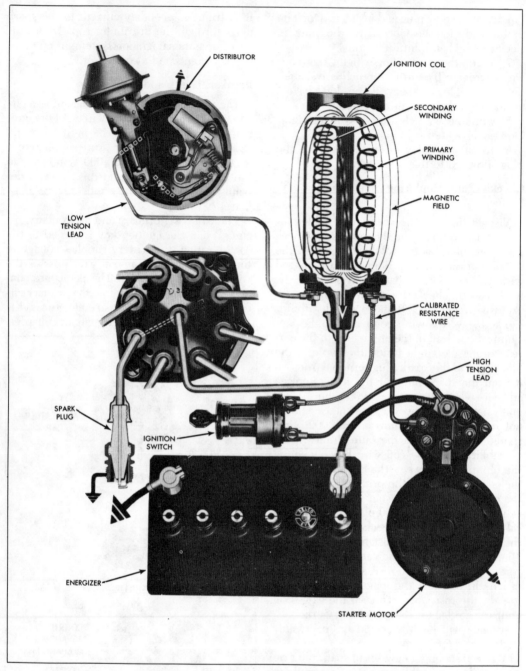

Ignition system—note primary and secondary sides.

The magnetic force in the primary circuit of the coil cuts through the secondary circuit and increases the voltage in the secondary circuit to a level that is sufficient to fire the spark plugs. When the points open, the electrical charge contained in the primary circuit jumps the gap that is created between the two open contacts of the points. If this electrical charge was not transferred elsewhere, the material on the contacts of the points would melt and that all-important gap between the contacts would start to change. If this gap is not maintained, the points will not break the primary circuit. If the primary circuit is not broken, the secondary circuit will not have enough voltage to fire the spark plugs. Enter the condenser.

The function of the condenser is to absorb the excessive voltage from the points when they open and thus prevent the points from becoming pitted or burned.

If you have ever wondered why it is necessary to tune-up your engine occasionally, consider the fact that the ignition system must complete the above cycle each time a spark plug fires. On a six-cylinder, four-cycle engine, 3 of the six plugs must fire once for every engine revolution. If the idle speed of your engine is 800 revolutions per minute (800 rpm), the breaker points open and close two times for each revolution. For every minute your engine idles, your points open and close 1,600 times ($2 \times 800 = 1600$). And that is just at idle. What about at 65 mph?

There are two ways to check breaker point gap: with a feeler gauge or with a dwell meter. Either way you set the points, you are adjusting the amount of time (in degrees of distributor rotation) that the points will remain open. If you adjust the points with a feeler gauge, you are setting the maximum amount the points will open when the rubbing block on the points is on a high point of the distributor cam. When you adjust the points with a dwell meter, you are measuring the number of degrees (of distributor cam rotation) that the points will remain closed before they start to open as a high point of the distributor cam approaches the rubbing block of the points.

There are two rules that should always be followed when adjusting or replacing points. *The points and condenser are a matched set; never replace one without replacing the other. If you change the point gap or dwell of the engine, you also change the ignition timing. Therefore, if you adjust the points, you must also adjust the timing.*

Points Inspection and Replacement

Remove the distributor cap and the rotor. Insert a screwdriver between the stationary and breaker arms of the points and examine the condition of the contacts. Replace the

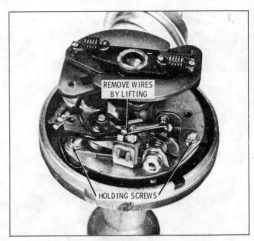

General Motors V8 distributor. Note that a ⅛ in. allen wrench is necessary to adjust the points.

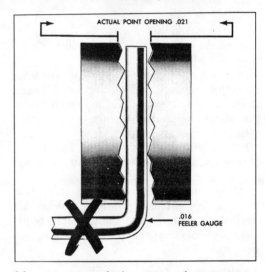

If the points are pitted, it's easy to get the gap wrong.

points if the contacts are blackened, pitted, or if the metal transfer exceeds that of the specified point gap. Also replace the points if the breaker arm has lost its tension or if the rubbing block is excessively worn. Contact points that have become slightly burned (light gray) may be cleaned with a point file. In order for the points to function properly, the contact faces must be aligned. The alignment must be checked with the points closed. If the contact faces are not centered, bend the stationary arm to suit. Never bend the breaker arm. Discard the points if they cannot be centered correctly.

Inspect the Secondary Ignition Circuit

Inspect the inside surface of the distributor cap for cracks, carbon tracks, or badly burned contacts. To remove carbon tracks, wash the

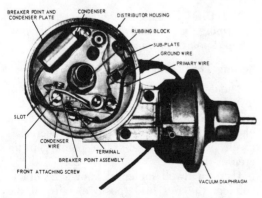

Top view of distributor showing points and condenser.

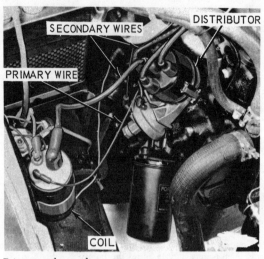

Primary and secondary wiring

Setting the point gap on a conventional distributor

cap in soap and water and dry thoroughly. Replace the cap if it is cracked or if the contacts are badly eroded.

Inspect the rotor for cracks, excessive burning of the contacts, and mechanical damage, and replace as necessary. Slightly burned contacts should be sanded smooth.

Inspect the spark plug leads and distributor-to-coil high-tension lead for cracks, brittleness, or damaged rubber boots. Replace any deteriorated parts.

While primary wiring is less perishable than the secondary circuit, it should be checked for cracked insulation or loose connections. Tighten connections or replace wires as necessary.

Adjusting Point Gap

This is a good method of making a preliminary setting of the dwell angle even if a dwell meter is available. Install the points and condenser, making sure all connections are pushed on or screwed together securely. If the mounting screw on the ignition points as-

sembly is also used to make the gap adjustment, tighten it just enough to hold the contacts apart. Rotate the engine until the tip of one of the distributor cams sits squarely under the cam follower on the movable contact arm. Using a leaf type feeler gauge (gap the points as specified in the manual), move the base plate of the point assembly back and forth until the gauge just slips between the two contacts when it is forced straight through. If the mounting screw serves as the adjusting lock, the contact assembly may usually be moved by wedging a screwdriver blade between a slot in the contact base plate and a protrusion on the surface of the distributor plate. In assemblies with an adjusting screw which is accessible from outside the distributor, an allen wrench is inserted into the head of the adjusting screw and rotated to make the adjustment. When the points are pitted, make sure the gauge does not come in contact with the built-up portion on one of the contact surfaces. A wire feeler gauge may help to make the most accurate adjustment when the points are pitted.

NOTE: *Make sure all gauges are clean in gapping the points. An oily gauge will cause rapid point burning.*

Setting Dwell Angle

The dwell angle is the number of degrees of distributor cam rotation through which the breaker points remain fully closed (conducting electricity). Increasing the point gap decreases dwell, while decreasing the point gap increases dwell.

Using a dwell meter of known accuracy, connect the red lead (positive) wire of the meter to the distributor primary wire connec-

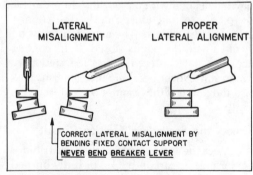

Proper and improper point alignment

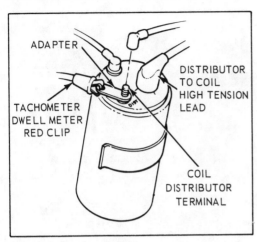

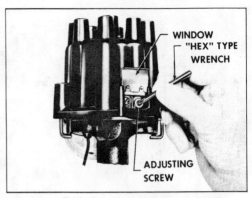

Setting the dwell on a General Motors V8 distributor

Typical dwell-tach connections

tion on the positive (+) side of the coil, and the black ground (negative) wire of the meter to a good ground on the engine (e.g. thermostat housing nut).

The dwell angle may be checked either with the distributor cap and rotor installed and the engine running, or with the cap and rotor removed and the engine cranking at starter speed. The meter gives a constant reading with the engine running. With the engine cranking, the reading will fluctuate between zero degrees dwell and the maximum figure for that angle. While cranking, the maximum figure is the correct one for that setting. Never attempt to change dwell angle while the ignition is on. Touching the point contacts or primary wire connection with a metal screwdriver may result in a 12 volt shock.

To change the dwell angle, loosen the point retaining screw slightly and make the approximate correction. Tighten the retaining screw and test the dwell with the engine cranking. On General Motors V8 engines, dwell angle is set with an allen wrench through the window

in the distributor. If the dwell appears to be correct, install the breaker point protective cover, if so equipped, the rotor and distributor cap, and test the dwell with the engine running. Take the engine through its entire rpm range and observe the dwell meter. The dwell should remain within specifications at all times. Great fluctuation of dwell at different engine speeds indicates worn distributor parts.

Following the dwell angle adjustment, the ignition timing must be checked. A 1° increase in dwell results in the ignition timing being retarded 2° and vice versa.

IGNITION TIMING

Ignition timing is the measurement in degrees of crankshaft rotation of the instant the spark plugs in the cylinders fire, in relation to the location of the piston, while the piston is on its compression stroke.

Ignition timing is adjusted by loosening the

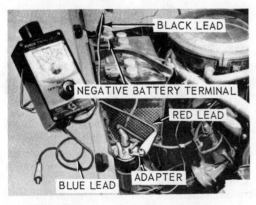

Dwell-tach hookup on a Ford four cylinder

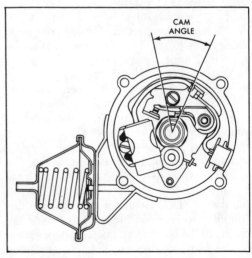

Dwell angle

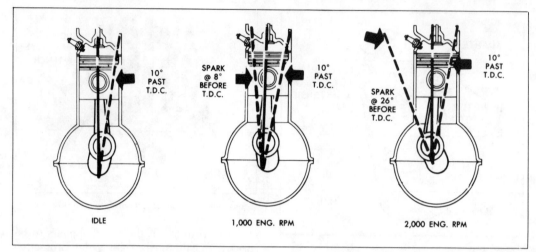

Ignition timing vs. engine speed

distributor locking device and turning the distributor in the engine.

Ideally, the air/fuel mixture in the cylinder will be ignited (by the spark plug) and just beginning its rapid expansion as the piston passes top dead center (TDC) of the compression stroke. If this happens, the piston will be beginning the power stroke just as the compressed (by the movement of the piston) and ignited (by the spark plug) air/fuel mixture starts to expand. The expansion of the air/fuel mixture will then force the piston down on the power stroke and turn the crankshaft.

It takes a fraction of a second for the spark from the plug to completely ignite the mixture in the cylinder. Because of this, the spark plug must fire before the piston reaches TDC, if the mixture is to be completely ignited as the piston passes TDC. This measurement is given in degrees (of crankshaft rotation) *before* the piston reaches *top dead center* (BTDC). If the ignition timing setting for your engine is six degrees (6°) BTDC, this means that the spark plug must fire at a time when the piston for that cylinder is 6° before top dead center of its compression stroke. However, this only holds true while your engine is at idle speed.

As you accelerate from idle, the speed of your engine (rpm) increases. The increase in rpm means that the pistons are now traveling up and down much faster. Because of this, the spark plugs will have to fire even sooner if the mixture is to be completely ignited as the piston passes TDC. To accomplish this, the distributor incorporates means to advance the timing of the spark as engine speed increases.

The distributor in your car has two means of advancing the ignition timing. One is called

centrifugal advance and is actuated by weights in the distributor. The other is called vacuum advance and is controlled by that large circular housing on the side of the distributor.

In addition, some distributors have a vacuum-retard mechanism which is contained in the same housing on the side of the distributor as the vacuum advance. The function of the mechanism is to retard the timing of the ignition spark under certain engine conditions. This causes more complete burning of the air/fuel mixture in the cylinder and consequently lowers exhaust emissions.

Because these mechanisms change ignition timing, it is necessary to disconnect and plug the one or two vacuum lines from the distributor when setting the basic ignition timing.

If ignition timing is set too far advanced (BTDC), the ignition and expansion of the air/fuel mixture in the cylinder will try to force the piston down the cylinder while it is still traveling upward. This causes engine "ping," a sound which resembles marbles being dropped into an empty tin can. If the ignition timing is too far retarded (after, or ATDC), the piston will have already started down on the power stroke when the air/fuel mixture ignites and expands. This will cause the piston to be forced down only a portion of its travel. This will result in poor engine performance and lack of power.

Ignition timing adjustment is checked with a timing light. This instrument is connected to the number one (no. 1) spark plug of the engine. The timing light flashes every time an electrical current is sent from the distributor, through the no. 1 spark plug wire, to the spark plug. The crankshaft pulley and the front cover of the engine are marked with a timing pointer and a timing scale. When the timing pointer is aligned with the "0" mark on the timing scale, the piston in no. 1 cylinder is at TDC of its compression stroke. With the engine running, and the timing light aimed at the timing pointer and timing scale, the stroboscopic flashes from the timing light will allow you to check the ignition timing setting of the engine. The timing light flashes every time the spark plug in the no. 1 cylinder of the engine fires. Since the flash from the timing light makes the crankshaft pulley seem stationary for a moment, you will be able to read the exact position of the piston in the no. 1 cylinder on the timing scale on the front of the engine.

Timing the Engine with a Timing Light

1. If the timing light operates from the battery, connect the red lead to the battery positive terminal, and the black lead to a ground. With all lights, connect the trigger lead in series with no. 1 spark plug wire.

2. Disconnect and plug the required vacuum hoses, as in the manufacturer's specifications. Connect the red lead of a tachometer to the distributor side of the coil and the black lead to ground. Start the engine, put the (automatic) transmission in gear (if required), and read the tachometer. Adjust the carburetor idle screw to the proper speed for setting the timing. Aim the timing light at the crankshaft pulley to determine where the timing point is. If the point is hard to see, it may help to stop the engine and mark it with chalk.

3. Loosen the distributor holding clamp and rotate the distributor slowly in either direction until the timing is correct. Tighten the

When you're timing the engine, try and stay out of strong light. It only makes it difficult to see the timing marks.

clamp and observe the timing mark again to determine that the timing is still correct. Readjust the position of the distributor, if necessary.

4. Accelerate the engine in Neutral, while watching the timing point. If the distributor advance mechanisms are working, the timing point should advance as the engine is accelerated. If the engine's vacuum advance is engaged with the transmission in Neutral, check the vacuum advance operation by running the engine at about 1,500 rpm and connecting and disconnecting the vacuum advance hose.

Static Timing

1. Make sure the engine is at the correct temperature for timing adjustment (either fully warmed or cold, as specified in the factory manual or a Chilton repair manual).

2. Locate no. 1 cylinder and trace its wire back to the distributor cap. Then, remove the cap.

3. Rotate the engine until the proper timing mark on the crankshaft pulley is lined up with the timing mark on the block. Observe the direction of distributor shaft rotation when the engine is turned in its normal direction of rotation.

4. Connect a test lamp from the coil terminal (the distributor side) to ground. Make sure the tip of the rotor lines up with no. 1 cylinder. If it does not, turn the engine one full revolution and line up the timing marks again.

5. Loosen the clamp that holds the distributor in position and turn the distributor body in the direction of normal shaft rotation until the points close and the test lamp goes out. Now turn the distributor in the opposite direction very slowly, just until the test lamp comes on. Tighten the distributor clamp.

6. To test the adjustment, turn the engine backward until the light again goes out, and then forward just until the light comes back on.

NOTE: *Engines with a belt-driven camshaft must not be rotated backward.*

If the timing marks are lined up, the engine is accurately timed. If the timing is too far advanced, loosen the distributor and turn it just slightly in the direction of shaft rotation, and retighten the clamp. If the timing is retarded, turn the distributor in the opposite direction and then repeat the test. Repeat this procedure until the light comes on just as the two timing marks are aligned.

CARBURETOR ADJUSTMENTS

Carburetors are fairly complex instruments, but since they have relatively few moving parts, they are not normally as vulnerable to the ravages of time as are distributor components. It is safe to say that modern carburetors are quite reliable and a correctly set-up carburetor is probably good for 50,000 maintenance-free miles. Any recurring carburetor problems indicate incorrect set-up or faulty repair work, since carburetor wear is very gradual.

Essentially, there are only two carburetor adjustments which may be necessary during the course of a normal tune-up. It is entirely possible that no adjustments will be necessary at all. Nonetheless, it is always a good idea to check.

When the engine in your car is running, air/fuel mixture from the carburetor is being drawn into the engine by a partial vacuum that is created by the downward movement of the piston on the intake stroke of the four-stroke cycle of the engine. The amount of air/fuel mixture that enters the engine is controlled by a throttle plate or plates in the bottom of the carburetor. When the engine is not running, the throttle plates are closed, completely blocking off the bottom of the carburetor from the intake manifold and thus the combustion chambers. The throttle plates are connected, through the throttle linkage, to the gas pedal. After you start the engine and put the transmission in gear, you depress the gas pedal to start the car moving. What you actually are doing when you depress the gas pedal is opening the throttle plate in the carburetor to admit more of the fuel/air mixture to the

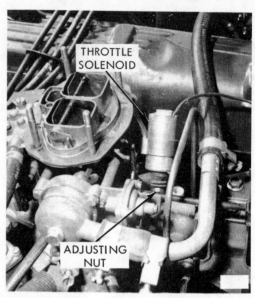

Solenoid equipped carburetor showing nut

engine. The further you open the throttle plates in the carburetor, the higher the engine speed becomes.

As previously stated, when the engine is not running, the throttle plates in the carburetor are closed. When the engine is idling, it is necessary to open the throttle plates slightly. To prevent having to keep your foot on the gas pedal when the engine is idling, an idle speed adjusting screw was added to the carburetor. This screw has the same effect as keeping your foot slightly depressed on the gas pedal. The idle speed adjusting screw contacts a lever (the throttle lever) on the outside of the carburetor. When the screw is turned in, it opens the throttle plate on the carburetor, raising the idle speed of the engine. This screw is called the curb idle adjusting screw and the procedures in this section will tell you how to adjust it.

Since the early seventies, most engines have been equipped with throttle solenoids. Due to the power-robbing effects of emission control systems, car manufacturers have found it necessary to raise the idle speed on almost all engines in order to obtain a smooth idle. Ordinarily, when the key is turned to "off," the current to the spark plugs is cut off, and the engine normally stops running. However, if an engine has a high operating temperature and a high idle speed (conditions common to emission-controlled engines), it is possible for the temperature of the cylinder instead of the spark plug to ignite the fuel/air mixture. When this happens, the engine continues to

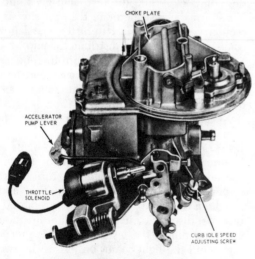

Carburetor showing idle speed screw.

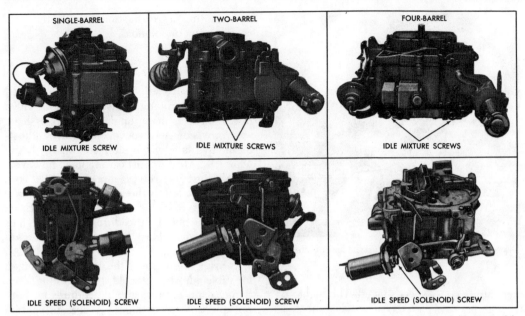

Various carburetors showing idle speed and mixture screws. Note that mixture screws are always at the bottom of the carburetor body.

run after the key is turned off. To solve this problem, a throttle solenoid was added to the carburetor. The solenoid is a cylinder with an adjustable plunger and an electrical lead. When the ignition key is turned to "on," the solenoid plunger extends to contact the carburetor throttle lever and raise the idle speed of the engine. When the ignition key is turned to "off," the solenoid is de-energized and the solenoid plunger falls back from the throttle lever. This allows the throttle lever to fall back and rest on the curb idle adjusting screw. This drops the engine idle speed back far enough so that the engine will not "run-on."

Since it is difficult for the engine to draw the fuel/air mixture from the carburetor with the small amount of throttle plate opening that is present when the engine is idling, an idle mixture passage is provided in the carburetor. This passage delivers fuel/air mixture to the engine from a hole which is located in the bottom of the carburetor below the throttle plates. This idle mixture passage contains an adjusting screw which restricts the amount of fuel/air mixture that enters the engine at idle. The idle mixture screws are capped on late-model cars due to emission-control regulations.

Idle Speed Adjustment

Generally, the idle speed is adjusted before the idle mixture is adjusted. You will need a tachometer to adjust the carburetor to the specified rpm. Connect the tachometer red lead to the negative terminal of the coil and connect the black lead to ground. This procedure is for conventional ignition systems only. Electronic ignition systems generally have specific tach hook-up procedures, and in addition, will not necessarily work with all tachometers. See Chapter Three for tach hook-up for the various types of electronic ignition systems. Locate the idle speed screw or the idle solenoid. With the engine at operating temperature, adjust the screw or the solenoid until the correct idle speed is reached. Ordinarily, on cars equipped with idle solenoids,

Adjusting the idle speed.

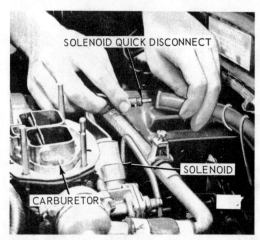

SOLENOID QUICK DISCONNECT

SOLENOID

CARBURETOR

Disconnecting the solenoid to adjust the lower of the two idle speeds.

there are two idle speeds listed. The higher of the two speeds is with the solenoid connected, while the lower is obviously with the solenoid disconnected. Set both speeds and then go on to the mixture adjustment.

Idle Mixture Adjustment

Locate the idle mixture screw or screws. All vehicles manufactured after 1972 have their idle mixture screws capped in accordance with Federal emission control regulations. As a result of this, there is only a very limited range of adjustment possible on these carburetors. To comply with emission regulations, the caps should not be removed or the mixture adjusted without them. After you have found the mixture screws, adjust them according to the manufacturer's instructions. These instructions vary, but in general, the procedure is this:

1. On early vehicles without capped mixture screws, adjust the mixture screw or screws for the highest idle speed you can obtain on the tachometer. An alternative method is to use a vacuum gauge and adjust the screws until the highest possible vacuum reading is obtained.

2. On vehicles with capped mixture screws, adjust the mixture screws (within the limits imposed by the caps) until the highest possible idle is obtained. Then adjust the screws inward from highest idle until the specified rpm drop is obtained.

After the mixture has been adjusted, it is quite often necessary to reset the idle speed with the idle speed screw or solenoid. As a general rule, idle mixture adjustments will raise the idle above that which is called for,

necessitating a readjustment with the idle speed screw or solenoid.

VALVE ADJUSTMENT

Periodic valve adjustments are not required on most modern engines with hydraulic valve lifters. In fact, many engines no longer have any provision whatsoever for valve adjustment, hydraulic valve lifter technology being what it is. Most import car engines, however, have adjustable valves, since a tightly controlled valve lash is the key to wringing horsepower out of these smaller motors. Exact valve adjustment procedures for all engines cannot be given here, but here are some general guidelines:

A. Bring the engine to the condition specified for valve adjustment (cold, hot, running, etc). Some manufacturers give procedures for both hot and cold adjustment. A note of caution about hot valve adjustment: oil temperature is far more critical to valve adjustment than water temperature; if the adjustment procedure calls for the engine to be at operating temperature, make sure the engine runs for at least fifteen minutes to allow the oil temperature to stabilize and parts to reach their full expansion.

B. Remove the valve or cam cover. If the valves are to be adjusted while the engine is running, oil deflector clips are available which install on the rocker arms and prevent oil spray.

C. If the valves must be adjusted with the engine stopped, follow the manufacturer's instructions for positioning the engine properly. For example, on Volkswagens, number one cylinder is adjusted while it is on the compression stroke at TDC, number two with the crankshaft turned 180 backward, etc.

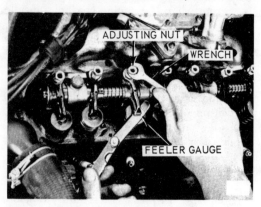

ADJUSTING NUT

WRENCH

FEELER GAUGE

Adjusting the valve clearance on an overhead valve engine

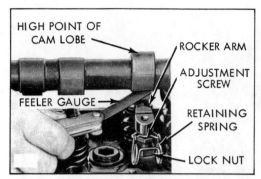

HIGH POINT OF CAM LOBE

FEELER GAUGE →

ROCKER ARM

ADJUSTMENT SCREW

RETAINING SPRING

LOCK NUT

Adjusting the valves on an overhead cam engine. Note that this is a rocker arm type OHC engine.

J-23587

Adjusting the valves on an OHC engine using lifters. This is a Vega engine. Note the special tool required.

D. Generally on overhead camshaft engines, valve adjustment is fairly simple. Turn the engine over (either manually or with a remote starter switch) until the highest part of the cam lobe is pointing directly *away* from the rocker arm or lifter. In the event you are unsure of how to do it, consult a service manual.

E. Adjust solid lifters by pushing a leaf type feeler gauge of the specified thickness (consult the manual) between the valve stem and rocker arm. Loosen the locking nut and tighten the screw until a light resistance to the movement of the feeler blade is encountered. Hold the adjusting screw while tightening the locking nut. Some adjusting screws are fitted snugly into the rocker arm so no locknut is required. If the feeler is too snug, the adjustment should be loosened to permit the passage of the blade. Remember that a slightly loose adjustment is easier on the valves than an overly tight one, so adjust the valves accordingly. Always recheck the adjustment after the locknut has been tightened.

Refer to a service manual for details on hydraulic valve lifter adjustment.

F. Replace the valve cover, cleaning all traces of old gasket material from both surfaces and installing a new gasket. Tighten valve cover nuts alternately, in several stages, to ensure proper seating.

Chapter 3

Troubleshooting the Engine Electrical System

Understanding just a little about the basic theory of electricity will make electrical system troubleshooting much easier. Several gauges are used in electrical troubleshooting to see inside the circuit being tested. Without a basic understanding, it will be difficult to understand testing procedures.

Electricity is defined as the flow of electrons. Electrons are hypothetical particles thought to constitute the basic "stuff" of electricity. In a comparison with water flowing in a pipe, the electrons would be the water. As the flow of water can be measured, the flow of electricity can be measured. The unit of measurement is amperes, frequently abbreviated "amps." An ammeter will measure the actual amount of current flowing in the circuit.

Just as water *pressure* is measured in units such as pounds per square inch, electrical pressure is measured in volts. When a voltmeter's two probes are placed on two "live" portions of an electrical circuit with different electrical pressures, current will flow through the voltmeter and produce a reading which indicates the difference in electrical pressure between the two parts of the circuit.

While increasing the voltage in a circuit will increase the flow of current, the actual flow depends not only on voltage, but on the resistance of the circuit. The standard unit for measuring circuit resistance is an ohm, measured by an ohmmeter. The ohmmeter is somewhat similar to an ammeter, but incorporates its own source of power so that a standard voltage is always present.

An actual electric circuit consists of four basic parts. These are: the power source, such as a generator or battery; a hot wire, which

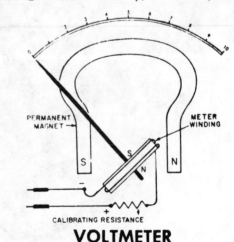

VOLTMETER

Voltmeter circuitry

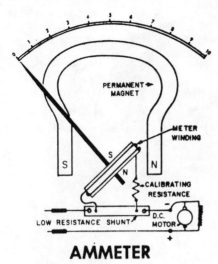

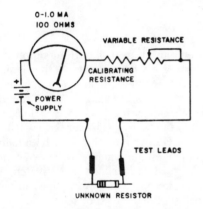

AMMETER

Ammeter circuitry

OHMMETER

Ohmmeter circuitry

conducts the electricity under a relatively high voltage or pressure to the electrical appliance supplied by the circuit; the load, such as a lamp, motor, resistor, or relay coil; and the ground wire, which carries the current back to the source under very low electrical pressure. In such a circuit, the bulk of the resistance exists between the point where the hot wire is connected to the load, and the point where the load is grounded. In an automobile, the vehicle's frame, which is made of steel, is used as a part of the ground circuit for many of the electrical devices.

Remember that, in electrical testing, the voltmeter is connected in parallel with the circuit being tested (without disconnecting any wires) and measures the difference in voltage between the locations of the two probes; that the ammeter is connected in series with the load (the circuit is separated at one point and

the ammeter inserted so it becomes a part of the circuit); and that the ohmmeter is self-powered, so that all the power in the circuit should be off and the portion of the circuit to be measured contacted at either end by one of the probes of the meter.

Battery and Starting System

BASIC OPERATING PRINCIPLES

The battery is the first link in the chain of mechanisms which work together to provide cranking of the automobile engine. In most modern cars, the battery is a lead-acid electrochemical device consisting of six two-volt (2 V) subsections connected in series so the unit is capable of producing approximately 12 V of electrical pressure. Each subsection, or cell, consists of a series of positive and negative plates held a short distance apart in a solution of sulfuric acid and water. The two types of plates are of dissimilar metals. This causes a chemical reaction to be set up, and it is this reaction which produces current flow from the battery when its positive and negative terminals are connected to an electrical appliance such as a lamp or motor. The continued transfer of electrons would eventually convert the sulfuric acid in the electrolyte to water, and make the two plates identical in chemical composition. As electrical energy is removed from the battery, its voltage output tends to drop. Thus, measuring battery voltage and battery electrolyte composition are two ways of checking the ability of the unit to supply

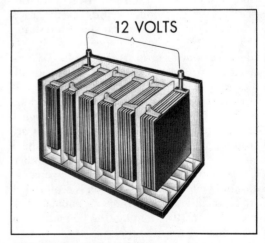

Cutaway view—twelve volt battery

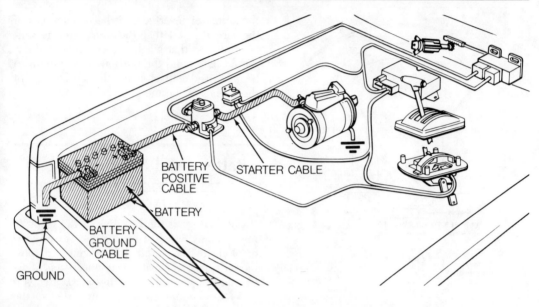

BATTERY POSITIVE CABLE

STARTER CABLE

BATTERY

BATTERY GROUND CABLE

GROUND

Starting system schematic. Not all starter systems use a relay.

power. During the starting of the engine, electrical energy is removed from the battery. However, if the charging circuit is in good condition and the operating conditions are normal, the power removed from the battery will be replaced by the generator (or alternator) which will force electrons back through the battery, reversing the normal flow, and restoring the battery to its original chemical state.

The battery and starting motor are linked by very heavy electrical cables designed to minimize resistance to the flow of current. Generally, the major power supply cable that leaves the battery goes directly to the starter, while other electrical system needs are supplied by a smaller cable. During starter operation, power flows from the battery to the starter and is grounded through the car's frame and the battery's negative ground strap.

The starting motor is a specially designed, direct current electric motor capable of producing a very great amount of power for its size. One thing that allows the motor to produce a great deal of power is its tremendous rotating speed. It drives the engine through a tiny pinion gear (attached to the starter's armature), which drives the very large flywheel ring gear at a greatly reduced speed. Another factor allowing it to produce so much power is that only intermittent operation is required of it. Thus, little allowance for air circulation is required, and the windings can be built into a very small space.

The starter solenoid is a magnetic device

which employs the small current supplied by the starting switch circuit of the ignition switch. This magnetic action moves a plunger which mechanically engages the starter and electrically closes the heavy switch which connects it to the battery. The starting switch circuit consists of the starting switch contained within the ignition switch, a transmission neutral safety switch or clutch pedal switch, and the wiring necessary to connect these in series with the starter solenoid or relay.

A pinion, which is a small gear, is mounted to a one-way drive clutch. This clutch is splined to the starter armature shaft. When the ignition switch is moved to the "start" position, the solenoid plunger slides the pinion toward the flywheel ring gear via a collar and spring. If the teeth on the pion and flywheel match properly, the pinion will engage the flywheel immediately. If the gear teeth butt one another, the spring will be compressed and will force the gears to mesh as soon as the starter turns far enough to allow them to do so. As the solenoid plunger reaches the end of its travel, it closes the contacts that connect the battery and starter and then the engine is cranked.

As soon as the engine starts, the flywheel ring gear begins turning fast enough to drive the pinion at an extremely high rate of speed. At this point, the one-way clutch begins allowing the pinion to spin faster than the starter shaft so that the starter will not operate at excessive speed. When the ignition switch is released from the starter position, the solenoid

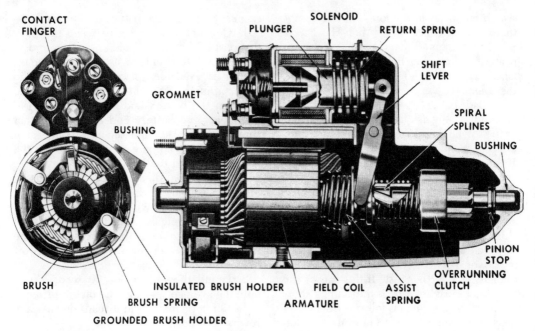

Starter—cutaway view

is de-energized, and a spring contained within the solenoid assembly pulls the gear out of mesh and interrupts the current flow to the starter.

Some starters employ a separate relay, mounted away from the starter, to switch the motor and solenoid current on and off. The relay thus replaces the solenoid electrical switch, but does not eliminate the need for a solenoid mounted on the starter used to mechanically engage the starter drive gears. The relay is used to reduce the amount of current the starting switch must carry.

STARTING SYSTEM TROUBLESHOOTING

A. Inspect the System:

1. Turn off all accessories. Place manual transmissions in Neutral; automatic transmissions in Park. Depress the clutch pedal all the way on cars with manual transmissions.

2. Turn the ignition switch firmly to the start position. If the engine cranks, hold it there for 15 seconds.

3. If you are familiar with the vehicle, listen for normal starting sounds. If they are unfamiliar, cranking may be checked by looking at the vibration damper on the front of the engine. It should turn steadily at about ⅓ normal idle speed. Turn on the headlights and check brightness during cranking.

Generally a problem falls into one of the following categories:

a. Starter drive mechanical problems: The starter turns, possibly with a gear clashing noise, but the engine does not turn. The trouble is in the starter pinion or its engagement mechanism, or possibly in the flywheel ring gear. The starter must be removed and the faulty parts repaired or replaced.

b. Engine mechanical problems: The starter turns the engine briefly and then stops very suddenly, or hums but does not turn the engine at all. The engine is hydrostatically locked or has some other severe mechanical defects. Attempt to turn the engine over using an 18 in. flex drive and socket on the crankshaft pulley mounting nut. Inability to turn the engine using this technique confirms the existence of mechanical engine problems. If the engine can be turned but the symptoms above apply, remove the starter and check for starter drive mechanical problems.

c. Malfunction in solenoid switch: The solenoid clicks loudly and the headlights remain bright, but there is no action or noise from the starter motor. The problem is in the solenoid switch and its wiring. Remove the starter and repair the switch.

d. Starter switch circuit: There is no click or other response from starter, but the headlights work normally. Check the starter switch circuit as in section J. If that is not the problem, check G and then H.

e. Bad solenoid: The starter clicks repeatedly, but the lights burn brightly. Check H and I. If no fault is found, replace the solenoid.

f. Bad battery, wiring, or starter: If cranking is sluggish and the lights are dim or the solenoid clicks and the lights are dim, or there is no response at all, follow checks B through J in alphabetical order.

B. Make Quick Checks:

1. Check both battery terminal connections for corrosion. Turn on the headlight switch and watch the headlights while twisting a screwdriver between the cable clamps and terminals, as a further test. If this causes the headlights to brighten, or if the clamps show corrosion, service them as follows: disconnect both clamps, remove corrosion from conducting surfaces, reinstall them securely, and then coat them with petroleum jelly or grease. Avoid the use of force in every way possible. If clamps are bolted together, loosen the nuts and force the terminals open before removing them. Clamps which are not bolted should be forced on with gentle strokes of a soft mallet. If the starter now cranks properly, return the vehicle to service.

2. Check the tension and condition of the belt(s) which drive the alternator or generator. If there is inadequate tension and belt surfaces are heavily glazed—indicating slippage—replace the belts, tighten them to specifications, recharge the battery, and return the vehicle to service.

3. Evaluate recent operating conditions. If your accessory load has been unusually heavy and the vehicle has been operated at moderate speeds with frequent stops, recharge the battery, and return the vehicle to service. If this is a recurrent problem, the electrical system should be checked for proper generator and regulator performance. In some cases, the regulator can be readjusted to reduce the severity of this problem.

NOTE: *During the tests below, the coil-to-distributor low-tension lead should be disconnected and securely grounded to prevent the vehicle from starting and to protect the ignition system from damage.*

C. Test Amperage and Voltage:

Checking starter amperage draw in conjunction with voltage during cranking will give excellent clues to the nature of the problem.

1. Connect a voltmeter between the positive post of the battery and a good ground.

2. If an induction type starter amperage indicator is available, place the yoke of the meter around a straight section of the cable between the battery and starter. Otherwise, disconnect the battery end of the lead that runs to the starter and securely connect an ammeter of 300 ampere capacity between the battery post and the lead.

A carbon pile rheostat can also be used. Measure voltage during cranking and then connect it in series with the ammeter across the battery terminals. Turn the rheostat until voltage is the same as during cranking. The reading on the ammeter will then show starter draw.

3. Crank the engine for 20 seconds and note the average readings. If you are using an induction type meter and it reads down-scale, reverse the position of the yoke.

4. Evaluate the readings according to the chart below. On 12 V systems, voltage should be 9.6 or more; on 6 V, 4.8 or more. On 12 V systems, amperage should be 100–200, depending on the size of the engine and its compression ratio. Double the amperages for 6 V systems.

Condition	Voltage	Amperage	Check Section
1	low	normal or low	D
2	near normal	high	E, F °
3	near normal	normal or low	G, H

° NOTE: If sections E and F do not reveal the problem, remove the starter for repair of ground or short circuit.

D. Check Specific Gravity of Battery Cells:

1. Test the specific gravity of each of the battery cells with a battery hydrometer. Do so before attempting to charge the battery. If the battery has been recently charged, or if the electrolyte level is below the level of the plates and requires replenishment, special procedures must be followed to ensure an accurate test. See the section on testing the electrical system for these procedures. Take

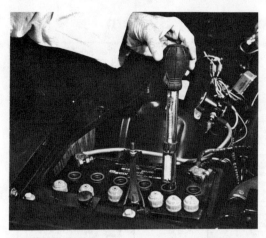

Testing the battery with a hydrometer

your measurements carefully, filling and emptying the hydrometer several times to ensure adequate removal of material left in the hydrometer and allowing time for the temperature to come to an accurate reading. Read the gravity scale from the liquid level at the center of the column, not from around the edges where it seeks an abnormally high level. Correct the readings according to the temperature scale on the hydrometer. If a hydrometer and battery thermometer must be used independently, this means subtracting 0.004 for each 10° below 80° F, and adding 0.004 for every 10° above that temperature. Readings not corrected according to temperature are meaningless.

2. Evaluate the readings. A fully charged battery will read between 1.260 and 1.280. Readings must be over 1.220 for the battery to be capable of cranking the engine. If any are below 1.220, or if the readings are far apart, see the section on testing the electrical system for information on evaluating the need for battery replacement or recharging dead batteries. If the battery requires replacement or recharging, be sure to test the charging system before placing the vehicle back in service.

E. Check for Engine Mechanical Problems:

Where amperage is high, a problem may exist in the engine itself or in the starter drive mechanism. If ambient temperature is below freezing, the engine oil should be a multigrade or light straight grade approved for winter use. Normal-weight oil can cause improper cranking in cold weather without any mechanical or electrical malfunction.

1. If improper lubrication is suspected, change the oil (and filter) and refill with the proper grade for the weather conditions. Return the vehicle to service if this permits good cranking.

2. If cranking is accompanied by a mechanical grinding or scraping noise and is very rough and unsteady (not merely sluggish), attempt to rotate the engine using an 18 in. flex drive and socket on the crankshaft pulley mounting nut. If the engine cannot be rotated or if extreme roughness, or tightness in a sporadic pattern is encountered, mechanical damage is evident. Remove the starter and check for mechanical problems in the starter drive. If none are found, major engine mechanical problems are indicated.

F. Check Mechanical Condition of Starter and Drive:

Where amperage is high and no engine mechanical problems are evident, remove the starter assembly and inspect the pinion and ring gears for sticking or severe wear due to lubrication problems, etc. Also check the starter motor armature shaft bearings. If no mechanical problems are evident, the problem is caused by starter motor or solenoid electrical problems.

G. Check Condition of Wiring Between Battery and Starter:

Normal voltage with low amperage indicates a poor connection somewhere in the starter circuit. The circuit between the battery and starter may be checked as below.

1. Connect the positive lead of a voltmeter (reverse the leads for a negative ground system) to the positive battery terminal. Connect the negative lead to the connector which carries power from the solenoid switch to the starting motor. Crank the engine and take note of the voltmeter reading. The reading should be 0.3 V or less. If the reading is acceptable, proceed to H. Otherwise proceed to step 2.

2. Isolate the faulty component by repeating the test with the voltmeter negative lead connected to each of the following:

  a. The starter motor terminal of the solenoid;

  b. The battery terminal of the solenoid;

  c. Starter terminal of starter relay (if your vehicle has one);

  d. Battery terminal of starter relay.

(If the vehicle has a starter relay, it will usually be mounted on one of the fender wells.) The voltage reading should drop slightly as each component is eliminated from the portion of

Troubleshooting the Starting System

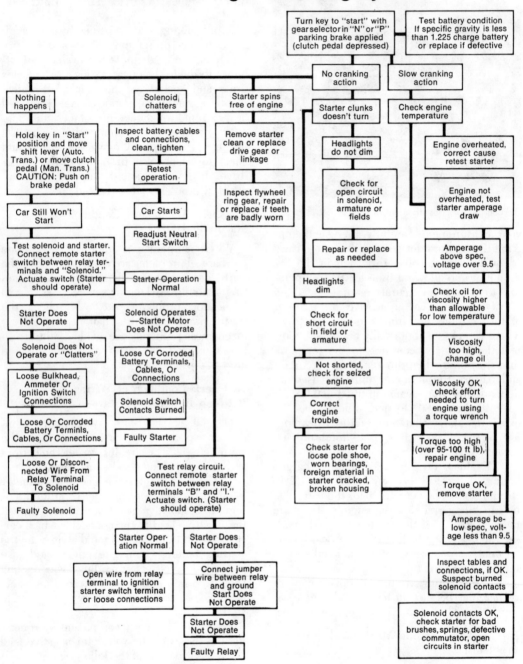

the circuit being tested. If the voltage drops more than 0.1 V when eliminating the solenoid switch or the relay, the unit is faulty. (Check for burned contacts inside; this is the most common problem.) The resistance of the battery cable should not exceed 0.2 V. Individual connections may be tested for high resistance by placing the probe of the negative lead first on the stud to which the connection is made, and then on the connector on the end of the cable leading to the connection. A measurable difference in the voltage drop indicates a bad connection which must be disassembled and cleaned. Usually bad connections will also be corroded or oil-covered. Be sure, when cleaning, to remove all the oxidized material and to reassemble the connection snugly. A wire brush or sandpaper will help.

H. Check Starter Ground Circuit:

1. Connect the negative lead of the voltmeter to the negative post of the battery (reverse hook-ups for positive ground systems) and the positive lead to a clean, unpainted spot on the starter housing. Crank the engine and note the voltmeter reading. If the reading is higher than 0.2 V, the system may be at fault, and step 2 should be followed. If no defects in the engine, battery, or wiring have been found, the starter should be removed for repair of its electrical circuitry.

2. Repeat the test outlined in step 1 with the positive voltmeter probe connected to:

    a. The ground cable to engine or frame connection;

    b. The battery negative cable to engine or frame connection;

Individual connections should be tested as in G. The ground cables should have resistances that cause the reading to change less than 0.2 V. Resistance of connections should be negligible.

J. Check Starter Switch Circuit:

1. If the system has a separate starter relay, locate the wire from the starter switch circuit to the relay and disconnect it. If the system uses only a solenoid, locate the wire from the starter switch circuit to the solenoid and disconnect it.

2. If the vehicle has an automatic transmission, make sure it is fully in Neutral or Park. If the vehicle has a manual transmission, the clutch pedal will have to be fully depressed during testing.

3. Connect the positive lead of the voltmeter to the end of the disconnected cable. Have someone turn the ignition switch to the start position and test for voltage. If about 12 V are present, the solenoid or relay is at fault, in most cases. Also check the ground for the relay, or the solenoid-to-starter connection and starter motor ground circuit in systems using a solenoid only.

4. If there is low or no voltage, the problem is in the starter switch circuit. Check for voltage at either side of the neutral safety or clutch pedal safety switch, and for voltage at the ignition switch connection that feeds the starter relay or solenoid. (If the warning lights work, current is getting to the ignition switch.) When working from the ignition switch toward the starter, the faulty component or connection is between the last point where voltage is detected and the first point which is dead. If the neutral safety switch is a combination type with four prongs, use a jumper cable to find the two prongs which operate the back-up lights, and then test the other prongs only. If the faulty component proves to be the neutral safety switch or clutch switch, remember to check the linkage for proper operation before condemning it. The linkage may be disconnected and moved through the full travel of the switch mechanism while checking for voltage to find out whether or not the fault is in the linkage.

The Charging System

BASIC OPERATING PRINCIPLES

The automobile charging system provides electrical power for operation of the vehicle's ignition and starting systems and all the electrical accessories. The battery serves as an electrical surge or storage tank, storing (in chemical form) the energy originally produced by the engine-driven generator. The system also provides a means of regulating generator output to protect the battery from being overcharged and to avoid excessive voltage to the accessories.

The storage battery is a chemical device incorporating parallel lead plates in a tank containing a sulfuric acid-water solution. Adjacent plates are slightly dissimilar, and the chemical reaction of the two dissimilar plates produces electrical energy when the battery is connected to a load such as the starter motor. The

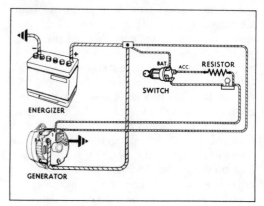

Charging system circuitry

chemical reaction is reversible, so that when the generator is producing a voltage (electrical pressure) greater than that produced by the battery, electricity is forced into the battery, and the battery is returned to its fully charged state.

The vehicle's generator is driven mechanically, through V belts, by the engine crankshaft. It consists of two coils of fine wire, one stationary (the "stator"), and one movable (the "rotor"). The rotor may also be known as the "armature," and consists of fine wire wrapped around an iron core which is mounted on a shaft. The electricity which flows through the two coils of wire (provided initially by the battery in some cases) creates an intense magnetic field around both rotor and stator, and the interaction between the two fields creates voltage, allowing the generator to power the accessories and charge the battery.

There are two types of generators; the earlier is the direct current (DC) type. The current produced by the DC generator is generated in the armature and carried off the spinning armature by stationary brushes contacting the commutator. The commutator is a series of smooth metal contact plates on the end of the armature. The commutator plates, which are separated from one another by a very short gap, are connected to the armature circuits so that current will flow in one direction only in the wires carrying the generator output. The generator stator consists of two stationary coils of wire which draw some of the output current of the generator to form a powerful magnetic field and create the interaction of fields which generates the voltage. The generator field is wired in series with the regulator.

Newer automobiles use alternating current generators or "alternators", because they are more efficient, can be rotated at higher speeds, and have fewer brush problems. In an alternator, the field rotates while all the current produced passes only through the stator windings. The brushes bear against continuous slip rings rather than a commutator. This causes the current produced to periodically reverse the direction of its flow. Diodes (electrical one-way switches) block the flow of current from traveling in the wrong direction. A series of diodes is wired together to permit the alternating flow of the stator to be converted to a pulsating, but unidirectional flow at the alternator output. The alternator's field is wired in series with the voltage regulator.

The regulator consists of several circuits.

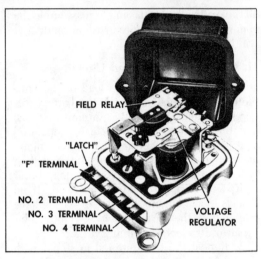

Typical voltage regulator

Each circuit has a core, or magnetic coil of wire, which operates a switch. Each switch is connected to ground through one or more resistors. The coil of wire responds directly to system voltage. When the voltage reaches the required level, the magnetic field created by the winding of wire closes the switch and inserts a resistance into the generator field circuit, thus reducing the output. The contacts of the switch cycle open and close many times each second to precisely control voltage.

While alternators are self-limiting as far as maximum current is concerned, DC generators employ a current regulating circuit which responds directly to the total amount of current flowing through the generator circuit rather than to the output voltage. The current regulator is similar to the voltage regulator except that all system current must flow through the energizing coil on its way to the various accessories.

Safety Precautions

Observing these precautions will ensure safe handling of the electrical system components, and will avoid damage to the vehicle's electrical system:

A. Be *absolutely* sure of the polarity of a booster battery before making connections. Connect the cables positive to positive, and negative to negative. Connect positive cables first and then make the last connection to a ground on the body of the booster vehicle so that arcing cannot ignite hydrogen gas that may have accumulated near the battery. Even momentary connection of a booster battery with the polarity reserved will damage alternator diodes.

B. Disconnect both vehicle battery cables before attempting to charge a battery.

C. Never ground the alternator or generator output or battery terminal. Be cautious when using metal tools around a battery to avoid creating a short circuit between the terminals.

D. Never ground the field circuit between the alternator and regulator.

E. Never run an alternator or generator without load unless the field circuit is disconnected.

F. Never attempt to polarize an alternator.

G. Keep the regulator cover in place when taking voltage and current limiter readings.

H. Use insulated tools when adjusting the regulator.

I. Whenever DC generator-to-regulator wires have been disconnected, the generator *must* be repolarized. To do this with an externally grounded, light duty generator, momentarily place a jumper wire between the battery terminal and the generator terminal of the regulator. With an internally grounded heavy duty unit, disconnect the wire to the regulator field terminal and touch the regulator battery terminal with it.

CHARGING SYSTEM TROUBLESHOOTING

A. Inspect the System

Check the alternator mounts for cracks or loose mounting bolts, and tighten or replace parts as necessary. Check the condition and tension of the drive belt. Replace the belt if it is frayed or cracked. Tighten the belt if there is play or inadequate tension. If manufacturer's specifications and a strand tension gauge are not available, the belt should be tightened so that it can be depressed about ½ in. for each 10 in. of length with moderate (10–15 lbs) thumb pressure.

Check the level of electrolyte in the battery cells and fill them, if necessary, with distilled water to the level of the indicator ring. Clean the surface of the battery with a rag. Replace the battery if there is a sizable crack.

Check the condition of the battery terminals. If there is corrosion, disconnect the terminals and clean them with a baking soda and water solution. Thoroughly clean the corroded material from the conducting surfaces with a wire brush. Reconnect the terminals snugly. Even if no cleaning was required, carefully tighten the terminals. Coat the terminals with clean petroleum jelly to prevent further corrosion.

All the visible wires in the charging system should then be checked for cracked or frayed insulation and loose or corroded connections. Clean any corroded connections with a wire brush or sandpaper, and reconnect them snugly. Replace any frayed wiring.

B. Check the Battery

Check the capacity of the battery as indicated by a rating on the label in wattage or ampere-hours. Recommended battery rating for the vehicle may be found in the owner's manual. The battery capacity should be at least equal to the recommended rating.

A quick check of battery condition may be made by connecting a voltmeter across the battery posts and cranking the engine for about 15 seconds. If the voltage at the positive terminal remains at approximately 9.6 or above, the battery is most likely in good condition.

If the battery does not pass this test, test the specific gravity of the electrolyte in each of the cells. If the battery requires addition of water to bring the cells to the proper level, this should be done first. If water had to be added, the battery should be charged at a high enough rate to cause gasing (hydrogen emission) of the cells for 15 minutes to ensure thorough mixing of the electrolyte.

Test the specific gravity of each cell with a clean hydrometer. If the hydrometer has a thermometer, draw in and expel the fluid several times to make a thermometer reading. Otherwise use a battery thermometer, allowing time for the thermometer to reach the temperature of the electrolyte. Correct the hydrometer reading by adding 0.004 to it for each 10° over 80° F, and subtracting 0.004 for each 10° below 80° F.

If the readings are more than 50 points apart, the battery should be replaced. The battery is fully charged if gravity is 1.260–1.280, half charged at about 1.210, and fully discharged at about 1.120. If the readings are inconclusive, the battery should be charged at a rate that will not bring the electrolyte to a temperature over 125° F. This should be done until the specific gravity remains constant for two hours. If at this point, all the cells are not between 1.260 and 1.280, especially if the variations exceed 50 points, the battery should be replaced.

There are various commercial battery testers available that measure output voltage while subjecting the battery to a load. They will do an excellent job.

C. Test the Output of the Generator (Alternator)

A quick and simple output test may be made using a voltmeter. Simply connect the voltmeter between the positive and negative battery terminals and measure the voltage. Then start the engine and run it at fast idle. Check the voltage again. If it has risen (usually about 2 V), the generator (alternator) and regulator are functioning.

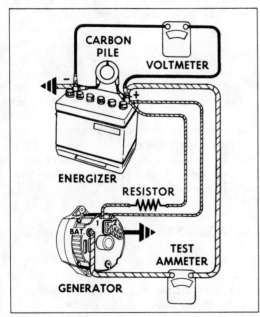

Generator output test hookup

The regulator may be easily bypassed if a field rheostat is available, in order to see whether an inadequate voltage rise as measured in the above test is due to problems in the generator (alternator) or regulator. Proceed as follows:

1. Disconnect the field wire from the F or FLD terminal on the regulator. Connect the field rheostat between the IGN terminal of the regulator and the disconnected field wire.

2. Turn the rheostat to the maximum resistance position (the low side of the scale).

3. Start the engine and operate it at fast idle. Gradually turn the rheostat control toward the decreased resistance side of the scale while watching the voltmeter. Turn the knob until the voltage read on the meter equals the manufacturer's specified maximum voltage for the generator (alternator). If it will not pro-

duce the specified voltage, it requires repair or replacement.

In cases of questionable performance, a more accurate test of generator (alternator) condition is an amperage output test. A DC generator may be tested as described below:

a. Remove the armature and field leads from the generator. Place a jumper wire between these two terminals. Connect a 100 amp capacity ammeter between the generator armature terminal, and whichever battery lead is not grounded, with the positive ammeter lead on the generator.

b. Start the engine, and with the engine idling, move the negative ammeter lead to the positive terminal of the battery.

c. Run the engine at fast idle and note the generator output as measured on the ammeter. Compare with manufacturer's specifications. Output should be about 30 amps for regular-duty equipment, and about 50 amps for heavy-duty units.

NOTE: *Disconnect all leads as soon as the engine stops or else battery current will flow through the generator.*

Alternator output tests very according to the design of the alternator and regulator in use. For the details of testing an alternator-powered charging system, it is recommended that a Chilton manual or factory repair manual be consulted. The alternator output test is generally accomplished as follows:

a. Place an ammeter in series between the battery terminal of the alternator and the disconnected battery lead.

b. Hook up a voltmeter between the battery lead on the alternator and the battery negative terminal. Ground or connect the alternator field terminal to the battery positive post. (This will depend on the internal design of the regulator.)

c. Hook a carbon pile rheostat between the two battery posts. Connect a tachometer to the engine.

d. Start the engine and adjust to the speed specified in the test instructions. Adjust the carbon pile rheostat so the voltage at which the test is to be performed registers on the voltmeter, then read the amperage on the ammeter.

e. If amperage is below specifications, the alternator requires repairs. Some test instructions include procedures for evaluating the alternator condition and locating the problem based on the difference between rated amperage and what is found in the test.

D. Test the Charging Circuit Resistance

The charging circuit resistance test is very similar to the output test for both generators and alternators. A manual should be consulted for details of instrument hook-up and amperage settings, as well as the maximum permissible voltage drop (usually less than 1 V).

The test differs in that the voltmeter is connected between the generator battery terminal and the positive terminal of the vehicle's battery. The engine is operated at fast idle, and the carbon pile rheostat adjusted until a specified amperage is flowing to the battery. The voltage drop is then compared to specifications. If voltage drop is excessive, the connections must be carefully inspected and, if necessary, cleaned and tightened. If this fails to bring the voltage drop down to specifications, wiring must be replaced.

E. Check Voltage and Current Regulator Performance

A very simple test of regulator performance may be made as follows:

1. Remove the high-tension lead from the coil and ground it. Crank the engine for about 30 seconds.

2. Disconnect the battery terminal of the regulator, or the alternator-to-battery cable on alternators with integral regulators, and insert an ammeter. The ammeter leads will have to be reversed (with the engine off) if the ammeter reads downscale.

3. Reconnect the distributor high-tension lead and start the engine, running it at fast idle. Watch the ammeter. The amperage reading should be high at first, and then, after two or three minutes of operation, it should fall off to a very low reading, assuming that all vehicle accessories are turned off.

If this test reveals problems, the regulator should be further tested. General test instructions follow. Manufacturer's specifications should be consulted for the exact voltage output required at various regulator temperatures.

Voltage Regulator Test

This test requires a voltmeter and ammeter. For Delco units, a 0.25 ohm resistor of 25 watt capacity is required. In the case of the Chrysler mechanical regulator with alternator, a carbon pile rheostat is required.

A. Hook up the test equipment as described below. Delco DC Generator: Connect the resistor in series between the battery and regulator by removing the line to the regulator "Batt" terminal and inserting the resistor between the terminal and the wire connection. Connect a voltmeter between the regulator terminal and a good ground.

Autolite or Ford DC Generator: Connect an ammeter between the battery and the regulator by disconnecting the line to the "Batt" terminal and inserting the ammeter. Connect the voltmeter between the armature connection on the regulator and ground.

Chrysler Mechanical Regulator with Alternator: Connect the voltmeter between the ignition terminal no. 1 of the ballast resistor and ground. Connect a carbon pile rheostat between the two battery terminals, with the resistance adjusted to the highest level.

Chrysler Electronic Regulator: Disconnect the battery during hook-up. Connect the ammeter between the alternator and battery by disconnecting the battery-to-alternator lead and inserting the ammeter (with the positive side toward the alternator). Connect the voltmeter between the "Ign" terminal of the regulator and a good ground.

Delco 5.5 and 6.2 alternators: Connect the resistor between the battery cable (with the cable disconnected) and the battery cable connection on the junction block. Connect the voltmeter between that junction block connection and a ground on the body of the relay.

B. Start the engine and run it at fast idle (about 1,600 rpm) for 15 minutes to bring all components to operating temperature. If you are testing a Chrysler alternator with a mechanical regulator, adjust the engine speed to 1,250 rpm with a tachometer, and adjust the carbon pile rheostat so the charging rate is 15 amps. With Delcotron alternators, turn on the headlights and heater blower. With Ford DC units, turn on accessories until the generator is producing 8–10 amps. With Autolite DC units, turn accessories until one half of the generator output is being produced.

C. Place a thermometer on the regulator to measure its temperature. Stop and start the engine after 15 minutes to cycle the regulator off and on.

D. Read the voltage and temperature, and compare each with manufacturer's specifications. On Chrysler mechanical units with an alternator, the lower contacts must also be tested by bringing the engine speed to 2,200 rpm and adjusting the carbon pile for 7 amps charging rate.

If the results of this test do not meet specifications, or if the battery is overcharged (loses water continuously), or if starting problems are encountered with no problems in the battery or starting system, the regulator should be adjusted and serviced or, if necessary, replaced.

REGULATOR ADJUSTMENT

Nonadjustable regulators that do not meet specifications must be replaced.

All mechanical units may be adjusted by either turning an adjusting screw or bending a spring mount to increase the tension of a spring to increase the voltage and decreasing the tension of the spring to lower the output voltage. General Motors solid-state regulators which are separate from the alternator may be adjusted by removing a pipe plug in the top of the regulator and turning the adjusting screw underneath.

Specific manufacturer's instructions and specifications for each type of regulator should be consulted. All final regulator checks must be accomplished with the regulator cover in place.

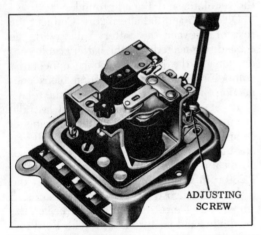

ADJUSTING SCREW

Typical regulator adjustment

If the regulator contact points are burned or pitted, they should be cleaned with a riffler file and the gap should be adjusted according to the manufacturer's specifications. This is done by closing the contacts and then measuring the distance between the armature and core of the regulator with a round feeler gauge. Bend the contact arm at the specified spot until the gap is correct.

In the case of DC regulators which fail to produce adequate output only under heavy load conditions, the current regulator may be checked. An ammeter is placed in series with the battery, and the amperage is read just after a very heavy load has been placed on the battery by cranking the engine for 30 seconds with the high-tension lead to the coil grounded. All accessories should be turned on for the test. The current should meet manufacturer's specifications. The current regulator is adjusted in the same way as the voltage regulator.

If the regulator produces insufficient voltage or does not regulate the voltage properly, and cannot be adjusted, it should be replaced. If voltage output is inadequate, the connections in the field circuit between the regulator and generator (alternator) should be cleaned and tightened, and the wires should be checked for continuity. Rectify any problems found by replacing wires or cleaning and tightening connections before condemning the regulator.

Point-Type Ignition Systems

BASIC OPERATING PRINCIPLES

There are two basic functions the automotive ignition system must perform: (1) it must control the spark and the timing of the firing to match varying engine requirements; (2) it must increase battery voltage to a point where it will overcome the resistance offered by the spark plug gap and fire the plug.

To accomplish this, an automotive ignition system is divided into two electrical circuits. One circuit, called the primary circuit, is the low voltage circuit. This circuit operates only on battery current and is controlled by the breaker points and the ignition switch. The second circuit is the high voltage circuit, and is called (logically enough) the secondary circuit. This circuit consists of the secondary windings in the coil, the high tension lead between the distributor and the coil (commonly called the coil wire), the distributor cap and rotor, the spark plug leads and the spark plugs.

The coil is the heart of the ignition system. Essentially, a coil is nothing more than a transformer which takes the relatively low voltage available from the battery and increases it to a point where it will fire the spark plug. This increase is quite large, since modern coils produce on the order of about 40,000 volts. The term "coil" is perhaps a misnomer

Troubleshooting The Charging System

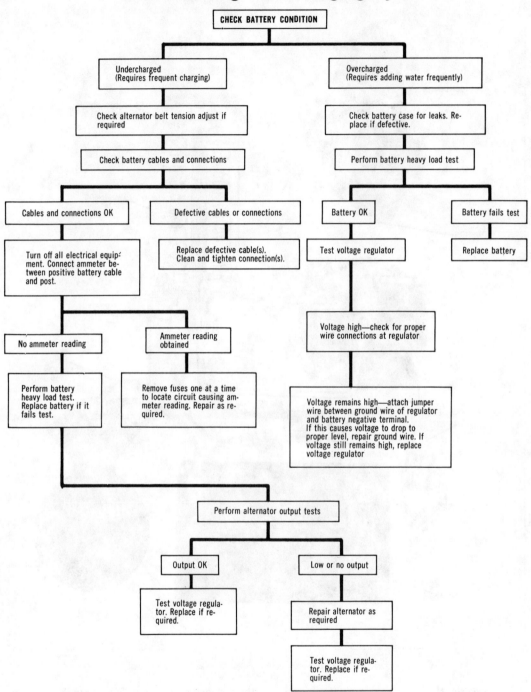

since a coil consists of *two* coils of wire wound about an iron core. These coils are insulated from each other and the whole assembly is enclosed in an oil-filled case. The primary coil is connected to the two primary terminals located on top of the coil and consists of rela-tively few turns of heavy wire. The secondary coil consists of many turns of fine wire and is connected to the high tension connection on top of the coil. This secondary connection is simply the tower into which the coil wire from the distributor is plugged.

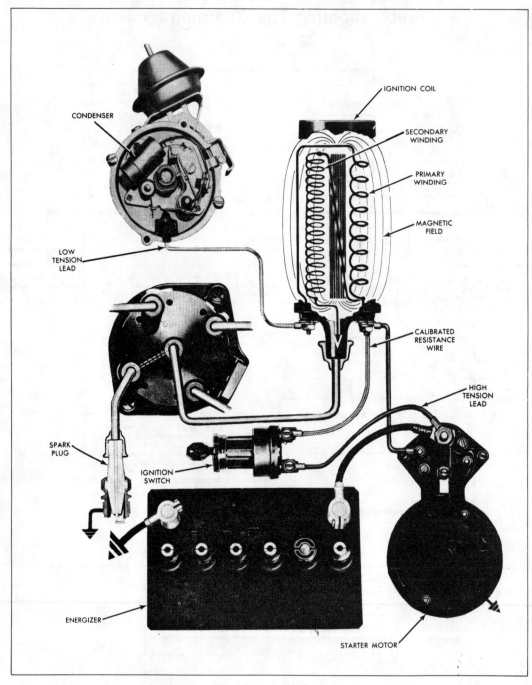

Ignition system schematic

Energizing the coil primary with battery voltage produces current flow through the primary windings. This in turn produces a very large, intense magnetic field. Interrupting the flow of primary current causes the field to collapse. Just as current moving through a wire produces a magnetic field, moving a field across a wire will produce a current. As the magnetic field collapses, its lines of force cross

the secondary windings, inducing a current in them. The force of the induced current is concentrated because of the relative shortness of the secondary coil of wire.

The distributor is the controlling element of the system, switching the primary current on and off and distributing the current to the proper spark plug each time a spark is produced. It is basically a stationary housing sur-

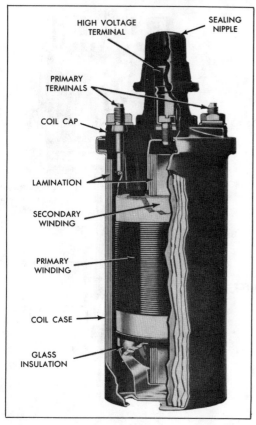

HIGH VOLTAGE TERMINAL

SEALING NIPPLE

PRIMARY TERMINALS

COIL CAP

LAMINATION

SECONDARY WINDING

PRIMARY WINDING

COIL CASE

GLASS INSULATION

Coil—cutaway view

about 60 crankshaft degrees before the firing of the spark plug. Current will begin flowing through the primary wiring to the positive connection on the coil, through the primary winding of the coil, through the ground wire between the negative connection on the coil and the distributor, and to ground through the contact points. Shortly after the engine is ready to fire, the current flow through the coil primary will have reached a near maximum value, and an intense magnetic field will have formed around the primary windings. The distributor cam will separate the contact points at the proper time for ignition and the primary field will collapse, causing current to flow in the secondary circuit. A capacitor, known as the "condenser," is installed in the circuit in parallel with the contact points in order to absorb some of the force of the electrical surge that occurs during collapse of the magnetic field. The condenser consists of several layers of aluminum foil separated by insulation. These layers of foil, upon an increase in voltage, are capable of storing electricity, making the condenser a sort of electrical surge tank. Voltages just after the points open may reach 250 V because of the vast amount of energy stored in the primary windings and their magnetic field. A condenser which is defective or improperly grounded will not absorb the shock from the fast-moving stream of electrons when the points open and these electrons will force their way across the point gap, causing burning and pitting.

The very high voltage induced in the secondary windings will cause a surge of current to flow from the coil tower to the center of the distributor, where it will travel along the connecting strip along the top of the rotor. The surge will arc its way across the short gap between the contact on the outer end of the rotor and the connection in the cap for the high-tension lead of the cylinder to be fired. After passing along the high-tension lead, it will travel down the center electrode of the spark plug, which is surrounded by ceramic insulation, and arc its way over to the side electrode, which is grounded through threads which hold the plug in the cylinder head. The heat generated by the passage of the spark will ignite the contents of the cylinder.

rounding a rotating shaft. The shaft is driven at one-half engine speed by the engine's camshaft through the distributor drive gears. A cam which is situated near the top of the shaft has one lobe for each cylinder of the engine. The cam operates the ignition contact points, which are mounted on a plate located on bearings within the distributor housing. A rotor is attached to the top of the distributor shaft. When the bakelite distributor cap is in place, on top of the unit's metal housing, a spring-loaded contact connects the portion of the rotor directly above the center of the shaft to the center connection on top of the distributor. The outer end of the rotor passes very close to the contacts connected to the four, six, or eight high-tension connections around the outside of the distributor cap.

Under normal operating conditions, power from the battery is fed through a resistor or resistance wire to the primary circuit of the coil and is then grounded through the ignition points in the distributor. During cranking, the full voltage of the battery is supplied through an auxiliary circuit routed through the solenoid switch. In an eight-cylinder engine, the distributor cam will allow the points to close

Most distributors employ both centrifugal and vacuum advance mechanisms to advance the point at which ignition occurs for optimum performance and economy. Spark generally occurs a few degrees before the piston reaches top dead center (TDC) in order that very high

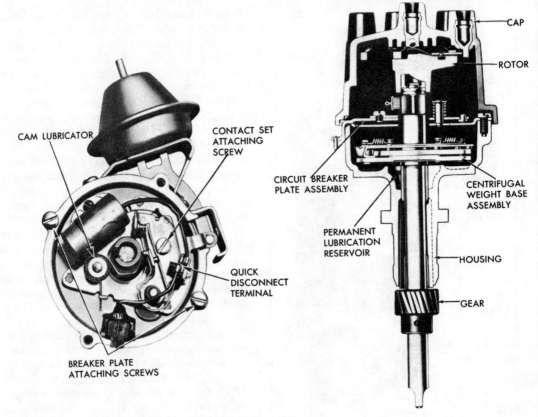

Typical conventional distributor

pressures will exist in the cylinder as soon as the piston is capable of using the energy—just a few degrees after TDC. Centrifugal advance mechanisms employ hinged flyweights working in opposition to springs to turn the top portion of the distributor shaft, including the cam and rotor, ahead of the lower shaft. This advances the point at which the cam causes the points to open. A more advanced spark is required at higher engine speeds because the speed of combustion does not increase in direct proportion to increases in engine speed, but tends to lag behind at high revolutions. If peak cylinder pressures are to exist at the same point, advance must be used to start combustion earlier.

Vacuum advance is used to accomplish the same thing when part-throttle operation reduces the speed of combustion because of less turbulence and compression, and poorer scavenging of exhaust gases. Carburetor vacuum below the throttle plate is channeled to a vacuum diaphragm mounted on the distributor. The higher the manifold vacuum, the greater the motion of the diaphragm against spring pressure. A rod between the diaphragm and the plate on which the contact points are mounted rotates the plate on its bearings causing the cam to open the points earlier in relation to the position of the crankshaft.

TROUBLESHOOTING POINT-TYPE IGNITION SYSTEMS

A. Check for Normal Cranking

Turn the ignition switch to the "start" position and check for normal cranking. If cranking is not normal, repair any problems in the

Condenser

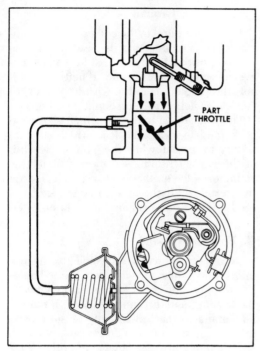

Vacuum advance schematic

starting system before inspecting the ignition system. Low voltage, whether caused by excessive battery drain or poor battery performance, and/or other starter system malfunctions, can affect the performance of the ignition system.

B. Check for an Adequate Spark

Pull off a spark plug lead and hold it about $3/16$ in. from a good ground. If possible, pull back the rubber boot covering the end of the lead so bare metal is exposed. A good fat spark should appear at regular intervals. Try at least two leads so you can be sure the problem is not just a bad individual cable. If the spark is good, proceed to O. Otherwise, proceed with the checks below.

C. Inspect the System for Visible Deficiencies

1. Inspect the primary wiring, cap, rotor, and secondary wiring. Look for bad connections, frayed insulation, and grounds in the primary wiring. Look for brittleness, cracks, and carbon tracking in the secondary circuit. Make sure all secondary connections are fully pressed in. Correct any deficiencies. Bad wiring must be replaced. A distributor cap or rotor with no cracks and contacts that are still intact may be cleaned in soap and water to remove carbon tracks. Wiring that is wet may

be dried with a clean, dry rag or treated with a spray made especially for that purpose.

2. Crank the engine with the distributor cap removed and the high-tension lead to the distributor grounded. Check to see that the distributor turns and the points open and close. If the distributor shaft does not turn, the problem is in the drive gear at the lower end of the shaft, and the entire distributor assembly will have to be removed and repaired or replaced.

If the points are severely burned and pitted or they do not have an adequate gap (they should open visibly), remove them, clean them with a point file, and reinstall them. If they are in extremely bad shape, replace them. Repeated excessive burning in less than approximately 12,000 miles points to a faulty condenser or use of the wrong type of condenser. Replace the condenser, if necessary. It may be checked for a short by removing it, and connecting an ohmmeter's leads at the pigtail lead and to the body of the condenser, if malfunction is suspected. The resistance reading will be infinite if the condenser is usable. Points can also burn if the gap (or dwell) is improper, or if an oily gauge has been used to adjust them.

Check the fiber block on the contact points assembly for excessive wear. Excess wear is indicated if it is difficult to adjust the points for a proper gap upon reinstallation, as described below. Make sure the fiber block and cam have a light coating of clean, high-temperature grease. If they do not, clean and lubricate them carefully. If the fiber block is worn excessively in spite of proper lubrication, or if there is evidence that excessive wear is a problem (timing and dwell go out of adjustment, and the car goes out of tune rapidly), suspect distributor mechanical troubles. Carefully check the cam for roughness or scoring after wiping it clean if this type of problem is suspected. The shaft and bushing wear should also be tested by checking the play in the shaft with a dial indicator. Mechanical problems may also be detected on an electronic distributor tester.

Reinstall the ignition points in their proper position. Using a clean feeler gauge, adjust the position of the stationary contact with the fiber block on the high part of the distributor cam to the specified gap. Unless you are adjusting new points, it will be necessary to avoid contact with built-up material on one of the contact surfaces. A wire gauge may be of help but, in any case, the proper gap must be measured between two parallel surfaces that are neither pitted nor built up with transferred material.

D. Test for Voltage at Points with Points Open

When the distributor cam is in a position which will hold the points open, the ignition switch is on, and the electrical system is functioning normally in all other respects, there will be approximately 12 V all the way from the battery to the movable contact point. This may be checked by placing the positive probe of a voltmeter on the movable breaker arm and grounding the negative probe. Reverse the polarity for positive ground systems. A test lamp may also be connected between these two spots to make this check. If voltage is good at this point (there should be nearly 12 V if you are using a voltmeter) the primary circuit is in acceptable shape to produce a spark, in most cases, provided the ignition points are not too badly burned. If rotating the distributor until the points close causes the voltage to drop to zero, the points are in functional condition.

If the system passes these two tests, proceed to J. Otherwise, it will be necessary to perform the tests in E. through H. to track down the problem in the primary circuit.

E. Test for Voltage to Coil

Connect a voltmeter between the positive terminal of the coil and ground following the polarity of the battery. Make sure the ignition switch is turned on. If there is no voltage, jiggle the key, leaving the switch in the "on" position. If voltage appears only when the key is jiggled, the ignition switch is faulty. If jiggling the key has no effect, turn the key to the start position. If this produces voltage at the coil, the problem is most likely the resistor wire that carries current to the coil only when the switch is in the normal running position. If the oil and generator lights do not come on, the problem is most likely in the ignition switch or in the connections on the switch. The switch should be removed and checked for continuity with the internal mechanism set for the "on" position. A wiring diagram will indicate which terminal of the switch receives voltage from the battery and which terminals receive voltage when the switch is on. The connections and the wiring from the battery will have to be checked if the switch has continuity between the proper terminals.

F. Test for a Ground

Test for a ground in the coil or another component by disconnecting the lead or leads to the coil positive terminal. Test for voltage between each lead and ground. If neither lead is hot, the problem is in the wiring, resistor, or ignition switch, and you should go on to H.

The voltage test in the paragraph above was performed to locate the lead which supplies voltage to the coil while the ignition switch is in the normal running position. Connect an ammeter between that lead and the coil positive terminal. If there is no amperage, proceed to H. If there is amperage, go on to G.

G. Find the Ground

Reconnect the wires to the coil positive terminal. Disconnect the wire from the coil negative terminal and check for amperage between the terminal and disconnected lead. If there is no amperage, the coil is faulty because of an internal ground and should be replaced.

If there is amperage flowing from the coil to the rest of the system, then there is a ground in the coil-to-distributor wire, or in the points, the condenser or their wiring. Inspect the wires that lead to the points and condenser from the connection inside the distributor. Grounds frequently occur in these wires because they are twisted whenever the vacuum advance diaphragm changes the position of the mounting plate. Grounds will be evidenced by frayed and burned insulation at a spot where the wire contacts the body of the distributor.

If this test reveals no ground, check the condenser for a ground by removing its lead wire and checking for amperage between the connection on the end of the lead and the terminal on the inside of the distributor. If there is any amperage, the condenser is faulty and should be replaced.

If these tests have not located the ground, it is probably in the wire from the coil to the distributor at a spot where it touches metal; in the rubber grommet which carries the primary circuit through the wall of the distributor, in the insulated terminal on the contact points assembly, or in the hinge on the contact points. In most cases, close examination for burning should reveal the location of the problem. If not, testing for amperage as described below may help locate the ground.

Remove the lead from the coil where it connects to the contact point assembly. Test for amperage between the lead's connection and the terminal on the contact assembly. If there is no amperage, the ground must be in the grommet where the primary circuit passes through the distributor, or in the coil-to-distributor wire. Replacing these two parts, which are generally supplied as an assembly, should rectify the problem.

H. Test for Voltage

The tests above will have revealed whether or not there is voltage to the coil, and will have eliminated the possibility of a ground existing in the circuit. If there is voltage to the positive terminal of the coil, there is an open circuit between there and the ignition points. Otherwise, the problem must be between the ignition coil's positive terminal and the battery.

Proceed in the appropriate direction from the coil positive terminal, checking for voltage at each connection. The faulty component is between a hot connection and a dead one. For example, if voltage exists at the coil positive terminal, but not at the negative terminal of the coil, the coil must be faulty. Before replacing a component, it might be wise to check it for continuity with an ohmmeter. This will eliminate the chance of mistaking a bad connection for a faulty component. Wiring should have very low resistance (but not zero), and the coil should behave as in K. Keep a sharp eye open for bad connections. Any connection which is dirty, corroded, loose, or burned should be cleaned and tightened.

J. Check Coil Polarity

While a coil that is connected backward will still produce a spark, weakened ignition system performance will result from improper polarity. If the top of the coil indicates positive and negative terminals, the polarity can be checked visually. The wire coming from the ignition switch should be the same polarity (positive or negative) as the wire going from the battery to the starter, while the coil-to-distributor wire should be the same polarity as the battery ground. If the coil is unmarked, remove the high-tension lead from the coil tower, contact the metal portion of the coil tower with the positive lead of a voltmeter, and ground the voltmeter's negative lead. Crank the engine until a spark is produced. The spark should move the voltmeter's needle downscale. Otherwise, reverse the leads to the coil.

K. Check Coil Primary Resistance

A weak spark or no spark at all can occur because of an open circuit or ground in either circuit of the coil. The coil can have a very small short or ground which might not show up in general primary system testing but which would have a significant effect on primary circuit resistance.

Disconnect wiring to both primary terminals of the coil. Connect an ohmmeter to the primary circuit—one lead to each primary terminal. The resistance of the coil will depend on whether or not it uses an external ballast resistor. Most coils are externally resisted to permit full battery voltage to be used during cranking. If there are two wires to the positive terminal of the coil, this is a sure sign that the coil is externally resisted. A small component wired in series with the coil in the wire to the positive terminal is another sure sign.

Coils that are externally resisted should have a resistance of approximately 1.0 ohms. Coils that have no external resistor should have about 4.0 ohms resistance. If the resistance is greatly above this figure, or zero (infinite) resistance is indicated, the coil must be replaced.

L. Check Coil Secondary Resistance

Even if the primary circuit checks out as in K, the coil could be faulty. With the primary leads disconnected, attach an ohmmeter across the secondary circuit of the coil to check for a short or open secondary winding. One proble should go to the metal connector inside the coil tower, while the other *must* go to the positive terminal of the primary circuit. The negative side cannot be used because the secondary is not connected to that side of the primary winding. The resistance should be between approximately 4,000 and 10,000 ohms. These figures are typical of normal-duty coils, but do not apply to heavy-duty equipment. If the resistance is much higher or lower than this, or if it reads zero, replace the coil.

The coil tower should also be checked very carefully for evidence of cracked or burned plastic, or burned metal in the connector inside the tower. Evidence of damage here indicates that the coil should be replaced. If the only burned spot is on the metal conductor, it may be sanded and the coil may be reused, provided the metal is not burned through and a smooth surface can be created.

In cases of coil tower damage, the coil-to-distributor high-tension lead must either be replaced or very carefully checked for burned connectors. If the surface can be smoothed by sanding, the lead may be reused. Use of a bad lead with a new coil can cause recurrence of the burning problem.

M. Inspect Rotor and Cap

The cap must be gone over with a fine tooth comb to properly check its condition. First, if there is any evidence of carbon, clean the cap carefully in a mild detergent and water solution. After a thorough drying, inspect it very carefully, looking for the following:

1. Looseness of any of the terminals.
2. Excessive burning of any of the terminals.
3. Hairline cracks due to breakage or prolonged arcing.
4. Failure of the spring to push a button type center contact firmly downward.

If the cap is serviceable, sand away any roughness on any of the contacts before reusing it.

Inspect the rotor for any signs of burning, cracking, or breakage. If it uses a spring type of pick-up to contact the carbon button in the center of the cap, make sure there is sufficient tension in the spring for firm contact, bending the pick-up slightly, if necessary. Make sure the contact at the outer end of the rotor is in good condition and will come within about $3/16$ in. of the inner surfaces of the terminals in the cap. If the contact surface cannot be smoothed by sanding, replace the rotor.

N. Inspect Secondary Wiring and Check its Resistance

Inspect all wiring for badly burned connectors, brittleness, or cracks, and replace if any such wear is found. Remove slight burning or roughness with sandpaper.

Connect the probes of an ammeter to either end of each wire to check resistance. It should be approximately 8,000 ohms per foot. Replace high-resistance wire. This, of course, includes wire that shows zero resistance, indicating a completely open circuit.

O. Clean and Gap the Spark Plugs

Badly burned spark plugs can cause misfiring, poor gas mileage, and difficult starting. Clean any carbon and lead deposits off both electrodes so a good inspection can be made. A relatively soft wire brush is the best tool for this job and is available as a part of many combination feeler gauge and spark plug tools.

The side electrode should be square and uniform in shape along its entire length and should extend well over the center of the center electrode. Burning will shorten this electrode and round it off near the free end. The center electrode should be uniform in diameter (not burned thinner near the top) and should form a relatively flat surface under the side electrode. A very round top surface, or only slight extension above the insulator, indicates extreme burning. The insulator should be smooth and round, entirely free of cracks, and tightly molded in place. If shaking the plug up and down causes the insulator to move up and down, it is severely damaged. Replace plugs which show any evidence of burning or damaged insulators.

The outer insulator should also be inspected for cracks after a thorough cleaning. Any evidence of cracking or arcing here means the plug is defective.

If the plugs are severely burned, the problem is usually one of the four below:

1. Improper torquing in the head, meaning poor cooling.
2. Use of a plug of too high a heat range.
3. Advance ignition timing, or lean carburetion.
4. Extremely prolonged use.

See the section on correcting poor engine operation for additional information.

If the plugs are in good condition, they may be reused if they are thoroughly cleaned and properly gapped to the manufacturer's specifications. A wire feeler gauge must be used to set the gap. The gap is correct when a slight pull is required to free the gauge from between the two electrodes. Bend the side electrode only when closing or opening the gap, using a spark plug tool. The gap should be set according to the manufacturer's specifications, which can be found on the sticker under the hood on post-1967 cars. Reinstall the plugs.

P. Adjust Timing and Dwell

The dwell angle is the amount of time, measured in degrees of distributor shaft rotation, that the contact points remain closed. Dwell angle is an indirect measurement of point gap. Increasing the point gap will decrease the dwell angle, as the cam will then separate the points earlier and allow them to close later. Decreasing the point gap will increase the dwell angle as the points will then be in contact with the distributor cam for a shorter period of time.

Ignition timing refers to the point in the rotation of the engine when ignition occurs. It is measured in degrees of crankshaft rotation in relation to TDC in number one cylinder when the cylinder is on the compression stroke. Timing is generally set at an engine speed which requires no centrifugal or vacuum advance, although in some cases vacuum retarding action is in effect.

The dwell angle *must* be set before the timing is adjusted and must *never* be disturbed unless timing is reset immediately thereafter. While ignition timing has no effect on dwell angle, a dwell change will affect timing because the distributor cam will separate the points at a different point in the rotation of the distributor shaft after the dwell adjustment.

Adjust timing and dwell as follows:

1. Connect a dwell-tach to the ignition system with the engine off. The negative or black clip goes to a good ground, while the positive or red clip should be attached to the negative (distributor) terminal of the coil primary circuit.

2. Make sure the wires are away from the fan and other engine auxiliaries. Start the engine and place it in or out of gear, as the manufacturer recommends on the engine compartment sticker or in a manual. If setting the timing requires disconnecting the vacuum lines, etc., perform these operations before setting the dwell. Switch the dwell tach to the tachometer function and to the proper setting for the number of cylinders in the engine. Making sure you are reading the right scale, check to see if the idle speed is as specified for setting the timing. Dwell should be set at this speed because some distributors on late-model cars change their dwell settings as rpm changes. Adjust the idle speed if it is not as specified.

3. Switch the dwell-tach over to the dwell function and read the dwell angle. If the dwell is outside the range specified by the manufacturer, adjust it.

4. Readjust the dwell, increasing the point gap if the dwell angle is too large, and decreasing it if the angle is too small. On some distributors, this may be done with an allen wrench through a window in the side of the distributor while the engine is running.

5. Turn off the engine and locate number one (no. 1) cylinder. Most engine blocks (or intake manifolds) are marked. Number one cylinder is usually the front one on inline engines, or the right front one on V8 engines. The timing light is usually connected by inserting a high-tension connection between the no. 1 plug and its wire and then connecting two 12 V leads to the battery—red to positive; black to negative. Making sure that no wires are near the fan, start the engine and, if necessary, put the transmission in gear.

6. Aim the timing light at the pulley on the front of the engine. The timing mark, which is usually a groove in the outer flange of the pulley, should be visible each time the timing light flashes. It may be necessary to stop the engine and mark the groove with chalk if visibility is poor.

7. Line up the timing mark with the scale, pointer, or mark on the engine. If necessary, loosen the distributor locking bolt and turn it until the pulley mark aligns with the proper mark on the engine. (Check the manufacturer's specifications.) Tighten the locking bolt and recheck the timing before shutting off the engine.

Electronic Ignition Systems

BASIC OPERATING PRINCIPLES

Electronic Ignition systems are not as complicated as they may first appear. In actual fact, they differ only slightly from conventional ignition systems. Like conventional ignition systems, electronic systems have two circuits: a primary circuit, and a secondary circuit. *The entire secondary circuit is exactly the same as the secondary circuit in a conventional ignition system. Also, the section of the primary circuit from the battery to the BAT terminal at the coil is exactly the same as a conventional ignition system.*

Electronic ignition systems differ from conventional ignition systems in the distributor component area. Instead of a distributor cam, breaker plate, points, and condenser, an electronic ignition system has an armature (called variously a trigger wheel, reluctor, etc.), a pickup coil (stator, sensor, etc), and an electronic control module. Essentially, all electronic ignition systems operate in the following manner:

With the ignition switch turned on, primary (battery) current flows from the battery through the ignition switch to the coil primary windings. Primary current is turned on and off by the action of the armature as it revolves

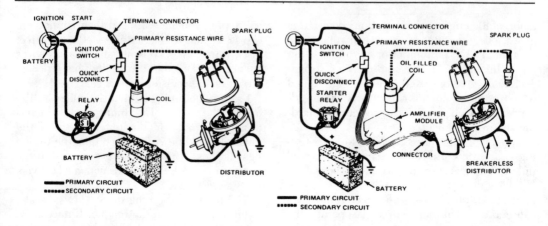

CONVENTIONAL   BREAKERLESS

Conventional ignition vs. solid-state ignition

the armature nears the pickup coil, it induces a voltage which signals the electronic module to turn off the coil primary current. A timing circuit in the module will turn the current on again after the coil field has collapsed. When the current is off, however, the magnetic field built up in the coil is allowed to collapse, inducing a high voltage in the secondary windings of the coil. It is now operating on the secondary ignition circuit, which, as noted, is exactly the same as a conventional ignition system.

Troubleshooting electronic ignition systems ordinarily requires the use of a voltmeter and/or an ohmmeter. Sometimes the use of an ammeter is required also. Because of differences is design and construction, troubleshooting is specific to each system. Due to space limitations, only the most common systems are covered here.

General Motors High Energy Ignition (HEI) System

The General Motors HEI system is a pulse-triggered, transistored-controlled, inductive discharge ignition system. Except on inline four- and six-cylinder models, the entire HEI system is contained within the distributor cap. Inline six-cylinder engines and all four-cylinders have an external coil. Otherwise, the systems are the same.

The distributor in addition to housing the mechanical and vacuum advance mechanisms,

contains the ignition coil (except on four and inline six engines), the electronic control module, and the magnetic triggering device. The magnetic pick-up assembly contains a permanent magnet, a pole piece with internal "teeth," and a pick-up coil (not to be confused with the ignition coil).

In the HEI system, as in other electronic ignition systems, the breaker points have been replaced with an electronic switch—a transistor—which is located *within* the control module. This switching transistor performs the same function the points did in a conventional ignition system; it simply turns coil primary current on and off at the correct time.

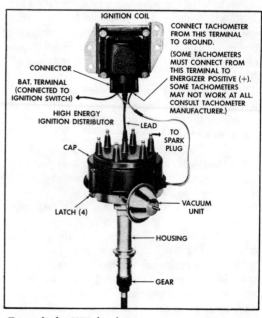

Four cylinder HEI distributor

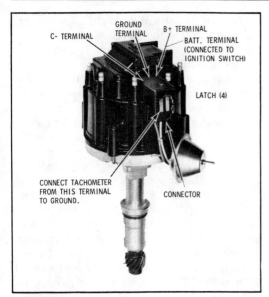

V6 and V8 HEI distributor

Essentially then, electronic and conventional ignition systems operate on the same principle.

The module which houses the switching transistor is controlled (turned on and off) by a magnetically generated impulse induced in the pick-up coil. When the teeth of the rotating timer align with the teeth of the pole piece, the induced voltage in the pick-up coil signals the electronic module to open the coil primary circuit. The primary current then decreases, and a high voltage is induced in the ignition coil secondary windings which is then directed through the rotor and high voltage leads (spark plug wires) to fire the spark plugs.

In essence then, the pick-up coil module system simply replaces the conventional breaker points and condenser. The condenser found within the distributor is for radio suppression purposes only and has nothing to do

HEI distributor showing module (arrow)

with the ignition process. The module automatically controls the dwell period, increasing it with increasing engine speed. Since dwell is automatically controlled, it cannot be adjusted. The module itself is non-adjustable and non-repairable and must be replaced if found defective.

HEI System Precautions

Before going on to troubleshooting, it might be a good idea to take note of the following precautions:

TIMING LIGHT USE

Inductive pick-up timing lights are the best kind to use if your car is equipped with HEI. Timing lights which connect between the spark plug and the spark plug wire occasionally (not always) give false readings.

SPARK PLUG WIRES

The plug wires used with HEI systems are of a different construction than conventional wires. When replacing them, make sure you get the correct wires, since conventional wires won't carry the voltage. Also, handle them carefully to avoid cracking or splitting them and *never* pierce them.

TACHOMETER USE

Not all tachometers will operate or indicate correctly when used on a HEI system. While some tachometers may give a reading, this does not necessarily mean the reading is correct. In addition, some tachometers hook up differently from others. If you can't figure out whether or not your tachometer will work on your car, check with the tachometer manufacturer. Dwell readings, of course, have no significance at all.

HEI SYSTEM TESTERS

Instruments designed specifically for testing HEI systems are available from several tool manufacturers. Some of these will even test the module itself. However, the tests given in the following section will require only an ohmmeter and a voltmeter.

HEI SYSTEM TACHOMETER HOOKUP

There is a terminal marked TACH on the side of the V8 HEI distributor. Connect one tachometer lead to this terminal and the other to ground. On some tachometers, the leads must be connected to the Tach terminal and the battery positive terminal. The hookup is the same for the six cylinder HEI system, ex-

HEI distributor showing TACH terminal (arrow)

cept that the TACH terminal is opposite the BAT terminal on the connector plug on the remote-mounted coil.

CAUTION: *Never ground the TACH terminal; serious system damage will result. If there is any doubt as to the correct tachometer hookup, check with the tachometer manufacturer.*

TROUBLESHOOTING THE HEI SYSTEM

The symptoms of a defective component within the HEI system are exactly the same as those you would encounter in a conventional system. Some of these symptoms are:

Hard or no Starting
Rough Idle
Poor Fuel Economy
Engine misses under load or while accelerating

If you suspect a problem in your ignition system, there are certain preliminary checks which you should carry out before you begin to check the electronic portions of the system. First, it is extremely important to make sure the vehicle battery is in a good state of charge. A defective or poorly charged battery will cause the various components of the ignition system to read incorrectly when they are being tested. Second, make sure all wiring connections are clean and tight, not only at

the battery, but also at the distributor cap, ignition coil, and at the electronic control module.

Since the only change between electronic and conventional ignition systems is in the distributor component area, it is imperative to check the secondary ignition circuit first. If the secondary circuit checks out properly, then the engine condition is probably not the fault of the ignition system. To check the secondary ignition system, perform a simple spark test. Remove one of the plug wires and insert some sort of extension in the plug socket. An old spark plug with the ground electrode removed makes a good extension. Hold the wire and extension about ¼ in. away from the block and crank the engine. If a normal spark occurs, then the problem is most likely *not* in the ignition system. Check for fuel system problems, or fouled spark plugs.

If, however, there is no spark or a weak spark, then further ignition system testing will have to be done. Troubleshooting techniques fall into two categories, depending on the nature of the problem. The categories are (1) Engine cranks, but won't start or (2) Engine runs, but runs rough or cuts out. To begin with, let's consider the first case.

Engine Fails to Start

If the engine won't start, perform a spark test as described earlier. This will narrow the problem area down considerably. If no spark occurs, check for the presence of normal battery voltage at the battery (BAT) terminal in the distributor cap. The ignition switch must be in the "on" position for this test. Either a voltmeter or a test light may be used for this test. Connect the test light wire to ground and the probe end to the BAT terminal at the distributor. If the light comes on, you have voltage to the distributor. If the light fails to come on, this indicates an open circuit in the ignition primary wiring leading to the distributor. In this case, you will have to check wiring continuity back to the ignition switch using a test light. If there is battery voltage at the BAT terminal, but no spark at the plugs, then the problem lies within the distributor assembly. Go on to the distributor components test section.

Engine Runs, But Runs Rough or Cuts Out

1. Make sure the plug wires are in good shape first. There should be no obvious cracks or breaks. You can check the plug wires with

HEI Plug Wire Resistance Chart

Wire Length	Minimum	Maximum
0–15 inches	3000 ohms	10,000 ohms
15–25 inches	4000 ohms	15,000 ohms
25–35 inches	6000 ohms	20,000 ohms
Over 35 inches		25,000 ohms

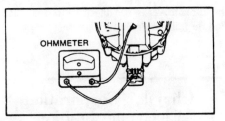

Checking coil secondary resistance

an ohmmeter, but *do not* pierce the wires with a probe. Check the chart for the correct plug wire resistance.

2. If the plug wires are OK, remove the cap assembly, and check for moisture, cracks, chips, or carbon tracks, or any other high voltage leaks or failures. Replace the cap if you find any defects. Make sure the timer wheel rotates when the engine is cranked. If everything is all right so far, go on to the distributor components test section.

Distributor Components Testing

If the trouble has been narrowed down to the units within the distributor, the following tests can help pinpoint the defective component. An ohmmeter with both high and low ranges should be used. These tests are made with the cap assembly removed and the battery wire disconnected.

1. Connect an ohmmeter between the Tach and Bat terminals in the distributor cap. The primary coil resistance should be less than one ohm.

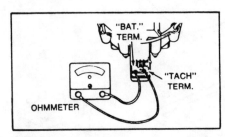

Checking coil primary resistance

2. To check the coil secondary resistance, connect an ohmmeter between the rotor button and either the BAT or Tach terminals. The resistance should be between 6,000 and 30,000 ohms.

3. Replace the coil *only* if the readings in step one and two are infinite.

NOTE: *These resistance checks will not disclose shorted coil windings. This condition can only be detected with scope analysis or a suitably designed coil tester. If these in-*

struments are unavailable, replace the coil with a known good coil as a final coil test.

4. To test the pick-up coil, first disconnect the white and green module leads. Set the ohmmeter on the high scale and connect it between a ground and either the white or green lead. Any resistance measurement *less* than infinity requires replacement of the pick-up coil.

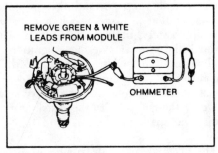

Testing pickup coil (step 4)

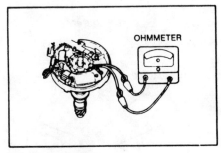

Checking pickup coil continuity

5. Pick-up coil continuity is tested by connecting the ohmmeter (on low range) between the white and green leads. Normal resistance is between 650 and 850 ohms. Move the vacuum advance arm while performing this test. This will detect any break in coil continuity. Such a condition can cause intermittent misfiring. Replace the pick-up coil if the reading is outside the specified limits.

6. If no defects have been found at this time, and you still have a problem, then the module will have to be checked. If you do not have access to a module tester, the only possi-

ble alternative is a substitution test. If the module fails the substitution test, replace it.

Chrysler Corporation Electronic Ignition

BASIC OPERATING PRINCIPLES

Chrysler Corporation has been using this system on all of its cars since 1973. The system consists of a magnetic pulse distributor, electronic control unit, dual element ballast resistor, and special ignition coil. The distributor outwardly resembles a standard breaker point unit, but is internally quite different. The usual breaker points, cam, and condenser are replaced with a reluctor and pick-up unit.

The ignition primary circuit is connected from the battery, through the ignition switch, through the primary side of the ignition coil, to the control unit where it is grounded. The secondary circuit is the same as in a conventional ignition system: the secondary side of the coil, the coil wire to the distributor, the rotor, the spark plug wires, and the spark plugs.

The magnetic pulse distributor is also connected to the control unit. As the distributor

Top view—Electronic Ignition System distributor

shaft turns, the reluctor rotates past the pick-up unit. As the relector turns by the pick-up unit, each of the six or eight teeth on the reluctor pass near the pick-up unit once during each distributor revolution (two crankshaft revolutions since the distributor turns at one half crankshaft speed). As the reluctor teeth move close to the pick-up unit, the rotating reluctor induces voltage into the magnetic pick-up unit. When the pulse enters the control unit, it signals the control unit to interrupt the ignition primary circuit. This causes the

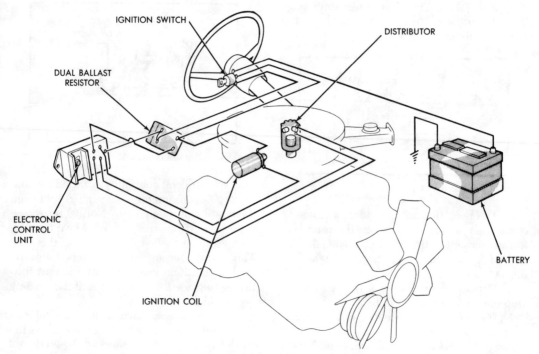

Chrysler Corporation electronic ignition schematic

HEAT SINK   TRANSISTOR   HARNESS PLUG

Electronic control unit. Don't touch it when the ignition is on, unless you want a healthy shock.

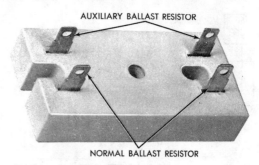

AUXILIARY BALLAST RESISTOR

NORMAL BALLAST RESISTOR

Dual ballast resistor

primary circuit to collapse and begins the induction of the magnetic lines of force from the primary side of the coil into the secondary side of the coil. This induction provides the required voltage to fire the spark plugs.

The advantages of this system are that the transistors in the control unit can make or break the primary ignition circuit much faster than the conventional ignition points can, and higher primary voltage can be utilized, since this system can be made to handle higher voltage without adverse effects, where standard breaker points would quickly burn. The quicker switching time of this system allows longer coil primary circuit saturation time and longer induction time when the primary circuit collapses. This increased time allows the primary circuit to build up more current and the secondary circuit to discharge more current.

TROUBLESHOOTING CHRYSLER CORPORATION ELECTRONIC IGNITION

A voltmeter with a 20,000 ohm/volt rating and a 1½ volt battery powered ohmmeter are required. Car battery voltage must be at least 12 volts.

1. Remove the wiring plug from the control unit.

CAUTION: *Make sure the ignition switch is off when removing or replacing the control unit connector.*

2. Turn the ignition switch on.

3. Ground the negative voltmeter lead.

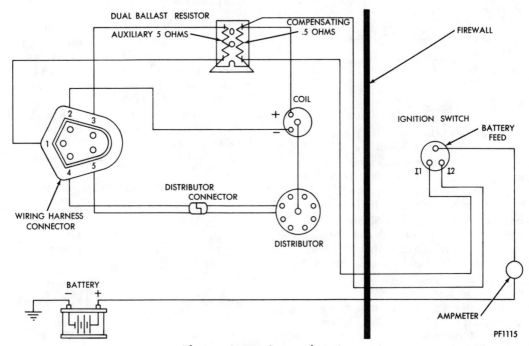

Electronic Ignition System schematic

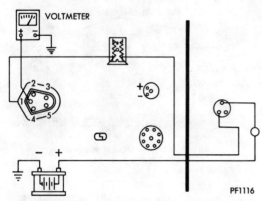

Testing cavity number one

PF1116

4. Connect the voltmeter positive lead to the harness connector cavity No. 1 (shown on the schematic). Voltage should be within 1 volt of battery voltage with all accessories off. If not, check the circuit through to the battery.

5. Connect the voltmeter positive lead to cavity No. 2. Voltage should be within 1 volt of battery voltage with all accessories off. If not, check the circuit through to the battery.

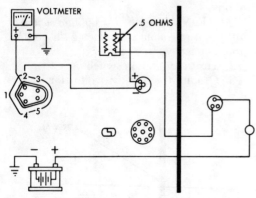

Testing cavity number two

6. Connect the voltmeter positive lead to cavity No. 3. Voltage should be within 1 volt of battery voltage with all accessories off. If not, check the circuit through to the battery.

7. Turn the ignition switch off.

8. Connect the ohmmeter leads to cavities No. 4 and 5. The resistance should be 150–900 ohms. If it isn't, detach the dual lead connector from the distributor. Check the resistance at the dual lead connector. If it still isn't within the range, replace the distributor pick-up coil.

9. Connect one ohmmeter lead to a ground and the other to either distributor connector. If the ohmmeter shows a reading, replace the distributor pick-up coil.

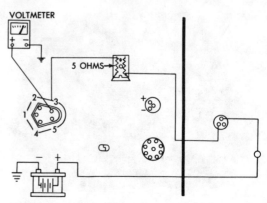

Testing cavity number three

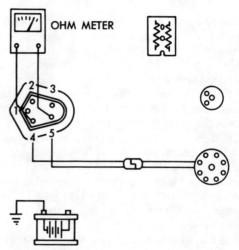

Testing pickup coil

10. Connect one ohmmeter lead to a ground and the other to the control unit pin No. 5. The ohmmeter should show continuity. If not, remove and remount the control unit and check again. Replace the control unit if no continuity can be established.

11. Make sure the ignition switch is off and replace the control unit connector plug and the distributor plug.

12. Check the air gap adjustment, as shown in the chart.

13. Remove the center wire from the dis-

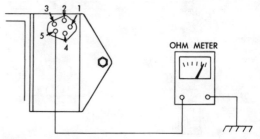

Testing cavity number five

tributor cap. Very cautiously, using insulated pliers and a very heavy glove, hold the cable about ³/₁₆ in. from the engine block and have the starter operated. If there is no spark, replace the control unit. Try the test again. If there is still no spark, replace the coil.

Troubleshooting Electronic Ignition

Condition	Possible Cause	Correction
ENGINE WILL NOT START (Fuel and carburetion known to be OK)	a) Dual Ballast Resistor	Check resistance of each section: Compensating resistance: .50–.60 ohms @ 70°–80° F Auxiliary Ballast: 4.75–5.75 ohms Replace if faulty. Check wire positions.
	b) Faulty Ignition Coil	Check for carbonized tower. Check primary and secondary resistances: Primary: 1.41–1.79 ohms @ 70°–80° F Secondary: 9,200–11,700 ohms @ 70°–80° F Check in coil tester.
	c) Faulty Pickup or Improper Pickup Air Gap	Check pickup coil resistance: 400–600 ohms Check pickup gap: .010 in. (.008 in. 1977 and later) *nonmagnetic* feeler gauge should not slip between pickup coil core and an aligned reluctor blade. No evidence of pickup core striking reluctor blades should be visible. To reset gap, tighten pickup adjustment screw with a .008 in. (.006 in. 1977 and later) *nonmagnetic* feeler gauge held between pickup core and an aligned reluctor blade. NOTE: *Lean-Burn engines through 1977 have 2 pickup air gaps. Gap is .008 in. for the "start" gap and .012 in. for the "run" gap.*

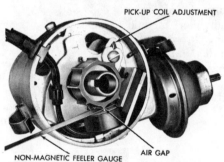

PICK-UP COIL ADJUSTMENT

NON-MAGNETIC FEELER GAUGE   AIR GAP

Condition	Possible Cause	Correction
	d) Faulty Wiring	Visually inspect wiring for brittle insulation. Inspect connectors. Molded connectors should be inspected for rubber inside female terminals.
	e) Faulty Control Unit	Replace if all of the above checks are negative. Whenever the control unit or dual ballast is replaced, make sure the dual ballast wires are correctly inserted in the keyed molded connector.
ENGINE SURGES SEVERELY (Not Lean Carburetor)	a) Wiring	Inspect for loose connection and/or broken conductors in harness.
	b) Faulty Pickup Leads	Disconnect vacuum advance. If surging stops, replace pickup.
	c) Ignition Coil	Check for intermittent primary.
ENGINE MISSES (Carburetion OK)	a) Spark Plugs	Check plugs. Clean and regap if necessary.
	b) Secondary Cable	Check cables with an ohmmeter.
	c) Ignition Coil	Check for carbonized tower. Check in coil tester.
	d) Wiring	Check for loose or dirty connections.
	e) Faulty Pickup Lead	Disconnect vacuum advance. If miss stops, replace pickup.
	f) Control Unit	Replace if the above checks are negative.

Ford Motor Company Solid-State Ignition

BASIC OPERATING PRINCIPLES

In mid 1974, Ford Motor Company introduced in selected models its new Solid-State Ignition System. In 1975, it became standard equipment on all cars in the Ford lineup. This system was designed primarily to provide a hotter spark necessary to fire the leaner fuel/air mixtures required by today's emission control standards.

The Ford Solid-State Ignition is a pulse-triggered, transistor controlled breakerless ignition system. With the ignition switch "On", the primary circuit is On and the ignition coil is energized. When the armature spokes approach the magnetic pick-up coil assembly, they induce a voltage which tells the amplifier to turn the coil primary current Off. A timing circuit in the amplifier module will turn the current on again after the coil field has collapsed. When the current is On, it flows from the battery through the ignition switch, the primary windings of the ignition coil, and through the amplifier module circuits to ground. When the current is off, the magnetic field built up in the ignition coil is allowed to collapse, inducing a high voltage into the secondary windings of the coil. High voltage is produced each time the field is thus built up and collapsed.

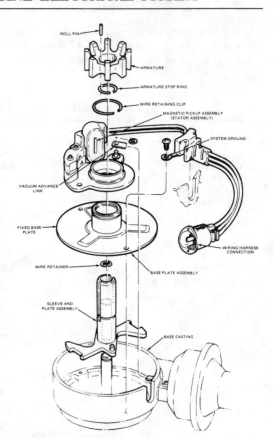

Breakerless distributor disassembled

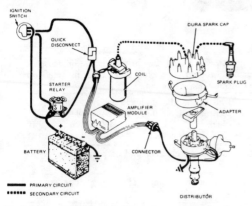

Ford Motor Company Solid-State Ignition schematic

Although the systems are basically the same, Ford refers to their solid-state ignition in several different ways. 1974–76 systems are referred to simply as Breakerless systems. In 1977, Ford named their ignition system Dura-Spark I and Dura-Spark II. Dura-Spark II is the version used in all states except California. Dura-Spark I is the system used in California V8's only. Basically, the only difference between the two is that the coil charging currents are higher in the California cars. This is necessary to fire the leaner fuel/air mixtures required by California's stricter emission laws. The difference in coils alters some of the test values.

Ford has used several different types of wiring harness on their solid-state ignition systems, due to internal circuitry changes in the electronic module. Wire continuity and color have not been changed, but the arrangement of the terminals in the connectors is different for each year. Schematics of the different years are included here, but keep in mind that the wiring in all diagrams has been simplified and as a result, the routing of your wiring may not match the wiring in the diagram. However, the wire colors and terminal connections are the same.

Wire color-coding is critical to servicing the Ford Solid-State Ignition. Battery current reaches the electronic module through either the *white* or *red* wire, depending on whether the engine is cranking or running. When the

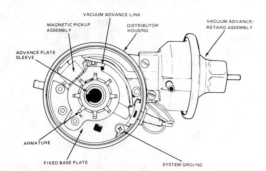

Top view—solid-state distributor

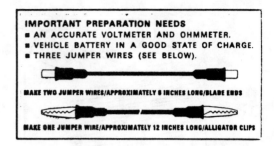

IMPORTANT PREPARATION NEEDS
- AN ACCURATE VOLTMETER AND OHMMETER.
- VEHICLE BATTERY IN A GOOD STATE OF CHARGE.
- THREE JUMPER WIRES (SEE BELOW).

MAKE TWO JUMPER WIRES/APPROXIMATELY 6 INCHES LONG/BLADE ENDS

MAKE ONE JUMPER WIRE/APPROXIMATELY 12 INCHES LONG/ALLIGATOR CLIPS

engine is cranking, battery current is flowing through the *white* wire. When the engine is running, battery current flows through the *red* wire. All distributor signals flow through the *orange* and *purple* wires. The *green* wire carries primary current from the coil to the module. The *black* wire is a ground between the distributor and the module. Up until 1975, a *blue*, wire provides transient voltage protection. In 1976, the *blue* wire was dropped when a zener diode was added to the module. The *orange* and *purple* wires which run from the stator to the module must *always* be connected to the same color wire at the module. If these connections are crossed, polarity will be reversed and the system will be thrown out of phase. Some replacement wiring harnesses were sold with the wiring crossed, which complicates the problem considerably. As previously noted, the *black* wire is the ground wire. The screw which grounds the black wire also, of course, grounds the entire primary circuit. If this screw is loose, dirty, or corroded, a seemingly incomprehensible ignition problem will develop. Several other cautions should be noted here. Keep in mind that on vehicles equipped with catalytic converters, any test that requires removal of a spark plug wire while the engine is running should be kept to a thirty second maximum. Any longer than this may damage the converter. In the event you are testing spark plug wires, do not pierce them. Test the wires at their terminals only.

TROUBLESHOOTING THE FORD SOLID-STATE IGNITION SYSTEM

This system, which at first appears to be extremely complicated, is actually quite simple to diagnose and repair. Diagnosis does, however, require the use of a voltmeter and an ohmmeter. You will also need several jumper wires with both blade ends and alligator clips.

The symptoms of a defective component within the solid state system are exactly the same as those you would encounter in a conventional system. Some of these symptoms are:

Hard or no starting

Rough Idle

Poor fuel economy

Engine misses while under load or while accelerating

If you suspect a problem in your ignition system, first perform a spark intensity test to pinpoint the problem. Using insulated pliers, hold the end of one of the spark plug leads about ½ in. away from the engine block or other good ground, and crank the engine. If you have a nice, fat spark, then your problem is not in the ignition system. If you have no spark or a very weak spark, then proceed to the following tests.

Stator Test

To test the stator (also known as the magnetic pickup assembly), you will need an ohmmeter. Run the engine until it reaches operating temperature, then turn the ignition switch to the "Off" position. Disconnect the wire harness from the distributor. Connect the ohmmeter between the orange and purple wires. Resistance should be between 400 and 800 ohms. Next, connect the ohmmeter between the black wire and a good ground on the engine. Operate the vacuum advance, either by hand or with an external vacuum source. Resistance should be zero ohms. Finally, connect the ohmmeter between the orange wire and ground, and then the purple wire and ground. Resistance should be over 70,000 ohms in both cases. If any of your ohmmeter readings differ from the above specifications, then the stator is defective and must be replaced as a unit.

If the stator is good, then either the electronic module or the wiring connections must be checked next. Because of its complicated electronic nature, the module itself cannot be checked, except by substitution. If you have access to a module which you know to be

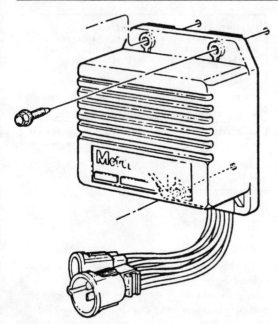

Electronic module. Don't make any tests at the module side of the connectors.

good, then perform a substitution test at this time. If this cures the problem, then the original module is faulty and must be replaced. If it does not cure the problem or if you cannot locate a known-good module, then disconnect the two wiring harnesses from the module, and, using a voltmeter, check the following circuits:

NOTE: *Make no tests at the module side of the connectors.*

1. Starting circuit—Connect the voltmeter leads to ground and to the corresponding female socket of the white male lead from the module (you will need a jumper wire with a blade end). Crank the engine over. The voltage should be between 8 and 12 volts.

2. Running circuit—Turn the ignition switch to the "On" position. Connect the volt-meter leads to ground and the corresponding female socket of the red male lead from the module. Voltage should be battery voltage plus or minus 0.1 volts.

3. Coil circuit—Leave the ignition switch "On." Connect the voltmeter leads to ground and to the corresponding female socket of the green male lead from the module. Voltage should be battery voltage plus or minus 0.1 volts.

If any of the preceding readings are incorrect, inspect and repair any loose, broken, frayed or dirty connections. If this doesn't solve the problem, perform a battery source test.

Battery Source Test

To make this test, *do not* disconnect the coil. Connect the voltmeter leads to the BAT terminal at the coil and a good ground. Connect a jumper wire from the DEC terminal at the coil to a good ground. Make sure all lights and accessories are off. Turn the ignition to the "On" position. Check the voltage. If the voltage is below 4.9 volts (11 volts for Dura-Spark I), then check the primary wiring for broken strands, cracked or frayed wires, or loose or dirty terminals. Repair or replace any defects. If, however, the voltage is above 7.9 volts (14 volts for Dura-Spark I), then you have a problem in the resistance wiring and it must be replaced.

It should be noted here that if you do have a problem in your electronic ignition system, most of the time it will be a case of loose, dirty or frayed wires. The electronic module, being completely solid-state, is not ordinarily subject to failure. It is possible for the unit to fail, of course, but as a general rule, the source of an ignition system problem will be somewhere else in the circuit.

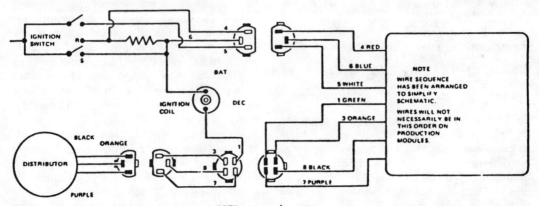

1975 wiring schematic

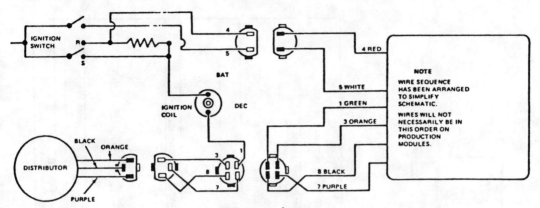

1976 wiring schematic

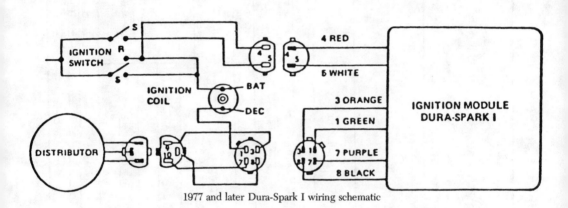

1977 and later Dura-Spark I wiring schematic

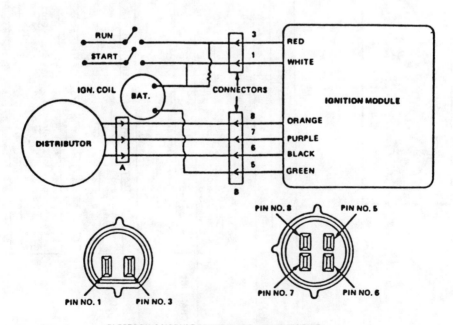

ELECTRONIC MODULE CONNECTORS – HARNESS SIDE

1977 and later Dura-Spark II wiring schematic

1974–76 Test Sequence

1974 CONNECTORS   1975 CONNECTORS   1976 CONNECTORS

Connector changes

IGNITION SWITCH POSITION	TEST VOLTAGE BETWEEN 1974	1975	1976	SHOULD BE	IF READING IS INCORRECT —
KEY ON	Ignition Coil Bat. Terminal and Engine Ground (Module Connected)			4.9 to 7.9 Volts	Less than Spec. — Check Primary Wiring. More than Spec. — Check Resistance Wire.
	Socket #3 and Engine Grd.	Socket #4 and Engine Grd.	Socket #4 and Engine Grd.	Battery Voltage ± 0.1 Volts	Check Supply Wire and Connectors Through Ignition Switch.
	Socket #5 and Engine Grd.	Socket #1 and Engine Grd.	Socket #1 and Engine Grd.	Battery Voltage ± 0.1 Volts	Check Wire to Ignition Coil and/or Ignition Coil.
CRANKING	Socket #1 and Engine Grd.	Socket #5 and Engine Grd.	Socket #5 and Engine Grd.	8 to 12 Volts	Check Supply Wire and Connectors Through Ignition Switch.
	Socket #5 and Engine Grd.	Socket #6 and Engine Grd.	Socket #1 and Engine Grd.	8 to 12 Volts	Check Solenoid By-Pass Circuit.
	Socket #7 and Socket #8	Socket #7 and Socket #3	Socket #7 and Socket #3	½ Volt Minimum A.C. or any D.C. Volt Variation	Perform Hardware Test (See Below)

IGNITION SWITCH POSITION	TEST RESISTANCE BETWEEN 1974	1975	1976	SHOULD BE	IF READING IS INCORRECT —
KEY OFF	Socket #7 and Socket #8	Socket #7 and Socket #3	Socket #7 and Socket #3	400 to 800 Ohms	If Any Test Fails, First Check for Defective Harness to Distributor.
	Socket #6 and Engine Grd.	Socket #8 and Engine Grd.	Socket #8 and Engine Grd.	0 Ohm	
	Socket #7 and Engine Grd.	Socket #7 and Engine Grd.	Socket #7 and Engine Grd.	70,000 Ohms or More	If Harness Checks Good, Distributor Stator Assembly Must be Replaced.
	Socket #8 and Engine Grd.	Socket #3 and Engine Grd.	Socket #3 and Engine Grd.	70,000 Ohms or More	
	Socket #3 and Coil Tower	Socket #4 and Coil Tower	Socket #4 and Coil Tower	7,000 to 13,000 Ohms	Check Coil on Coil Tester.
	Ignition Coil Primary Terminals			1.0 to 2.0 Ohms	Check Coil on Coil Tester.
	Socket #5 and Engine Grd.	Socket #1 and Engine Grd.	Socket #1 and Engine Grd.	More than 4.0 Ohms	Check for Short to Ground at DEC Terminal of Coil or in Primary Coil Winding.

Test sequences (1974–76)

1977 and Later Test Sequence

	Test Voltage Between	Should Be	If Not, Conduct °
KEY ON	Pin #3 and Engine Ground	Battery Voltage ± 0.1 volts	Module Bias Test
	Pin #5 and Engine Ground	Battery Voltage ± 0.1 volts	Battery Source Test
CRANKING	Pin #1 and Engine Ground	8 to 12 volts	Cranking Test
	Jumper #5 to #6— Read Coil "Bat" Term. & Engine Ground °°	More than 6 volts	Starting Circuit Test
	Pin #7 and Pin #8	½ volt minimum wiggle	Distributor Hardware Test

	Test Resistance Between	Should Be	If Not, Conduct °°
KEY OFF	Pin #7 and Pin #8 Pin #6 and Engine Ground Pin #7 and Engine Ground Pin #8 and Engine Ground	400 to 800 ohms 0 ohms More than 70,000 ohms More than 70,000 ohms	Magnetic Pick-up (Stator) Test
	Pin #3 and Coil Tower	7,000 to 13,000 ohms	Coil Test
	Pin #5 and Coil "Bat" Term.	1.0 to 2.0 ohms Dura Spark II 0.5 to 1.5 ohms Dura Spark I	
	Pin #5 and Engine Ground	More than 4 ohms	Short Test
	Pin #3 and Coil "Bat" Term. (Except Dura Dura Spark I)	0.7 to 1.7 ohms Dura Spark II	Resistance Wire Test

American Motors Corporation Breakerless Inductive Discharge(BID) Ignition System

BASIC OPERATING PRINCIPLES

NOTE: *Beginning in 1978, AMC uses the Ford Motor Company Solid-State Ignition.*

The AMC breakerless inductive discharge (BID) ignition system consists of five components:

Control unit
Coil
Breakerless distributor
Ignition cables
Spark plugs

The control unit is a solid-state, epoxy-sealed module with waterproof connectors. The control unit has a built-in current regulator, so no separate ballast resistor or resistance wire is needed in the primary circuit. Battery voltage is supplied to the ignition coil positive (+) terminal when the ignition key is turned to the "ON" or "START" position; low voltage is also supplied by the control unit.

The coil used with the BID system requires no special service. It works just like the coil in a conventional ignition system.

The distributor is conventional, except for the lack of points, condenser and cam. Advance is supplied by both a vacuum unit and a centrifugal advance mechanism. A standard cap, rotor, and dust shield are used.

In place of the points, cam, and condensor, the distributor has a sensor and trigger wheel. The sensor is a small coil which generates an electromagnetic field when excited by the oscillator in the control unit.

Standard spark plugs and ignition cables are used.

When the ignition switch is turned on, the control unit is activated. The control unit then sends an oscillating signal to the sensor which causes the sensor to generate a magnetic field.

When one of the trigger wheel teeth enters this field, the strength of the oscillation in the sensor is reduced. Once the strength drops to a predetermined level, a demodulator circuit operates the control unit's switching transistor. The switching transistor is wired in series with the coil primary circuit; it switches the circuit off when it gets the demodulator signal.

From this point on, the BID ignition system works in the same manner as a conventional ignition system.

TROUBLESHOOTING THE AMC BID IGNITION SYSTEM

1. Check all of the BID ignition system electrical connections.

2. Disconnect the coil-to-distributor high tension lead from the distributor cap.

3. Using insulated pliers and a heavy glove,

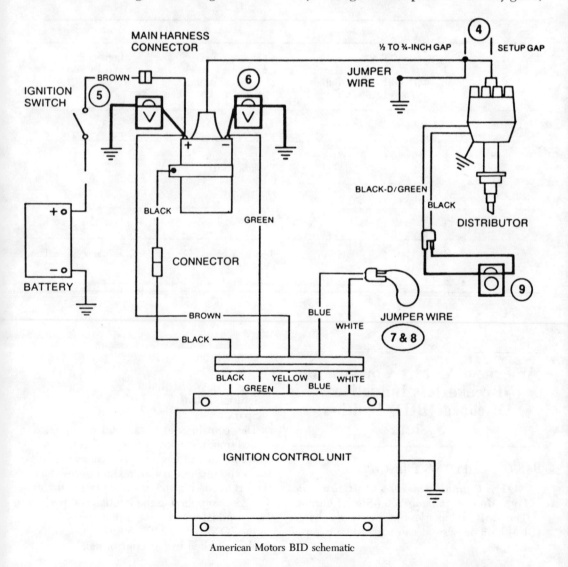

American Motors BID schematic

hold the end of the lead ½ in. away from a ground. Crank the engine. If there is a spark, the trouble is not in the ignition system. Check the distributor cap, rotor, and wires.

4. If there was no spark in step 3, connect a test light with a No. 57 bulb between the positive coil terminal (+) and a good ground. Have an assistant turn the ignition switch to "ON" and "START" (Do not start the engine). The bulb should light (battery voltage) in both positions; if it doesn't, the fault lies in the battery-to-coil circuit. Check the ignition switch and related wiring.

5. If the test light lit in step 4, disconnect the coil-to-distributor leads at the connector and connect the test light between the positive (+) and negative (−) coil terminals.

6. Turn the ignition switch on. If the test light doesn't come on, check the control unit's ground lead. If the ground lead is in good condition, replace the control unit.

7. If the bulb lights in step 6, leave the test light in place and short the terminals on the coil-to-distributor connector together with a jumper lead (connector separated) at the coil side of the connector. If the light stays on, replace the control unit.

8. If the test light goes out, remove it. Check for a spark, as in step 2, each time that the coil-to-distributor connector terminals are shorted together with the jumper lead. If there is a spark, replace the control unit; if there is no spark, replace the coil.

Coil Testing

Test the coil with a conventional coil checker or an ohmmeter. Primary resistance should be 1–2 ohms and secondary resistance should be 9–15 kilohms. The open output circuit should be more than 20 kilovolts. Replace the coil if it doesn't meet specifications.

Sensor Testing

Check the sensor resistance by connecting an ohmmeter to its leads. Resistance should be 1.6–2.0 ohms at 77°–200°F. Replace the sensor if it doesn't meet these specifications.

Chapter 4

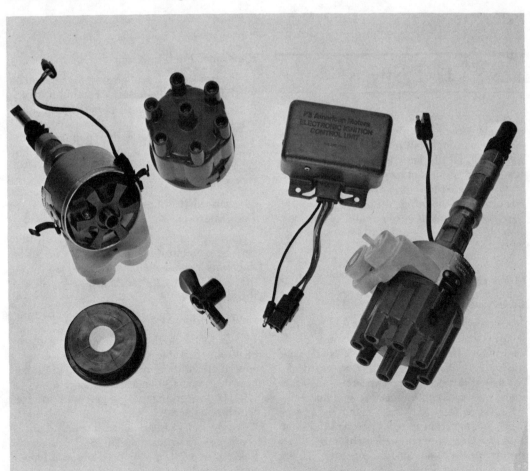

Fuel and Emission Control Systems

Fuel Systems

An automotive fuel system consists of everything between the fuel tank and the carburetor or fuel injection unit. This includes the tank itself, all the lines, one or more fuel filters, a fuel pump (either mechanical or electric) and the carburetor or fuel injection unit. Also, on late-model cars, some form of fuel vapor control unit is incorporated into the system.

FUEL INJECTION UNITS

Basic Operating Principles

There are two general types of fuel injection in use today. In one, the fuel/air delivery is controlled electronically; in the second type, the fuel/air delivery is controlled mechanically (air flow controlled). Mechanical fuel injection is also known as continuous flow fuel injection.

Although they are complicated in appearance, fuel injection systems perform the same basic job as a conventional carburetor. They simply provide an air/fuel mixture in the proper ratio under all operating conditions.

Electronic Fuel Injection

Electronic fuel injection systems depend on what is essentially a small computer which senses the determining factors for fuel delivery and adjusts the fuel flow accordingly. These systems were highly popular in the early seventies, but are now being replaced by the simpler, more reliable continuous flow type of fuel injection.

Mechanical (Continuous Flow) Fuel Injection

This type of fuel injection, which is steadily replacing electronic systems, relies on an air flow sensor to measure air volume and injects fuel continuously (in most cases) regardless of firing position.

Fuel Injection System Precautions

Due to the highly sensitive nature of the electronic fuel injection system, the following special precautions must be strictly adhered to in order to avoid damage to the system.

1. Do not operate the engine with the battery disconnected.

2. Do not utilize a high-speed battery charger as a starting aid. The Bosch computer box is protected by a diode which will blow if more than 15 volts is applied.

3. When using a high-speed battery charger to charge the battery while it is installed in the vehicle, at least one battery cable must be disconnected.

4. Do not allow the control unit to be subjected to temperatures exceeding 185°F, such as when the vehicle is being baked after painting. If there is a risk of the temperature exceeding 185°F, the control unit must be removed.

5. The engine must not be started when the ambient temperature exceeds 158°F, or damage to the control unit will result.

6. The ignition must be in the off position when disconnecting or connecting the control unit.

7. When working on the fuel system, take care not to allow dirt to enter the system. Small dust particles may jam fuel injectors.

DATSUN 280Z FUEL INJECTION

The 1975–77 280-Zs are equipped with electronic fuel injection built under Bosch patents. The Bosch L-Jetronic system precisely controls fuel injection to match engine requirements, reducing emissions and increasing driveability.

The electric fuel pump pumps fuel through a damper and filter to the pressure regulator. The six fuel injectors are electric solenoid valves which open and close by signals from the control unit. The control unit receives input from six sensors (seven on 1977 California models).

1. Air flow meter—measures the amount of intake air.

2. Ignition coil—engine rpm.

3. Throttle valve switch—amount of throttle opening.

4. Water temperature sensor—temperature of coolant.

5. Air temperature sensor—temperature of intake air.

6. Starting switch—signals that starter is operating.

7. Altitude switch—used on 1977 California cars to signal changes in atmospheric pressure.

The sensors provide the input to the control unit, which determines the amount of fuel to be injected by its present program.

Troubleshooting the 280Z Fuel Injection System

NOTE: *For the following tests, you will need a test light and an ohmmeter.*

CONTROL UNIT

1. Connect the test lamp to the harness-side connector of the injector.

2. Crank the engine. If the light flashes due to the pulse voltage applied to the injector, the control unit is operating.

NOTE: *Two different transistors are used. Test both the No. 1 and 4 cylinders.*

To confirm the test, remove the connector on the coolant sensor. The test lamp should flash more brightly. It is only necessary to run this test on the No. 1 or No. 4 cylinders.

POTENTIOMETER

CAUTION: *Before checking the air flow meter, remove the battery ground cable.*

1. Remove the air flow meter.

2. Measure the resistance between terminals 8 and 6. It should be 180 ohms.

3. Measure the resistance between terminals 8 and 9. The resistance should be 100 ohms.

4. Connect a 12-volt battery to terminals 9 (positive) and 6 (negative).

5. Connect the positive lead of a voltmeter to terminal 8 and the negative lead to terminal 7.

6. Reaching into the air flow meter, slowly open the flap so that the volt flow slowly decreases. If the indicator varies suddenly, the problem may be in the potentiometer.

AIR FLOW METER INSULATION

Connect an ohmmeter to any one terminal on the flow meter. Touch the meter body with the other connector. If any continuity is indicated, the unit is malfunctioning.

AIR FLOW METER FLAP

Reach into the air flow meter with your fingers. If the flap opens and closes smoothly, without binding, the mechanical portion of the unit is working.

FUEL PUMP CONTACT POINTS

Connect an ohmmeter to terminals 36 and 39 of the fuel pump, on the side of the air flow meter.

Reach into the meter and move the flap. A current flow should be indicated when you have opened the flap about 8 degrees. There should be no continuity with the flap closed. If the unit is not working, replace the entire air flow meter.

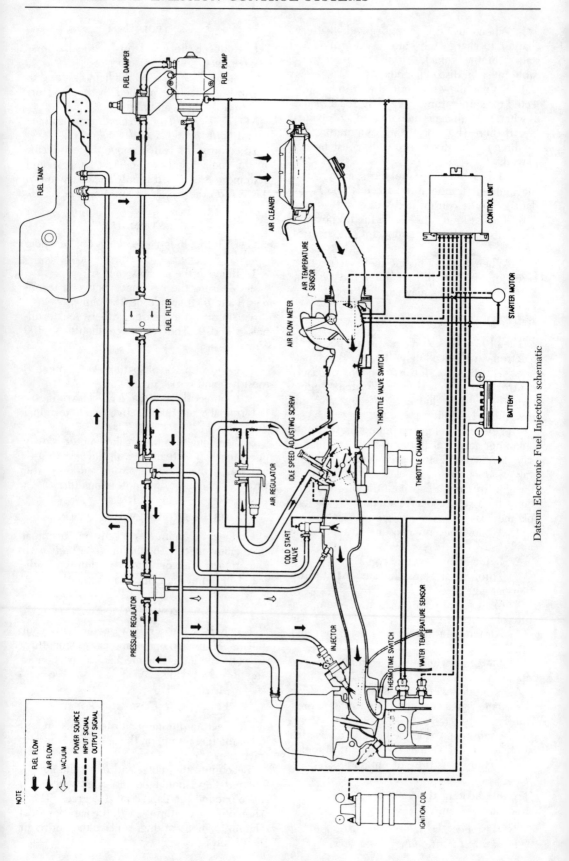

Datsun Electronic Fuel Injection schematic

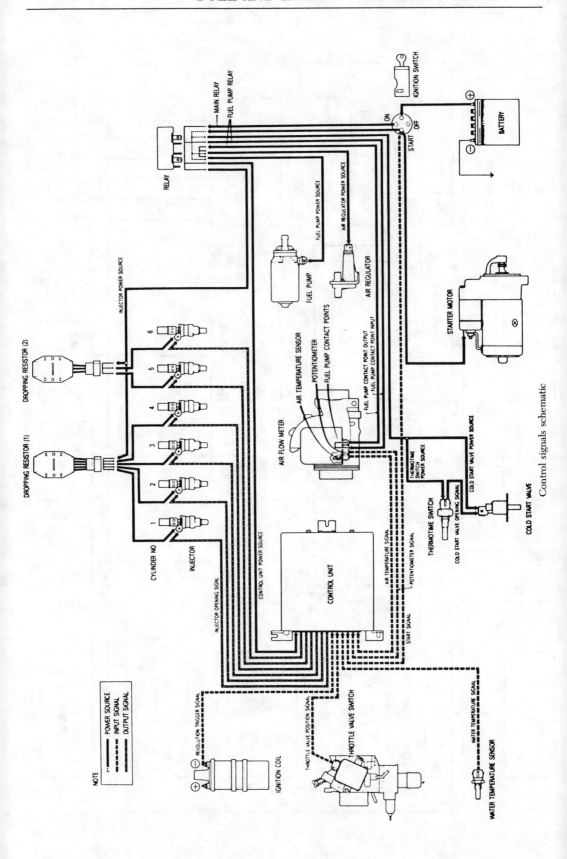

Control signals schematic

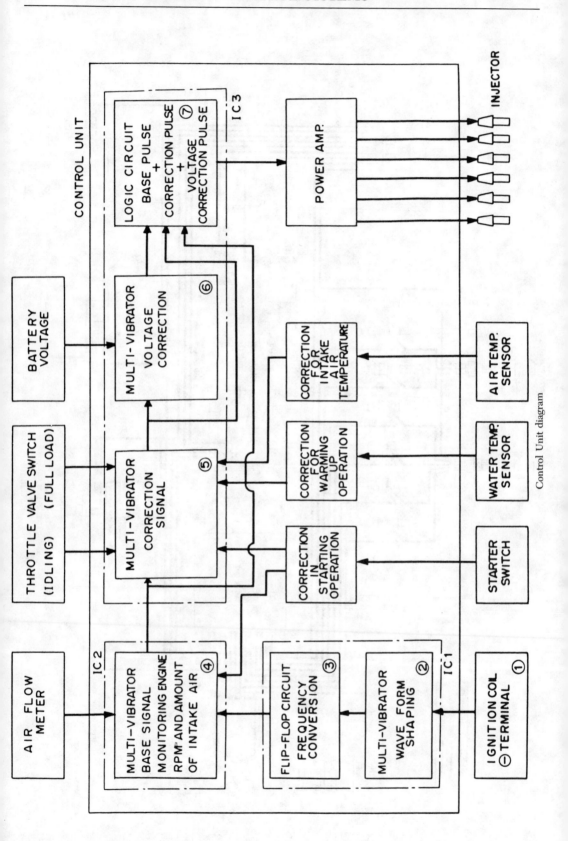

Control Unit diagram

AIR TEMPERATURE CONTINUITY

1. Disconnect the battery ground cable.
2. Remove the air flow meter.
3. Note the ambient temperature.
4. Connect an ohmmeter to terminals 27 and 8 on the air flow meter connector and note the resistance.

The resistance values should be as indicated in the chart. Should the test results vary far from the chart, replace the air temperature sensor and air flow meter as a unit.

INSULATION RESISTANCE

Connect an ohmmeter to terminal 27 of the air flow meter and touch the body with the other connector. Should continuity be indicated, replace the unit.

WATER TEMPERATURE SENSOR

This test may be done either on or off the vehicle. The test should be done with the coolant both hot and cold.

1. Disconnect the battery ground cable.
2. Disconnect the water temperature sensor harness.
3. Place a thermometer in the coolant when the engine is cold. Note the temperature.
4. Compare the resistance on the meter with that on chart for temperature/resistance values.

To measure the coolant temperature and resistance values when hot:

1. Connect the water temperature sensor harness.
2. Connect the battery ground cable.
3. Warm the engine and disconnect the harness and battery cable.
4. Read the sensor resistance as described in the cold process.

SENSOR CHECK OFF THE ENGINE

1. Remove the sensor and dip the unit into water at 68°F. Read the resistance.
2. Heat the water to 176°F and check the resistance.

In either type of check, should the resistance be far outside the ranges provided, replace the sensor unit.

SENSOR INSULATION CHECK

This check is done on the engine.

1. Disconnect the battery ground cable.
2. Disconnect the sensor harness connector.
3. Connect an ohmmeter to one of the ter-

minals on the sensor and touch the engine block with the other. Any indication of continuity indicates need to replace the unit.

THERMOTIME SWITCH

1. Disconnect the ground cable from the battery.
2. Disconnect the electric connector of the thermotime switch and measure the resistance between terminal No. 46 and the switch body.

The resistance should be zero with water temperatures less than 57°F.

The resistance should be zero or infinite with temperatures of 57°–72°F.

The resistance should be infinite with a temperature of 72°F.

3. Measure the resistance between terminal No. 45 and the switch body. It should be 70–86 ohms.

COLD START VALVE

1. Disconnect the "S" terminal of the starter motor.
2. Turn the ignition switch to START and make sure the fuel pump is working. You should be able to hear it.
3. Disconnect the battery ground.
4. Remove the cold start valve.
5. Disconnect the start valve electrical connector.
6. Put the start valve into a large glass container and plug the neck of the jar.
7. Connect the ground cable of the battery and turn the ignition switch to START. The valve should not inject fuel.
8. Turn the switch to OFF and connect a jumper wire between the valve and the battery terminals. Leave the valve in the jar.

At this point, the valve should inject fuel. If not, proceed to the next step.

9. With the ignition switch in the START position, and the jumper wire installed as described, check for fuel flow. If the fuel is injected to the jar, the unit is operating. If not, replace it.

MAIN INJECTION RELAY CHECK

Disconnect the battery and remove the relay. Connect a battery (12-volt) between the positive (86c) terminal and the negative (85). Clicks should be heard and continuity indicated between terminals 88z and 88a, and between 88z and 88b.

Connect the battery (12-volt) between positive (85) and negative (86c) terminals. No clicks should be heard.

If the results are not as described, the unit is faulty.

FUEL PUMP RELAY

Disconnect the battery and remove the relay.

1. Make sure there is continuity between terminals 88d and 88c and between 86a and 86.

2. Connect a 12-volt battery to positive (86a) and negative (85) terminals. Clicks should be heard and there should be continuity between 88y and 88d.

3. Connect the battery to positive (85) and negative (86a) terminals. No clicks should be heard.

4. If the test results are not as specified, the relay is faulty.

THROTTLE VALVE SWITCH

Disconnect the ground cable from the battery. Remove the throttle valve switch connector.

IDLE SWITCH

1. Connect an ohmmeter between terminals 2 and 18.

2. If continuity is indicated when the throttle valve is in the IDLE position, and does not exist when the valve opens about 4° the switch is normal.

FULL SWITCH CHECK

1. Connect an ohmmeter between terminals 3 and 18.

2. Gradually optn the throttle valve and read the indication when the valve is open about 34°. If the indication is higher at all settings other than 34°, the full switch is operating properly.

THROTTLE VALVE SWITCH INSULATION

Connect an ohmmeter between body metal and terminals 2, 3, and 18. Meter reading should be infinite.

DROPPING RESISTOR

Disconnect the ground cable from the battery. Disconnect the 4-pin and 6-pin connectors from the injection system harness and conduct resistance checks between the following points.

43/1 and No. 41—#4 cylinder
43/1 and No. 40—#3 cylinder
43/1 and No. 38—#2 cylinder

43/1 and No. 37—#1 cylinder
43/2 and No. 56—#6 cylinder
43/2 and No. 55—#5 cylinder
The resistance should be 6 ohms.

ALTITUDE SWITCH (CALIFORNIA MODELS ONLY)

Disconnect the ground cable from the battery and remove the switch.

Attach an ohmmeter to the connector and blow or suck through the discharge port. If a click is heard and continuity exists, the switch is in good order.

There is no adjustment possible on the switch. Should it be found to be defective, replace the unit.

Water Temperature Sensor Resistance Specifications

Cooling Water Temperature °C (°F)	Resistance (kΩ)
−30 (−22)	20.3 to 33.0
−10 (−14)	7.6 to 10.8
10 (50)	3.25 to 4.15
20 (68)	2.25 to 2.75
50 (122)	0.74 to 0.94
80 (176)	0.29 to 0.36

Air Flow Meter Resistance Specifications

Air Temperature °C (°F)	Resistance (kΩ)
−30 (−22)	20.3 to 33.0
−10 (−14)	7.6 to 10.8
10 (50)	3.25 to 4.15
20 (68)	2.25 to 2.75
50 (122)	0.74 to 0.94
80 (176)	0.29 to 0.36

VOLKSWAGEN FUEL INJECTION SYSTEMS

NOTE: *VW fuel injection systems are highly complex systems. Troubleshooting and repair should be left to the dealer.*

Electronic Fuel Injection—Non-Air Flow Controlled

The Bosch Electronic fuel injection system used on all Type 3 models, and on 1971–74 Type 4 models (except 1974 models equipped with an automatic), consists of two parts. One part consists of the actual injection components: the injectors, the fuel pump, pressure regulator, and related wiring and hoses. The second part consists of the injection controls and engine operating characteristics sensors: a manifold vacuum sensor that monitors engine load, trigger contacts used to determine when and which pair of injectors will operate, three temperature sensors used to control air fuel mixture enrichment, a cold starting valve for additional cold starting fuel enrichment, a throttle valve switch used to cut off fuel during deceleration, and the brain box used to ana-

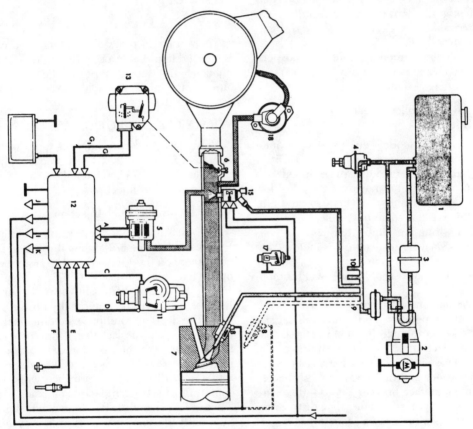

Air-flow controlled VW Electronic Fuel Injection schematic

1. Fuel tank
2. Fuel pump
3. Fuel filter
4. Pressure regulator
5. Pressure sensor
6. Intake air distributor
7. Cylinder head
8. Injectors
9. Fuel distributor pipe
10. Fuel distributor pipe with connection for cold starting device
11. Distributor with trigger contacts (distributor contact I, distributor contact II)
12. Control unit.
13. Throttle valve switch with acceleration enrichment

15. Cold starting valve
17. Thermostat for cold starting device
18. Auxiliary air regulator
A + B. from pressure sensor (load condition signal)
C + D. from distributor contacts (engine speed and releasing signal)
E + F. from temperature sensors (warmup signal)
G. from throttle valve switch (fuel supply cut-off when coasting)
G1. Acceleration enrichment
I. from starter, terminal 50 solenoid switch (signal for enrichment mixture when starting)
J. to the injectors, cylinders 1 and 4
K. to the injectors, cylinders 2 and 3

lyze information about engine operating characteristics and, after processing this information, to control the electrically operated injectors.

It is absolutely imperative that no adjustments other than those found in the following pages be performed. The controls for this fuel injection system are extremely sensitive and easily damaged when subject to abuse. Never attempt to test the brain box without proper training and the proper equipment. The dealer is the best place to have any needed work performed.

CAUTION: *Whenever a fuel injection component is to be removed or installed, the battery should be disconnected and the ignition turned OFF.*

It is not recommended that the inexperienced mechanic work on any portion of the fuel injection system.

Air Flow Controlled Electronic Fuel Injection

1974 Type 4 models equipped with automatic transmission, as well as all 1975–77 Type 1 and Type 2 models, are equipped with an improved system known as the Air Flow Controlled Electronic Fuel Injection System. With this system, some of the electronic sensors and wiring are eliminated, and the control box is smaller. Instead fuel is metered according to intake air flow.

The system consists of the following components;

Intake air sensor—measures intake air volume and temperature and sends voltage signals to the control unit (brain box). It also controls the electric fuel pump by shutting it off when intake air stops. It is located between the air cleaner and the intake air distributor.

Ignition contact breaker points—these are the regular points inside the distributor. When the points open, all four injectors are triggered. The points also send engine speed signals to the control unit. No separate triggering contacts are used.

Throttle valve switch—provides only for full load enrichment. This switch is not adjustable.

Temperature sensor I—senses intake temperature as before. It is now located in the intake air sensor.

Temperature sensor II—senses cylinder head temperature as before.

Control unit (brain box)—contains only 80 components compared to the old systems 300.

Pressure regulator—is connected by a vac-

uum hose to the intake air distributor and is no longer adjustable. It adjusts fuel pressure according to manifold vacuum.

Auxiliary air regulator—provides more air during cold warmup.

ELECTRONIC CONTROL (BRAIN) BOX

All work concerning the brain box is to be performed by the dealer. Do not remove the brain box and take it to a dealer because the dealer will not be able to test it without the vehicle. Do not disconnect the brain box unless the battery is disconnected and the ignition is OFF.

FUEL INJECTORS

There are two types of injectors. One type is secured in place by a ring that holds a single injector. The second type of injector is secured to the intake manifold in pairs by a common bracket.

VOLVO FUEL INJECTION SYSTEMS

Volvo has used two different types of fuel injection. Up until 1973, Electronic fuel injection was used. 1974 and later Volvos use Continuous flow fuel injection.

Volvo Electronic Fuel Injection

Volvo has made Bosch electronic fuel injection available since 1970, when it was standard equipment on the 1800 series. The system was optional on the 140 series in 1971, and on the 164 in 1972. For 1973, all Volvos imported into the U.S. will be equipped with the system. The decision to utilize electronic fuel injection, despite the fact that it has increased the base price of the cars, has been made by many European manufacturers who desire to retain a modicum of performance while still conforming to stringent federal emission regulations. The electronic fuel injection system is inherently cleaner than carbureted systems because of its precise regulation of fuel under varying conditions of atmospheric temperature, and engine temperature, load, and rpm.

The complete system contains the following components: electronic control unit (brain), electric fuel pump, fuel filter, fuel pressure regulator, fuel injectors, cold-start valve, inlet duct (for intake air), throttle valve switch, auxiliary air regulator, intake air temperature sensor, coolant temperature sensor, intake air pressure sensor, and the triggering contacts in the ignition distributor.

Briefly, the system operates as follows:

Fuel is drawn from the fuel tank by the

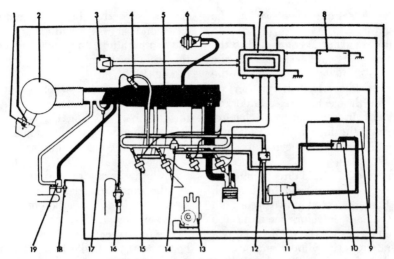

Volvo Electronic Fuel Injection schematic

1. Temperature sensor for induction air
2. Air cleaner
3. Throttle valve switch
4. Cold start valve
5. Inlet duct
6. Pressure sensor
7. Control unit (electronic)
8. Battery
9. Fuel tank
10. Fuel filter, suction side

11. Fuel pump
12. Fuel filter, discharge side
13. Triggering contacts in distributor
14. Pressure regulator
15. Injectors
16. Thermal timer contact
17. Idling adjusting screw
18. Temperature sensor for coolant
19. Auxiliary air regulator

electric fuel pump and forced through the fuel lines and filter to the pressure regulator. The pressure regulator supplies fuel at a constant pressure of 28 psi to the injectors. If the fuel pressure for some reason exceeds 28 psi, a relief valve opens, allowing the excess fuel to return to the fuel tank. The electromagnetic fuel injectors are mounted in the intake ports of the cylinder head.

The duration of fuel injection, and consequently, fuel quantity, is controlled by engine rpm and load. Engine rpm information is supplied to the electronic brain via the distributor triggering contacts. Engine load information is supplied by the intake air pressure sensor. The electronic brain uses this information to determine the length of time the injectors will remain open. During warm-up periods, the cold-start valve injects extra fuel into the intake air stream when the starter is operated. At the same time, the auxiliary air regulator supplies extra air until the engine reaches operating temperature.

When the engine is accelerated, the throttle valve switch sends electrical impulses to the brain to increase the time the injectors are open. When decelerating, the throttle valve switch sends another impulse to the brain, closing off the fuel flow. When engine speed

drops to approximately 1,000 rpm, the fuel supply is turned on again, allowing a smooth transition to idle speed.

Component

The electronic control unit (brain) receives electrical impulses from the intake air pressure and temperature sensors, and determines the duration of the opening interval for the injectors. In addition, on 1970–71 models, the control unit determines if, and for how long, the cold-start valve should be open. Another function of the control unit is to determine when the fuel pump should be operated. The control unit is located beneath the passenger's front seat on 140 series and 164 models, and behind the instrument panel on 1800 series models. Repair of the control unit requires the use of special test equipment which is available on the dealer level only.

The fuel pump relay receives impulses from the control unit to operate the electrical fuel pump. The main relay feeds current from the charging system to the control unit, and also protects the injection system from damage should the battery leads be switched. On 1970–71 models, a cold-start valve relay receives impulses from the control unit to operate the cold-start valve. The relays are located on the right front wheel well in the engine compartment.

The pressure regulator is connected to the fuel distributing pipe, and is located at the firewall on 1970–71 models, and between the second and third injectors (four-cylinder) on the third and fourth injectors (six-cylinder) on 1972–73 models. It is a purely mechanical unit, pressurizing the fuel to 28 psi for purposes of injecting it into the cylinders. The regulator is adjustable.

The fuel injectors pass fuel directly into the intake ports of the cylinder head (one for each intake port). Fuel is injected in two cycles. On four-cylinder engines, injectors one and three operate simultaneously, then injectors two and four operate. On six-cylinder engines, injectors one, three, and five operate together, then injectors two, four, and six operate. The injector operates when a pulse from the control unit energizes the magnetic winding of the injector, drawing the sealing needle up from the seat. When the pulse stops and the magnetic winding de-energizes, the sealing needle is pushed against the seat by the return spring. A valve opening time interval of 0.002–0.010 second regulates the amount of fuel injected.

The cold-start valve is located in the inlet duct downstream from the air throttle. Its purpose is to provide extra fuel during cold starts. On 1970–71 models, the cold-start valve is operated by the cold-start valve relay which receives information from the temperature sensor via the control unit. On 1970–71 models, the valve supplies additional fuel during starting for a period of 10 seconds when the coolant temperture is −4° F or colder, and stops providing the fuel during starting at a temperature of 132° F. On 1972–73 models, the cold-start valve is actuated by a temperature-sensitive thermal timer. On these models, extra fuel is provided during starting for a period of 12 seconds when the coolant temperature is −4° F or colder, and the additional fuel supply is cut off when the temperature reaches 95° F. On all models, the fuel is cut off when the starter stops running, regardless of the temperature.

The thermal timer is installed in 1972–73 models, on the right-hand side of the engine block. The timer, which is sensitive to engine temperature, supplies electrical current to the cold-start valve when the engne temperature is less than 95° F, and the starter is engaged. The duration of time that the timer feeds current to the cold-start valve varies from a fraction of a second at the higher temperatures to 12 seconds at −4° F and lower. Regardless of the temperature, the timer ceases operating the cold-start valve when the starter is disengaged.

The throttle valve switch is mounted at the mouth of the inlet duct and is connected to the throttle shaft. Its function is to increase the fuel supply during acceleration by sending additional and longer impulses to the electromagnetic fuel injectors, and to shut off the fuel supply during deceleration by withholding the impulses. At idle, the throttle valve switch regulates the carbon monoxide content of the exhaust gases.

The one-piece, cast aluminum inlet duct is bolted to the cylinder head. Its function is to supply intake air (and occasionally a few drops of fuel when the cold-start valve is activated) metered to the engine's needs by the throttle valve to each individual induction port in the cylinder head. The idle adjustment screw is located at the mouth of the inlet duct.

The auxiliary air regulator is located at the right front end of the cylinder head. It is a temperature-sensitive device with an expanding element projecting into the cooling system. The air regulator's operating range is from −13° F, fully open, to 140° F, fully closed. At the cold-start, the expanding element is temporarily contracted, allowing the auxiliary air hose to admit additional air into the inlet duct. Gradually, as the engine heats up, the element expands, closing off the auxiliary air hose.

The temperature sensor for the intake air provides the control unit with intake air temperature information so that the control unit can increase the injection frequency and duration somewhat at low intake air temperature. Compensation ceases when the temperature of the intake air becomes greater than 68 ° F (1970–71 models), or 86° F (1972–73 models). The sensor is located at the radiator crossbar, adjacent to the intake air hose on 140 and 1800 series Volvos, and at the radiator crossbar, near the right front headlight housing on the 164.

The coolant temperature sensor (not to be confused with the temperature gauge sensor) also provides the control unit with engine temperature information so that the control unit can regulate the injection interval and duration. On 1970–71 models, the sensor also provides the control unit with information determining if, and for how long, the cold-start valve will operate. This sensor is located in the cylinder head next to the auxiliary air regulator.

The pressure sensor monitors the atmospheric pressure present in the inlet duct, and supplies the control unit with information concerning engine load. The unit is located on the right front wheel housing and is connected to the inlet duct by means of a hose.

The triggering contacts supply the control unit information concerning engine speed (rpm). The control unit then determines when the injection shall begin, and what the duration will be, with the help of information received from the pressure sensor. The triggering contacts are located beneath the centrifugal governor in the distributor.

Component Testing and Adjustment

CONTROL UNIT

The idle mixture may be adjusted with the slotted knob on the control unit. This operation is best performed with the use of a CO meter, which is available on the dealer level.

The control unit may be tested only with the help of sophisticated test equipment available, again, only at the dealer level.

PRESSURE REGULATOR

The regulator may be adjusted with its adjusting nut. Pinch and disconnect the flexible fuel hose between the presure regulator and the header pipe and insert a tee fitting and pressure gauge. Tighten the fuel connections and start the engine. Slacken the locknut and adjust the pressure to 28 psi. If the regulator cannot be adjusted properly, it must be replaced. Remove the tee fitting and gauge, and connect the fuel hoses.

THROTTLE VALVE

The throttle valve may be adjusted with its stopscrew near the mouth of the inlet duct. Release the stopscrew locknut for the throttle valve switch, and back off the screw several turns so that it does not lie against the throttle valve spindle stop. Make sure that the valve is completely closed. Screw in the stopscrew so that it contacts the spindle stop. At this point, turn the stopscrew 1/4–1/3 additional turn and tighten the locknut. Check to see that the switch does not jam in the closed position. Proceed to adjust the throttle valve switch as follows.

NOTE: *The stopscrew must not be used for idle adjustment.*

THROTTLE VALVE SWITCH

The throttle valve switch may be adjusted with an ohmmeter. Connect the ohmmeter to the control unit (contacts 14 and 17 for four-cylinder, and contacts 9 and 14 for six-cylinder). Loosen the screws slightly so that the switch may be rotated. Scribe a mark at the upper switch screw on the inlet duct if one is not there already. Close the throttle valve by turning the switch clockwise as far as it will go. Then, observing the ohmmeter, carefully turn the switch counterclockwise until the ohmmeter registers 0 (zero). At this point, the switch is turned a further 1° counterclockwise (1/2 graduation mark at upper screw), and both switch screws are tightened. Check to make sure that the ohmmeter reading rises to infinity when the throttle valve opens approximately 1°.

AUXILIARY AIR REGULATIOR

To check the operation of the auxiliary air regulator, start the engine and allow it to reach operating temperature (176° F). Make a note of the idle speed and then disconnect the hose between the inlet duct and the regulator. While covering the hose operning with your hand, check to see that the idle speed does not drop significantly over the first reading. A drop in idle speed indicates a leak in the regulator, requiring its replacement.

Continuous Fuel Injection

Continuous fuel injection is standard on all 240, 260 and 1974 140 models. It differs from electronic fuel injection in that injection takes place continuously; controlled through variation of the fuel flow rate through the injectors, rather than variation of the fuel injection duration. This system has no electronic computer. It is an electro-mechanical system that will provide suitable air/fuel mixtures to accommodate differing driving conditions.

The complete system consists of the following components: air/fuel control unit (housing both air flow sensor and fuel distributor), electric fuel pump (and fuel pressure accumulator), fuel filter, control pressure regulator, continuous fuel injectors, auxiliary air valve, cold start injector, thermal time switch, main relay, and a fuel pump relay.

The fuel distributor, which controls and distributes the amount of fuel to the injectors consists of a line pressure regulator, a control plunger, and (4 or 6) presure regulator valves (one for each injector). The line pressure regu-

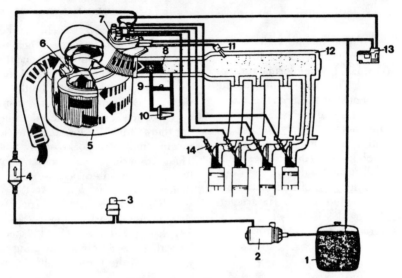

Volvo continuous flow schematic

1. Fuel tank	8. Throttle
2. Fuel pump	9. Idle adjustment screw
3. Fuel accumulator	10. Auxiliary air valve
4. Fuel filter	11. Cold start injector
5. Air cleaner	12. Intake manifold
6. Air flow sensor	13. Control pressure regulator
7. Fuel distributor	14. Injector

lator maintains the fuel distributor inlet pressure at about 65 psi., and will recirculate fuel to the tank if pressure exceeds this value. The pressure regulator valves maintain a constant fuel pressure differential (1.4 psi) between the inlet and outlet sides of the control plunger. This is independent of the amount of fuel passing through the valves, which varies according to plunger height.

The injectors themselves are spring loaded and calibrated to open at 47–51 psi. They are not electrically operated as on the older electronic fuel injection system.

The control pressure regulator, located on the intake manifold, acts to regulate the fuel/air mixture according to engine temperature. When the engine is cold, the control pressure regulator richens the mixture (4–5 minutes max.). On V-6 models, a vacuum feature is added to the regulator, whereby low vacuum situations, such as acceleration, temporarily lowers the control pressure and richens the mixture. At idle, full throttle, and steady state conditions, the vacuum is high and the mixture returns to normal.

The fuel accumulator, located adjacent to the fuel tank mounted electric fuel pump, has a check valve which keeps residual fuel pressure from dropping below 28 psi when the engine or fuel pump are shut off. Therefore,

the system is always pressurized, preventing vapor lock in hot start situations.

Component Testing and Adjusting

AIR-FUEL CONTROL UNIT

The air-flow sensor plate adjustment is critical. The distance between the sensor plate and the plate stop must be 0.002 in. The plate must also be centered in the venturi, and must not contact the venturi walls. Loosen the plate center screw to adjust. The plate should not bind, and although (due to the control pressure) the plate will offer some resistance when depressed, it should return to its rest position when released.

To check the air-flow sensor contact switch, depress the sensor plate by hand. The fuel injectors should buzz, and the fuel pump should activate. If the pump operates, but the injectors do not buzz, check the fuel pressures. If the pump does not operate, check for a short in the air-flow sensor connector.

FUEL PUMP

With the ignition switch on, disconnect the wire connector at the air flow sensor. The pump should work. If not, check fuse #7, and voltage across auxiliary air valve terminals.

Live terminals indicate a faulty fuel pump or wiring.

Fuel Distributor Line, Rest and Control Pressures, Auxiliary Air Valve and Control Pressure Regulator Operation

NOTE: *A special fuel pressure gauge with a three position tee-fitting is required to isolate the line, rest, and control pressure readings.*

Connect a pressure gauge and tee-fitting with 3-way valve in-line between the center of the fuel distributor (control pressure fuel line) and the control pressure regulator.

CAUTION: *Disconnect the coil wire (terminal 15) to prevent burning out the coil windings. Disconnect the wire connectors at the control pressure regulator and auxiliary air valve. Switch on the ignition and disconnect the wire connector at the air-flow sensor. The fuel pump should start.*

Check the line pressure first. With the tee-fitting lever pointing to the fuel distributor, check that the line pressure is 64–75 psi. If insufficient, check fuel lines for leakage, fuel pump for delivery capacity (25.3 fluid ounces in 30 sec.), or low line pressure adjustment. If too high, check for clogged fuel return line or high line pressure adjustment. Line pressure is adjusted along with rest pressure later in this procedure.

Check the control pressure. With the tee-fitting turned at a right angle to the hoses, check that the control pressure corresponds to those values given in the control pressure/coolant temperature graph. Depending on coolant temperature, the control pressure will be somewhere between 18–55 psi, lower for cool temperatures, higher for warm temperatures. If the control pressure is insufficient, try a new pressure regulator. If the pressure is too high, check for a clogged fuel return line, or try a new control pressure regulator. Reconnect the control pressure regulator electrical connector. After 4–5 minutes, the pressure should decrease to 44–50 psi. If not, disconnect the electrical connector at the control pressure regulator and check with a 12v test light across the terminals. No voltage indicates a defective wire. Voltage indicates a possible faulty regulator. Then, check across the terminals with an ohmmeter. Resistance indicates corroded terminals. No resistance indicates a defective control pressure regulator.

The vacuum function of the control pressure regulator on the V-6 engine is checked later in this test.

The auxiliary air valve is checked next. Disconnect the auxiliary air valve hoses. Using a mirror and a flashlight, check that the valve is partly open at room temperature. Then, reconnect the wire connector at the valve and, after 4–5 min., the valve should be fully closed. If not, tap on the valve and check again. If tapping closes valve, the valve is OK (engine vibrations will close valve in normal operation). If the auxiliary air valve still does not close, disconnect the connector and check the voltage across the wire connector terminals with a 12v test light. No voltage indicates a defective wire. Next, check across the auxiliary air valve terminals with an ohmmeter. Resistance indicates corroded contacts. No resistance indicates a faulty auxiliary air valve.

Check the rest pressure. Connect the wire connector at the air-flow sensor terminal to stop the fuel pump. With the pump stopped, and the pressure gauge tee-fitting lever at a right angle to the fuel lines, check that the rest pressure is 24 psi (14 psi minimum after 10 minutes). The rest pressure and line pressure are adjusted simultaneously by inserting or removing shims between the regulator plunger and plunger cap on the side of the fuel distributor. A 0.1mm shims makes an 0.8 psi difference, and an 0.5mm shim makes a 4.3 psi difference in both rest and line pressure. If the rest pressure drops noticeably within one minute, check for defective control pressure regulator, leaky line pressure regulator or O-ring, a defective fuel pump check valve, or some external fuel leak.

The vacuum function of the V-6 control pressure regulator is checked with the pressure gauge and tee-fitting installed, and all electrical connectors installed. On a running, warm engine, with the tee-fitting positioned at a right angle to the fuel hoses, fuel pressure should be 50–55 psi. When the vacuum hose is disconnected at the regulator, the pressure should drop to 44–50 psi. If not, the regulator is defective.

Cold Start Injector

Remove the cold start injector from the intake manifold and hold over a beaker. With a cold engine (95° F or lower coolant temperature), the injector should spray during starter operation (max. 12 seconds). If not, check the voltage between the terminals of the injector when the starter is on. Voltage indicates a bad cold start injector. No voltage indicates a faulty thermal time switch or wiring.

With the starter off, disconnect the wire connector at the air-flow sensor to operate fuel pump. Check for cold start injector leakage. Maximum allowable leakage is one drop per minute.

THERMAL TIME SWITCH

Remove the cold start injector and place over a beaker. With a hot engine (coolant temperature over 95° F), the injector should not operate. If it does, the thermal time switch is defective. Also, on a cold engine, the cold start injector should not inject fuel for more than 12 seconds (during starter cranking). If it does, the thermal time switch is defective.

CONTINUOUS FUEL INJECTORS

The injectors are simple spring-loaded atomizers, designed to open at 47–51 psi. Critical factors are spray pattern, fuel spray quantity, and leakdown after engine is shut off.

To check spray pattern, remove the injectors, one at a time, and hold over a beaker. Switch the ignition key on and disconnect the connector at the air-flow sensor to activate the fuel pump. Move the air-flow sensor plate. The injector should provide a healthy dose of uniformly atomized fuel at about a 15–25 degree wide angle.

To check injection quantity, connect the removed injectors via hoses to 4 (or 6) equal sized beakers. Switch on the ignition. Disconnect the connector at the air-flow sensor to activate the fuel pump. Run (the pump) for approximately 30 seconds to pressurize the system. Then connect the connector to stop the fuel pump. Lift (four-cylinder) or depress (V-6) the air-flow sensor plate halfway until one of the beakers fills up. Check the beakers. If injection quantity deviates more than 20% between injectors, isolate problem by swapping the lowest and highest (in fuel quantity) injectors and repeating the test. If the same injector still injects less, clean or replace that injector and fuel supply line. If the other injector is now faulty, the fuel distributor is defective.

The check for injector leak-down (when closed) can now be conducted. Injector leakage more than slight seepage may be due to air-flow sensor plate set to incorrect height, seizing of fuel distributor plunger, or internal leaks in the fuel distributor. Connect the air-flow sensor connector to deactivate the fuel pump and switch off the ignition. Check for injector leakage at rest pressure. Depress the sensor plate to open the fuel distributor slots. Maximum permissable leakage is one drop per 15 seconds. If all injectors leak, problem may be excessive rest pressure.

MERCEDES-BENZ FUEL INJECTION SYSTEMS

Several types of fuel injection are used on Mercedes-Benz gasoline engines. All 6-cylinder engines except the 280E and 280SE use mechanical fuel injection, while the 280E and 280SE use the CIS fuel injection. V-8's are equipped with electronic fuel injection. 1976– and later V8's use the Bosch K-Jetronic mechanical injection.

CAUTION: *Even a seemingly minor adjustment, such as idle speed, can necessitate adjustments to other portions of the fuel injection system. Be extremely careful when adjusting the system. If any difficulty at all is experienced, reassess the problem. Further attempts at adjustment will only upset the balance of an already delicate system.*

Mechanical Fuel Injection—280SE/8 (1972) and 280S/8 (1972)

This system is a mechanical system used on 6-cylinder engines. The injection pump is a 6-cylinder type with mechanical linkage. There is very little testing that can be done to this system without the use of special equipment. However, there are some adjustments that can be made.

Adjustments

REGULATING LINKAGE

NOTE: *Do not change the idle speed and full load stop on the injection pump.*

1. Disconnect the regulating rod.
2. Check the linkage for freedom of operation. There should be no play.
3. When checking the adjusting lever on the injection pump, it will not return to idling position each time. It is sufficiently free if it jumps back to idle position when the starter is activated for a few seconds.
4. Disconnect regulating rod from venturi control unit.
5. The throttle valve in the venturi should close completely with no binding.
6. Adjust the idle stop screw so that when the throttle valve lever is pressed tightly against the stop screw it will grip slightly without binding.
7. Loosen the regulating shaft ballhead.

8. If there is no bolt hole on six-cylinder models adjust the length of the regulating linkage to 233 mm between the center of the 2 ball heads.

9. Make the same adjustment on the regulating rod toward the venturi control unit so that the throttle valve lever rests against the idle speed stop.

10. Slowly move the regulating shaft and adjust the levers on the injection pump and throttle valves so that they are lifted simultaneously.

11. Connect the regulating rod.

12. On engines with progressive regulating linkage, adjust the regulating rod so that the roller is just resting against the end stop in the cam lever.

13. If equipped with regulating damper, the closing damper stroke should be 4–5 mm.

14. On automatic transmission cars, disconnect the control thrust rod on the guide lever. Disconnect the pull rod and connect it free of any tension. Push the control rod back to the idle position and connect the ball socket free of tension.

15. Step on the accelerator pedal. The adjusting lever on the injection pump should be against the full load stop with the pedal floored. Adjust the regulating shaft if necessary.

Bosch Electronic Fuel Injection—1972–75 V8 Engines

This system is a constant pressure, electronically controlled unit. The "brain" of the system, actually a small computer that senses the determining factors for fuel delivery, is located behind the passenger kick panel on the right-hand side.

A Bosch tester is necessary to accurately test the solid state circuitry and components, but there are a few checks that can be carried out independently of the tester.

Tests

DELIVERY PRESSURE

Temporarily reduce the pressure in the ring line by unplugging the connection at the starting valve. Connect the terminals of the starting valve to the battery for approximately 20 seconds. Reconnect the starting valve.

1. Remove the air filter and connect a pressure gauge at the branch connection at the ring line.

2. Run the engine and measure the pressure. It should be 26.5–29.5 psi.

3. Stop the engine. The fuel pressure may drop to 21 psi, after approximately 5 minutes. If the fuel pressure drops uniformly to 0, check the following points for leaks:

Starting valve—Switch on ignition and disconnect hose at starting valve. If there is no drop in pressure, the valve leaks.

Pressure regulator—switch on the ignition and disconnect the fuel return hose, as soon as the fuel pump stops. If there is no drop in pressure, the regulator leaks.

Ball valve in delivery connection of fuel pump—Switch on the ignition and disconnect the fuel hose in front of the ring line the moment the fuel pump stops. If there is no drop in pressure, replace the fuel pump.

Injection Valves—remove the kick panel and bridge terminals 1 and 3 of the relay shown. This will energize the fuel pump with the engine stopped, and ignition ON. Check the valves for leaks.

4. Before removing the gauge, reduce the pressure in the ring line.

Mechanical Fuel Injection (Air Flow Controlled)—1976–77 V8 Engines

This system replaces the electronic system of earlier years. In contrast to the intermittent type fuel injection, this system measures air volume through an air flow sensor and injects fuel continuously in front of the intake valves, regardless of firing position.

Testing

DELIVERY CAPACITY

Remove the fuel return hose from the fuel distributor. Connect a fuel line and hold the end in a measuring cup. Disconnect the plug from the safety switch on the mixture regulator and turn on the ignition for 30 seconds. If the delivery rate is less than 1 liter in 30 seconds, check the voltage at the fuel pump (11.5) and the fuel lines for kinks.

Disconnect the leak off line between the fuel accumulator and the suction damper. Check the delivery rate again. If it is low replace the accumulator.

Replace the fuel filter and test again. If still low, replace the fuel pump.

COLD START VALVE

1. Disconnect the plugs from the safety switch and mixture control regulator.

2. Remove the cold start valve with fuel line connected.

3. Hold the cold start valve in a container.

4. Turn on the ignition. Connect the valve to battery voltage. It should emit a cone shaped spray.

5. Dry the nozzle off. No fuel should leak out.

Hot Start System

Perform the test at coolant temperature 104°–1222° F.

1. Remove the coil wire.

2. Connect a voltmeter to hot-start terminal 3 and ground.

3. Actuate the starter. In approximately 3–4 seconds, the voltmeter should read about 11 volts for 3–4 seconds.

4. If 11 volts are not indicated, check fuse 10. Connect the plug of the 104° F. temperature switch and ground and repeat the test. If 11 volts are now indicated, replace the temperature switch. If 11 volts are not indicated, or if the time periods are wrong, replace the hot start relay.

Fuel Pump Safety Circuit

The pump will only run if the starter motor is actuated or if the engine is running.

1. Remove the air filter.

2. Turn on the ignition and briefly depress the sensor plate.

3. Remove the coil wire from the distributor.

4. Connect a voltmeter to the positive fuel pump terminal and ground.

5. Actuate the starter. Voltmeter should indicate 11 volts.

6. If the fuel pump runs only when the sensor plate is depressed or only when the engine is cranked, replace the fuel pump relay. If the pump is already running when the ignition is turned ON, replace the safety switch.

CADILLAC ELECTRONIC FUEL INJECTION (EFI)

The fuel injection system used as standard equipment on the 1976 and later Seville and now optional on other Cadillac models is the type that injects the gasoline into the intake manifold, close to the cylinder head intake port. The basic engine is unchanged from a carbureted engine. Most of the fuel injection parts mount on the special intake manifold. Basically, the system utilizes electronically actuated fuel metering valves or injectors to spray a carefully metered amount of fuel into the engine.

Testing & Troubleshooting

In case of trouble, there are three things that should be checked:

1. Wiring
2. Vacuum hoses
3. Injectors

The wiring and the hoses should be checked for loose connections or bad wires and hoses. The hose to the electronic control unit may be accidentally knocked off during work done under the instrument panel.

The injectors will not normally give any trouble, but they may clog up if the fuel is dirty, or if some dirt gets into the system while it is apart for any reason. If one cylinder is dead, and the ignition checks out OK, the chances are that the injector is plugged. Cadillac has not published any procedure for cleaning the injectors. More information will be available later.

Troubleshooting Cadillac's Fuel Injection System

ATTENTION: Before checking out fuel injection system problems be sure that the vehicle's other electrical systems are in good order and functioning properly.

The Problem	The Cause
Engine Cranks But Will Not Start	1. Blown 10 amp in-line fuel pump located below instrument panel near ECU jumper harness connectors.*
	2. Open circuit in 12 purple wire between starter solenoid and ECU.
	3. Open circuit in 18 dark green wire between generator BAT terminal and ECU (fusible link).*
	4. Poor connection at ECU jump harness (below instrument panel) or at ECU.
	5. Poor connection at fuel pump jumper harness (below instrument panel near ECU jumper harness) 14 dark green wire.*
	6. Poor connections at engine coolant sensor or open circuit in sensor or wiring (cold engine only).**
	7. Poor connection at distributor trigger (speed sensor).
	8. Distributor trigger (speed sensor) stuck closed.
	9. Malfunction in chassis-mounted pump.

Troubleshooting Cadillac's Fuel Injection System (cont.)

The Problem	The Cause
Engine Cranks But Will Not Start	10. Malfunction in throttle position switch (WOT section shorted). To check, disconnect switch—engine should start. 11. Fuel flow restriction.
Hard Starting	1. Open engine coolant sensor (cold or partially warm engine only starts OK hot).°° 2. Malfunction in throttle position switch (WOT section shorted). To check, disconnect switch—engine should start normally. 3. Malfunction in chassis-mounted fuel pump. (Check valves leaking back.) 4. Malfunction in pressure regulator.
Poor Fuel Economy	1. Disconnected or leaking MAP sensor hose. 2. Disconnected vacuum hose at fuel pressure regulator or at throttle body. 3. Malfunction of air or coolant sensor.°°°
Engine Stalls After Start	1. Open circuit in 12 black/yellow ignition signal wire between fuse block and ECU; or poor connection at connector (12 black/yellow wire) located below instrument panel near ECU jumper harness. 2. Poor connection at engine coolant sensor or open circuit in sensor or wiring (cold or warm engine only).°°
Rough Idle	1. Disconnected, leaking or pinched MAP sensor hose. If plastic harness line requires replacement, replace entire EFI engine harness. 2. Poor connection at air or coolant sensor or open circuit in sensor or wiring (cold engine only).°° 3. Poor connection at injection valve(s). 4. Shorted engine coolant sensor.°°°
Prolonged Fast Idle	1. Poor connection at fast idle valve or open circuit in heating element. 2. Throttle position switch misadjusted. 3. Vacuum leak.
Engine Hesitates or Stumbles on Acceleration	1. Disconnected, leaking or pinched MAP sensor hose. If plastic harness line requires replacement, replace entire EFI engine harness. 2. Throttle position switch misadjusted. 3. Malfunction in throttle position switch. 4. Intermittent malfunction in distributor trigger (speed sensor). 5. Poor connection at 6 pin connector or of ECU jumper harness or at ECU. 6. Poor connection at EGR solenoid or open solenoid (cold engine only).
Lack of High Speed Performance	1. Misadjusted throttle position switch (WOT only). 2. Malfunction in throttle position switch. 3. Malfunction of chassis-mounted fuel pump. 4. Intermittent malfunction in distributor trigger (speed sensor). 5. Fuel filter blocked or restricted. 6. Open circuit in 12 purple wire between starter Solenoid and ECU.

° To check, listen for chassis-mounted fuel pump whine (one second only) as key is turned to ON position (not to START position).

°° To check for an open circuit in an EFI temperature sensor, connect an ohmmeter to the sensor connector terminals. If the sensor resistance is greater than 1600 ohms, replace the sensor.

°°° To check for a closed (short) circuit in an EFI temperature sensor, connect an ohmmeter to the sensor connector terminals. If the sensor resistance is less than 700 ohms, replace the sensor.

WOT—wide open throttle
ECU—electronic control unit
EFI—electronic fuel injection
EGR—exhaust gas recirculation
MAP—manifold absolute pressure

Carburetors

BASIC OPERATING PRINCIPLES

Carburetors vary greatly in the way that they are made, but they are all basically the same in that their job is to mix the air with the fuel in the proportion that the engine needs. There are six different systems or fuel/air circuits in a carburetor that make it work. These systems are the Float System; Main Metering System; Idle and Low-Speed System; Accelerator Pump System; Power System; Idle and Low-Speed System; and the Choke System. The way these systems are arranged in the

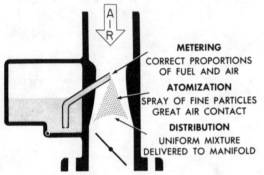

METERING
CORRECT PROPORTIONS OF FUEL AND AIR

ATOMIZATION
SPRAY OF FINE PARTICLES GREAT AIR CONTACT

DISTRIBUTION
UNIFORM MIXTURE DELIVERED TO MANIFOLD

Basic carburetor functions

carburetor determines what the carburetor looks like.

It's hard to believe that the little single-barrel carburetor used on 6 cylinder or 4 cylinder engines have all of the same basic systems as the enormous 4-barrel carburetors used on the big V8s. Of course, the 4-barrels have secondary throttle bores and a lot of other paraphernalia that you won't find on a single-barrel carburetor. But basically, all carburetors are the same and if you can understand a simple single-barrel, you can use that knowledge to understand the 4-barrel. Understanding the basic systems in a carburetor is important from the standpoint of diagnosis. If you have a lean-running engine, you must have enough knowledge about carburetors to know that it might be caused by a low float level or the wrong jet size. The more you know about carburetors, the easier it will be to make this kind of quick decision that will save you time when you are trying to find a problem.

Float System

When the fuel pump pushes fuel into the carburetor, it flows through a seat and past a needle which is a kind of shutoff valve. The fuel flows into the float bowl and raises a hinged float so that the float arm pushes the

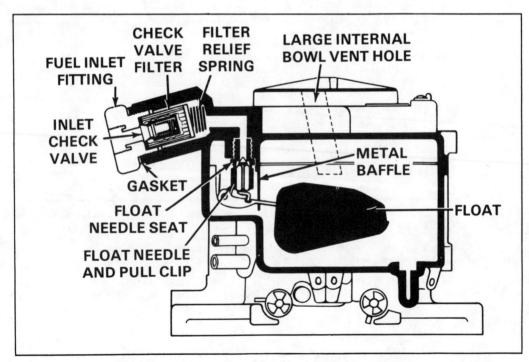

Typical float system

needle into the seat and shuts off the fuel. Floats have a large range of movement when you look at them in a disassembled carburetor, but in actual operation they move very little, as long as the fuel pump has enough capacity to keep up with the engine. If the engine uses more fuel than the pump can supply, then the float drops down, which allows the fuel to push the needle valve away from the seat and more fuel flows in. If the float system is properly designed, the fuel level will stay fairly constant which means that the engine gets the right mixture at all times. Floats are adjusted by bending a little tang on the float arm that bears against the needle.

All manufacturers give a float level specification. If the float is the type that is mounted in the bowl itself, the float level specification is a measurement from the top of the bowl to the top of the float. If the float is the type that is mounted on the bowl cover, then the measurement is taken from the cover to the top of the float. The float level measurement is always taken with the needle in the closed position and the float resting against it. If the float is in the bowl you can close it by filling the bowl with solvent or by turning the carburetor upside down. Some manufacturers recommend pushing on the little float tang to hold the float and needle in the closed position. We do not recommend this because it requires a delicate touch so that you don't push the soft rubber tip of the needle into the seat and make a groove in it. If the float is attached to the cover, then the way to close the needle is to turn the cover upside down, so that the float bears on the needle. Then make your measurement between the float and the underside of the bowl cover.

Fuel level is also given as a specification for some carburetors. The fuel level is the measurement from the top of the bowl to the surface of the fuel in the bowl. Of course, measuring the actual wet fuel level is more accurate than just measuring the float level, but the measurement of fuel level cannot be done on all carburetors. On some carburetors, there are holes in the top of the bowl that can be uncovered by removing parts of the carburetor, which will then allow you to stick a scale down through the hole and measure the actual wet fuel level. Other carburetors have sight holes covered up by plugs in the side of the bowl. When these plugs are removed with the engine idling, the fuel should just wet the threads in the bottom of the hole. If the fuel runs out, the fuel level is too high.

In some manuals and even in some shops, you may see a special gauge that is attached to the carburetor, so that the fuel in the bowl can run out into the gauge and tell you the actual wet fuel level. Whichever you use, fuel level or float level, you should make adjustments to the float according to the manufacturer's specifications. In most cases, the float level is set and the fuel level is an optional check that you can use if you feel it is necessary.

Float drop is the measurement of the amount that the float drops when there isn't any fuel in the bowl. Float drop is regulated by a second tang on the float arm which usually hits against the side of the brass seat. Float drop is not a precise measurement. As long as the float drops enough to allow the needle to open and fuel to enter, it will probably be alright. However, you must be sure that the float cannot drop so far that the needle jams against the float tang. Some carburetors have a boss in the bottom of the bowl that keeps the float from dropping too far. In those instances, there is no float drop adjustment because the boss takes care of it. In any case, follow the manufacturer's instructions. If he gives a float drop specification, then by all means check it when you have the carburetor apart.

A lot of development has gone into the needle and seat in most modern carburetors. Originally, needles were all steel and seats were all brass. The trouble with a steel needle on a brass seat is that it can be held open by a very small amount of dirt. The manufacturers have gone to great lengths to try to solve this problem, even using diaphragm needles that were very difficult to repair. Today, almost every carburetor uses a steel needle with a rubber or Viton® tip, or a complete steel needle that bears against a rubber or Viton® seat. This flexible needle tip or seat is the reason that you must be careful not to push too hard against the seat when checking float level. The needle can get a groove in it that will take several hours, if ever, to go back to its original shape.

Main Metering System

At cruising speed, most of the fuel for engine operation comes through the main metering system. When the engine is running, it constantly sucks air through the throat of the carburetor. The throat is made with a narrow portion in the middle, called the venturi. When the air passes through the venturi section of the throat, it creates a slight vacuum in

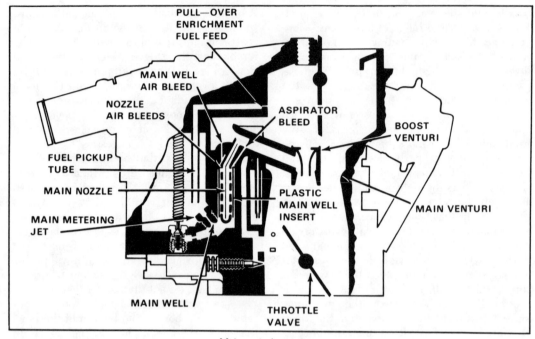

Main metering system

that area. The vacuum acts on the end of the main nozzle, which is a tube that runs at a slant from the bottom of the float bowl up into the venturi. The slant is necessary so that the fuel will not run out of the float bowl into the throat of the carburetor. Some carburetors use multiple venturis, with one inside the other and the end of the main nozzle inside the smallest venturi. These multiple venturis increase the suction effect on the end of the main nozzle.

Fuel would flow from the float bowl through the main nozzle in tremendous quantity if it were not for some type of metering. The fuel is metered by a calibrated hole called the main jet, located at the bottom of the float bowl. All of the fuel has to pass through the main jet before it can get to the main nozzle. In some carburetors, the jet is connected directly to the end of the main nozzle, but in most modern carburetors there is a main well between the jet and the bottom end of the nozzle. This main well contains screens or bars to break up the fuel and also is the area where air bleeds allow air to mix with the fuel and try to break it up before it goes out the end of the main nozzle. Raw fuel does not travel too well through an intake manifold. It has a tendency to fall out of the air stream. So everything in the carburetor is designed with the idea that the finer that you can break up the particles of fuel, the better the engine will

run and the better will be the fuel distribution.

Some carburetor designs use a main jet and let it go at that. Others have a main jet with a metering rod resting in the jet. The metering rod is simply a brass rod that hangs in the jet hole and limits the amount of fuel that can go through. Metering rods have tapers or steps on them. The rod gets thinner toward the bottom end. If the rod is lifted slightly, so that the center portion is in the jet hole, then more fuel will flow and the mixture will become richer. This richer mixture is needed as the engine goes faster. There are several ways to lift the metering rod in the jet. It can be done mechanically, through a connection with the throttle linkage or it can be done by vacuum, acting on a piston or a diaphragm. The vacuum arrangement is set up so that it holds the metering rod down in the jet. As the engine throttle is opened and more load is put on the engine, the vacuum reduces and the metering rod slowly rises up out of the jet from the force of a spring underneath the vacuum piston. Because the suction in the venturi that draws the fuel out of the end of the main nozzle is so small, the fuel level in the bowl is critical. The main nozzle slants upward with its venturi end higher than the fuel in the bowl, so that the fuel level in the bowl is also the level of fuel inside the main nozzle. Ideally, the fuel should stay just inside the tip of the nozzle, ready for the slight venturi vacuum to pull it out, but not dripping. If you have ever seen a carburetor that drips when the engine is off, it means that the fuel level in the bowl is too high. If the fuel level is too low, the fuel will be way down inside the main nozzle and the slight venturi vacuum will have difficulty pulling it out. This causes a lean mixture and makes a poor running car at cruising speed.

What we have been describing so far is the main metering system as it exists in a single throat carburetor.

The main metering system works very well at cruising speed, but it depends on the airflow in the venturi to have enough suction to draw the fuel out of the main nozzle. At very low speeds and at idle, the main metering system simply won't work. In order to have the car run at slow speeds, we have to have the Idle and Low Speed System.

Idle and Low-Speed System

The vacuum in the intake manifold at idle is high because the throttle is almost completely closed. This vacuum is used to draw fuel into the engine through the idle system and keep it running. The idle jet is usually a tube with a calibrated hole in the end, that sticks down from the top of the carburetor in the main well, below the fuel level. The upper end of the tube connects to a passageway above the fuel level, which crosses over and then travels

down inside the casting, to a hole in the throat of the carburetor below the throttle valve. Engine vacuum acts on the hole and sucks the fuel up into the idle jet, across, and down into the engine. As the fuel crosses over above the fuel level, it is mixed with air from air bleeds in the top of the carburetor. There may be some restrictions in the channel that help to break up the fuel and mix it with the air.

The fuel cannot be allowed to run uncontrolled into the engine, through the hole under the throttle valve, so an idle mixture needle is built into the carburetor with its point resting in the hole. When the needle is screwed in, it closes the hole off partway and limits the amount of fuel that can go into the engine. When the mixture is properly adjusted with the needle, it mixes with the air passing around the throttle blade and gives the engine the right fuel and air mixture for a good idle. There is usually one idle mixture needle for each throat in the carburetor, but there have been designs in the past that use a single mixture needle located high up on the carburetor that controls the mixture to more than one throat at a time.

Other designs of carburetors close the throttle valve completely at idle and use a large screw to allow the air to by-pass the throttle valve. Instead of opening the throttle to adjust engine speed at idle, you adjust the bypass air screw.

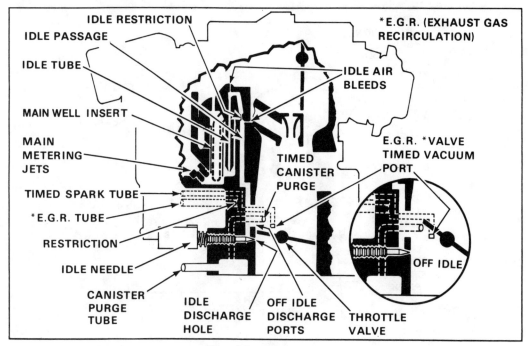

Idle and low speed system

As the throttle opens, the venturi main metering system does not take over immediately. The throttle has to be open fairly far before there is enough airflow through the venturi to suck fuel out of the main nozzle. To take care of this transition period and keep the engine running smoothly, there is what is known as an off idle port or an idle transfer port above the throttle valve. As the throttle valve opens, it exposes this port to engine vacuum and we have an additional flow of idle mixture.

The idle and low-speed system is commonly thought of as working only during idle, but actually it feeds fuel almost up to wide-open throttle. It's important to remember that the idle mixture needle does not change the mixture in the idle passageway from rich to lean. It only changes the *amount* of mixture coming through the passageway. The richness or leanness of the idle passageway mixture is controlled by the size of the idle jet, which in many carburetors is not replaceable. If the idle jet is the wrong size or damaged so that it limits the flow of fuel, you could compensate for this at idle by unscrewing the idle mixture needle and allowing more mixture to mix with the air coming around the throttle valve. However, as the throttle opens and exposes the idle transfer port, the restrictive idle jet would cause a lean mixture in the transition period, contributing to a stumble. It works the other way around too. If the idle jet is too big

it can cause a rich mixture throughout the cruising range, almost up to top speed.

Accelerator Pump System

When the throttle is open, the air flowing through the venturi starts moving faster almost instantly, but there is a lag in the flow of fuel out of the main nozzle. The result is that the engine runs lean and stumbles. It needs an extra shot of fuel just when the throttle is opened. This extra shot of fuel is provided by the accelerator pump. It's nothing more than a little pump operated by the throttle linkage that shoots a squirt of fuel through a separate nozzle into the throat of the carburetor. The accelerator pump jet, which is usually located in the pump nozzle, is calibrated so that it supplies the right amount of fuel.

The pump is usually a plunger working in a vertical cylinder, as the throttle is closed, the plunger rises and draws fuel into the cylinder, from the float bowl, which stays there ready for the next time the throttle is opened. When the throttle is opened the plunger is forced down the cylinder, which pushes the fuel up through the nozzle into the throat of the carburetor. When the pump is on the upstroke drawing fuel in from the float bowl, an intake check, usually a steel ball opens to allow the fuel to enter from the bowl. An outlet check closes at the same time so that the pump will not suck air back from the throat of the carbu-

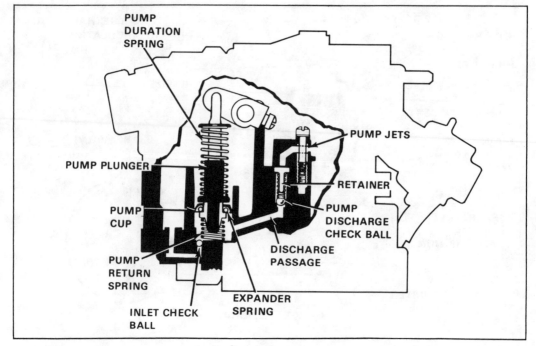

Accelerator pump system

retor. When the pump moves down to push the fuel into the throat, it opens the outlet check and closes the intake check so that fuel will not be forced back into the carburetor bowl.

The intake check is not on all pumps. Some allow the sides of the pump itself to collapse on the upstroke and the fuel flows past the lip of the cup, into the bottom of the pump well. A vertical plunger pump design can be operated directly by the throttle linkage or operated by a spring around the pump shaft. When the pump is operated by the spring, the throttle linkage holds the spring in a compressed position. When the throttle is opened, the linkage relaxes its hold on the spring and the spring pushes the pump plunger down. The spring gives the same rate of flow everytime the pump is operated and prevents an overly ambitious driver from bending the linkage by shoving the throttle down too fast.

Pumps can also be a rubber or neoprene diaphragm connected to the throttle linkage. The diaphragm has the disadvantage that it has to be placed below the fuel level, in order to receive fuel and stay full at all times. If the diaphragm develops a leak, as it will when it eventually wears out, fuel will leak out of the carburetor onto the intake manifold.

Most pumps can be adjusted for the length of the stroke with different holes in the pump link. If there are no optional holes, the linkage itself can be bent to change the stroke of the pump. A shorter stroke results in less fuel being squirted into the carburetor throat and a longer stroke more fuel. Flat spots in acceleration can be caused by too much accelerator pump fuel the same way they can be caused by too little. In the days before emission controls, such adjustments could be easily made to tailor the pump setting to the car so that all flat spots could be eliminated. In these days of emission controls, pump adjustments must be made according to the manufacturer's specifications. Unauthorized adjustments may change emission levels and should not be done unless the adjustment is factory authorized.

Power System

The main metering system works very well at normal engine loads, but when the throttle is in the wide-open position, the engine needs more fuel to prevent detonation and give it full power. The power system provides additional fuel by opening up another passageway

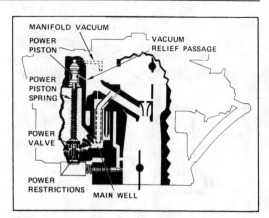

Power system

that leads to the main nozzle. On some carburetors, this extra passageway is controlled by a power valve. The power valve can be opened by a vacuum-operated metal plunger, a diaphragm, or by mechanical linkage from the throttle. If the power valve is vacuum-operated, the high vacuum in the engine keeps the valve closed above approximately 10 in. Hg. When the throttle is opened and the vacuum drops, the spring behind the plunger or diaphragm pushes the power valve open and allows the additional fuel to flow up to the main nozzle. If the power valve is operated by mechanical linkage from the throttle, then it is strictly a question of throttle position and has nothing to do with the actual load on the engine. Most of the power valves today are vacuum-operated.

Some carburetors do not use a separate power valve. They consider that lifting the metering rod or what they may call a "step-up" rod out of the jet is adequate without the need for a separate power valve. The lifting of the metering rod or step-up rod out of the jet is accomplished by a spring underneath a vacuum piston. When engine vacuum falls off, the spring pushes the rod up and the thinnest portion of the metering rod or step-up rod is in the jet, which allows more fuel to flow.

Choke System

A choke is necessary on a cold engine because the fuel condenses out of the air/fuel mixture on to the combustion chamber and cylinder walls. This means there is less fuel in the mixture to actually burn and some means must be used to get more fuel into the engine. The choke does this because it is a plate located at the top of the carburetor, above the venturi. When the choke is closed, very little air can enter the engine. This in itself would

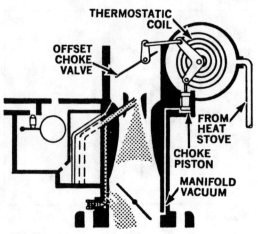

THERMOSTATIC COIL

OFFSET CHOKE VALVE

FROM HEAT STOVE

CHOKE PISTON

MANIFOLD VACUUM

Choke system

richen the mixture, but the main reason that the mixture is richened when the choke closes is that the entire vacuum suction from the engine acts on the main nozzle and literally sucks raw fuel right out of the carburetor bowl. Of course, we very seldom run an engine with a completely closed choke, but moving your choke just a few degrees toward the closed position will create a vacuum underneath it that will draw more fuel out of the main nozzle.

Chokes used to be manually controlled by the driver, which worked fine as long as he remembered to shut it off after the engine warmed up. Now most chokes are automatically controlled by a thermostatic spring, either on the carburetor or mounted on the engine and connected to the carburetor through a linkage. When the thermostatic spring is cold, it pushes the choke towards the closed position. If the spring is mounted on the carburetor, hot air from around the exhaust manifold is piped to the spring to make it open quickly. If the thermostatic spring is mounted in a well on the intake manifold or next to the intake manifold, it picks up heat from the exhaust crossover passage.

When a cold engine is being started, we need a completely closed choke for quick starting, but the instant the engine starts running, we need to get that choke open to give the engine enough air to keep going. The thermostatic spring does not heat quickly enough and open the choke as fast as needed, so that a piston or diaphragm, called a vacuum break diaphragm, is used to pull the choke open just a few degrees; enough so that the engine will keep running. The piston type of vacuum break use to be built into the choke

housing and it was common to have heat distort the housing and the piston to stick. Today, the vacuum break is a separate diaphragm which is much more reliable than the older piston.

Another device to keep the engine running after it starts is the fast idle. When the choke is closed, linkage connects to a fast idle cam and raises it underneath the throttle stop screw, so that the engine idles at a faster speed than normal. This fast idle cam must be set by depressing the throttle before starting a cold engine. In fact, the fast idle cam is connected to the choke plate itself so that if the fast idle cam is not set, the choke will not close.

The type of choke that mounts on the carburetor itself usually has a housing with marks on it and can be adjusted by lining up the marks according to factory specifications.

The type of choke coil that mounts off the carburetor is usually adjusted, if necessary, by bending a link connecting the choke coil to the choke plate. A close inspection of the choke coil that mounts off the carburetor will reveal marks on it and an adjustment nut on some models. However, this adjustment is usually for factory adjustment only. The way to adjust the choke in the field on this type is by bending the link. Other manufacturers, who have their chokes mounted off the carburetor, do not provide any adjustment specifications and they do not recommend that you reset the marks or bend the link. In all choke adjustments, you must follow the manufacturer's specifications.

Choke Unloader

If the driver accidently floods the engine by working the throttle too much and squirting too much fuel out of the accelerator pump, the engine won't start unless the choke can be opened. The unloader device takes care of this by providing a choke opening of a few degrees, just enough to get the engine started if the driver will shove the throttle all the way to the floor and hold it there. Unfortunately, many drivers don't know about the unloader feature and therefore the flooded carburetor still presents quite a few problems on a cold engine.

Secondary Carburetor Throats

At low engine speeds, a car runs best with a small carburetor and at high engine speeds, it puts out its best power with a large carburetor. The problem is to build both carburetors into the same engine. The solution is a system of primary and secondary throats. The primary throttles work in all normal, around town and low-speed driving. When the primary throttles are opened to about a ¾ opening, then the secondary throttles start to open and both primary and secondary throttles reach the wide-open position at the same time. The result is that the engine runs well at low-speed and puts out maximum power at high-speed. Most secondary throats have only a main metering system, but some of them may have a constant flow idle system that makes the engine idle smoother.

On domestic vehicles, a two-barrel carburetor has always meant a carburetor with two primary throats. However, imported cars have two-barrel carburetors on their small 4 cylinder engines that have primary and secondary throats.

Four-barrel carburetors are all of the primary/secondary design with two primary throats that are for normal running and two secondary throats that open at high-speed or high-load. The activating control to the secondary throttles can be either mechanical through throttle linkage, or through a venturi vacuum system. If a large enough diaphragm is used, the venturi vacuum is strong enough to actually open the throttle plates at high airflow.

Vacuum-operated secondaries only open when the engine needs them. It is impossible for the driver to get them open at low speeds. Mechanically-operated secondaries are different. If the driver doesn't know what he is doing, he can stick his foot all the way to the floor, opening all 4 barrels wide-open when the car is only going two mph. This can cause the engine to gasp and take several seconds to recover. To keep this from happening, some carburetors have a weighted or spring-loaded air valve in the secondary barrels, above the throttle plates. The air valve opens only if the airflow through the secondary throats is high enough to push it open.

Another problem with the driver, is that he sometimes insists on opening all 4 barrels when the engine is cold. Calling on a cold engine to produce maximum horsepower can be very damaging. Carburetors with secondaries get around this problem by using what is known as a "lock-out". A little lever connected to the choke drops down over the secondary and prevents their opening until the choke is fully opened. The lock-out on some 4-barrel carburetors is not on the throttle plates

themselves, but on the air valve above the throttle plates. The throttle plates open anytime the driver floors the gas pedal, but it doesn't do anything unless the choke is off because the little lock-out lever keeps the air valve closed.

Vacuum-operated secondaries don't need a lock-out mechanism because they would not open at low-speed anyway, as they depend upon airflow through the venturi to get enough vacuum to open the secondaries.

EMISSION-RELATED CARBURETOR CONTROLS

There are a number of devices on modern carburetors that, strictly speaking, are not necessary for the operation of the carburetor. Some of these devices are discussed in a general way in the following section. Unfortunately, the scope of this book does not permit specific analysis.

Bowl Vents

If you want to be technical about it, the suction in the venturi really does not draw the fuel out of the main nozzle. What happens is that atmospheric pressure, acting on the fuel in the bowl, pushes the fuel out of the main nozzle because there is less pressure at the end of the nozzle. We mention this because it will help to understand why bowl vents are necessary. If the atmospheric pressure can't get into the bowl to act on the fuel, then it can't push it out of the nozzle and the engine won't run, or at least it won't run very well. Bowl vents are sometimes necessary when an engine stops in order to get rid of evaporating fuel that might go down into the throat of the carburetor and make the engine hard to start.

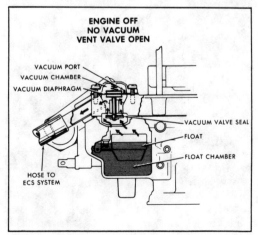

Bowl vent

When vapor emission controls came out, bowl vents on many carburetors were either eliminated or the vent was connected to the carbon canister so that the vapors could be collected. Some carburetors still use a bowl vent that goes into the atmosphere but it has a valve in it that only opens when there is high pressure in the bowl. This evidently doesn't happen very often, so that the system is considered non-polluting.

Bowl vents on some carburetors are what is known as an internal vent. The air space over the fuel in the bowl is connected by a slanting tube into the throat of the carburetor above the choke valve. This internal vent not only keeps the fuel vapors inside the air cleaner, but helps the fuel flow at high rpm by allowing the rush of air through the throat of the carburetor to go down the tube and help push the fuel up into the main nozzle.

Carburetor Heat

The mixture passages in the intake manifold under the carburetor have been heated for many years in both inline and V8 engines by exhaust passages that run through the manifold. This intake manifold heat is necessary to eliminate flat spots and get better fuel distribution because there is more complete vaporization of the fuel. Fuel does not vaporize as easily as you might think, and the heavy particles of fuel that tend to settle out of the air moving in the intake manifold can make some cylinders run rich, while a cylinder right next to it is running lean. Actually, carburetor heat, in part, makes up for deficiencies in intake manifold design. For many years, a heat valve was used in the exhaust manifold on both inline and V8 engines to send some of the exhaust through the heat passages in the intake manifold. The valve was spring-loaded with a thermostatically-controlled spring, so that at high engine temperatures it did not send as much exhaust through the heat passages. Now most engines use a heated air cleaner which sends hot air to the carburetor on a cold engine and shortens the warm-up time considerably. Many manufacturers have found that they can do away with the heat valve in the exhaust manifold when they have the heated air cleaner. In most cases, the heat passages are still in the intake manifold, but the valve has been eliminated from the exhaust manifold.

Hot Idle Compensators

When underhood temperatures get extremely high on a hot day, the fuel vaporizes much easier. This extra vaporization of the fuel can cause a rich mixture, particularly at idle. The hot idle compensator is a little valve which can be mounted on the carburetor or in a vacuum hose, such as the PCV hose. When underhood temperatures get extremely hot, the hot idle compensator valve opens and allows atmospheric air to flow into the intake manifold. This leans the excessively rich mixture down to where the engine will keep idling without stalling. The hot idle compensator opens at idle because that is the period when there is no airflow (or very little airflow) through the engine compartment and very high temperatures result. When the car starts moving, the airflow increases and that usually is enough to cool the compensator and close it.

Vacuum Control Ports

The carburetor not only has the job of mixing the air and the fuel, but also of regulating vacuum supply to various other parts of the engine, such as the distributor vacuum advance and emission controls.

PORTED VACUUM

Ported vacuum is a system of vacuum advance control that results in no spark advance

Hot idle compensator mounted in the PCV line

at idle. A vacuum port is located in the throat of the carburetor, so that it is above the throttle valve when the throttle is in the curb idle position. There is no vacuum above the throttle valve, so that the distributor vacuum advance goes to the neutral or no advance position at idle. When the throttle is opened above idle, the vacuum under the throttle blade acts on the spark port and advances the spark. The ported vacuum system is also used to operate exhaust gas recirculation valves. Sometimes, the EGR valve is operated from the same port that operates distributor advance. On other carburetors, there may be two separate ports. There are even emission control systems where the operation of the distributor advance is switched back and forth from the EGR port to the spark port.

Another system operated by a port over the throttle blade is the purge to the vapor control canister. Purge at idle might upset the engine idle, therefore the port is placed above the throttle blade and the canister is only purged when the throttle is opened.

Venturi Vacuum

Venturi vacuum is another control method that was formerly used to operate the Ford all-vacuum distributor several years ago. Venturi vacuum works from a port in the venturi of the carburetor. The low pressure or suction in the venturi area acts on the port the same way it does on the main nozzle. Venturi vacuum is not very strong, but when used with a distributor vacuum advance that is calibrated for it, it will operate the vacuum advance according to the amount of airflow that is rushing through the carburetor throat. This airflow is inversely proportional to the load on the engine. When the load is high, the throttle is wide-open. Therefore, the airflow is low, which means that venturi vacuum is low and the spark is retarded. When the load is light, the airflow is high and the spark advances.

On some emission controlled cars, the venturi vacuum system is used to operate an exhaust gas recirculation amplifier. The venturi vacuum turns on the amplifier valve and then the amplifier valve sends full manifold vacuum to open the EGR valve. Because there is no venturi vacuum at idle, the EGR valve stays closed. There is venturi vacuum at wide-open throttle, but manifold vacuum is so low that there isn't enough to open the EGR valve. Venturi vacuum is not necessarily any better or any worse than the vacuum system. It's just another way of trying to get precise control over the vacuum-operated units.

Anti-Stall Dashpots

When the driver of a car with an automatic transmission suddenly takes his foot off of the throttle, the throttle closes before the engine gets a chance to slow down. The engine is turning faster than it would at a normal curb idle, but the carburetor having its throttle in the idle position, is supplying a curb idle mixture. The result is the engine won't run and it stalls. An anti-stall dashpot, which is sometimes called a slow closing throttle, is used on the throttle linkage so that the throttle closes slowly whenever the driver lifts his foot. This gives the mixture a chance to stabilize and the engine keeps running. You will also find these dashpots on some manual transmission cars. In some cases, they have been used to prevent driveline whip which is damaging to the manual transmission driveline. In other cases, they have been used as an emission control device to prevent the excessively rich idle mixture from being pulled through the engine before it gets a chance to slow down to idle speed. When you see an anti-stall dashpot on a manual transmission car, the chances are that it was not a mistake, but it was put there for a definite purpose.

Anti-Dieseling Solenoids

When the emission controls came out, the manufacturers generally went to retarded spark and greater throttle openings at idle. This gave a better mixture that burned more completely for fewer emissions, but it created a problem of dieseling or after-running; i.e., the engine would keep going after the ignition switch was turned off. Lean mixtures, high combustion chamber temperatures and the increased throttle opening at idle all contributed to the dieseling problem. One way to stop dieseling is to shut off the air, or at least cut down on the air, that the engine receives. The anti-dieseling solenoid does this by providing one throttle setting for normal curb idle and another throttle setting which is considerably smaller. When the anti-dieseling solenoid is used, the normal curb idle is set with the solenoid adjustment. It can be a threaded stem, a solenoid that moves in a bracket, or is adjusted in some way to give the correct engine idle speed. The solenoid is connected so that it is on whenever the ignition switch is on. When the driver turns the ignition off, the anti-dieseling solenoid also goes off, allowing

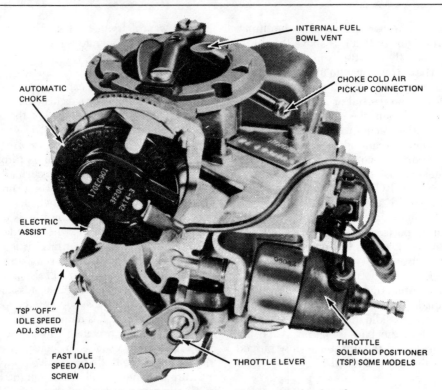

INTERNAL FUEL
BOWL VENT

AUTOMATIC
CHOKE

CHOKE COLD AIR
PICK-UP CONNECTION

ELECTRIC
ASSIST

TSP "OFF"
IDLE SPEED
ADJ. SCREW

FAST IDLE
SPEED ADJ.
SCREW

THROTTLE LEVER

THROTTLE
SOLENOID POSITIONER
(TSP) SOME MODELS

Typical one barrel carburetor. Note the throttle solenoid.

the throttle to drop that back to a much smaller opening. This cuts down on the air entering the engine and supposedly eliminates dieseling.

The manufacturers give idle speed specifications for anti-dieseling solenoid equipped cars as two numbers separated by a slash. The lower number is the speed that is set with the solenoid off. This adjustment is made with the normal throttle stop screw. When the solenoid is on, the stem of the solenoid holds the throttle open off the normal stop screw and the adjustment for curb idle is made with the solenoid itself.

Anti-dieseling solenoids are strictly an electrical unit. If you see a solenoid that looks like an anti-dieseling solenoid, but has vacuum hoses connected to it; it is there for another purpose entirely. The solenoid with vacuum hoses to it is the General Motors CEC valve, which is not for anti-dieseling, but for holding the throttle open during deceleration.

Throttle Openers

For several years General Motors has used a throttle opener called a CEC valve. The CEC valve is a Combined Emission Control that regulates the transmission controlled spark and also opened the throttle for a wider closed throttle opening during deceleration in High gear. Idle speed should never be set with the stem of the CEC valve. The valve can be recognized because there are vacuum hoses running to it. There is a specification of engine rpm for the CEC valve, but it has nothing to do with idle speed and it's only necessary to set it after carburetor overhaul or any other reason for disassembling the throttle linkage.

Imported cars also use deceleration throttle openers of varying designs. The throttle opener is used for only one reason, to prevent the excessively rich mixtures that come from decleration in High gear or at high speeds with a closed throttle. Imported car throttle openers are usually 100% vacuum-controlled although some of them are connected with a speed switch that shuts off the throttle opening below a certain speed.

If you drive a car with a throttle opener it feels as if it's trying to keep going when you take your foot off the gas in High gear. This is not a defect, it's designed that way deliberately. If the car feels like it is running away, it's possible that the throttle opener is set too high.

Deceleration Enrichers

Small engines have a problem with maintaining combustion when they decelerate under closed throttle. Many 4 cylinder engines use what is called a "deceleration enriching valve" or a "coasting enricher." In the case of the Pinto and the Capri, this valve is separate, mounted on the intake manifold. It sucks fuel and air out of the float bowl of the carburetor and allows it to enter the intake manifold to support combustion during deceleration. Imported cars use a similar system, but the deceleration enricher is built into the carburetor itself. It's similar to a diaphragm-operated power valve, but it only opens during deceleration.

FUEL SYSTEM TROUBLESHOOTING

A. Inspect the System

Make sure there is fuel in the tank. Turn on the ignition switch and look at the gauge. If the gauge responds normally and reads anywhere but at the extremes, there is probably fuel in the tank. Unless you're sure that there is fuel in the tank, gently push a clean, slender object down the tank filler to check. If fuel level cannot be clearly determined in this way, the best procedure is to put a gallon or two of fuel in to ensure the pick-up is covered.

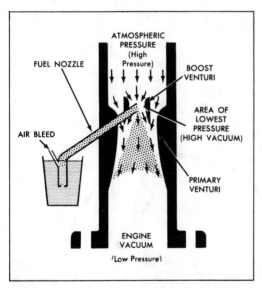

Carburetor venturi vacuum principle

Remove the air cleaner to check its condition. It should be possible to see a bright light through a paper element. If the element is dirty, blow the dirt off from the inside with air pressure. If this will not do an adequate cleaning job, the filter element should be replaced.

An oil bath unit will rarely clog enough to severely restrict air flow but it would be wise to clean a very dirty unit by dipping it in a solvent and moving it back and forth until the dirt has been effectively removed. Drain the oil from the base, remove the residue with solvent, and refill the base to the mark with clean engine oil. Do not reinstall the air cleaner until the fuel system problem has been found.

Open the throttle slightly to allow the automatic choke to set itself, and then check its position. If the engine is dead cold, and the outside temperature is as low as 70° F, the choke will generally close fully. The choke should be wide open at operating temperature. At temperatures in between these extremes, the choke should seek a middle position. After observing the position of the choke, move the flap very gently back and forth holding the throttle part-way open. If the choke does not come to an appropriate position, or if it does not move freely, see F.

Check for flooding next. Inspect the throttle bores for the presence of liquid fuel. If there is an obvious smell of raw fuel and the bores are lined with liquid, the engine is flooded. Flooding may be caused by improper starting technique—primarily, pumping of the throttle. If this is not suspected, tap the carburetor bowl firmly with a light but solid object, and then crank the engine for 20–30 seconds with the throttle held firmly to the floor. If this procedure allows the car to start, the problem is a stuck float. If the carburetor was flooded, see subsection C. on checking fuel pump pressure, and then go to subsection G.

To test for the presence of fuel in the carburetor, move the throttle from idle position to full throttle while watching for accelerator pump discharge. If there is no discharge, check further before assuming there is no fuel in the carburetor. Disconnect one of the spark plug leads. Crank the engine for 15–20 seconds with the throttle slightly open. Immediately pull the spark plug where the lead was disconnected. Check the electrodes for the presence of fuel. If the electrodes are dry, either the carburetor is malfunctioning or there is no fuel getting to it. Tap the carburetor bowl several times with a light but solid object, and then replace the spark plug and repeat the test. If this puts noticeable amounts of fuel on the plug's electrodes or enables the engine to start, the problem is a stuck float and subsection G. should be consulted without going through the others. Go to G. also, if the accelerator pump discharges fuel.

B. Check the Fuel Supply System

Disconnect the fuel line at the carburetor. Ground the distributor high-tension lead. Crank the engine for about 15 seconds with a clean glass container held under the open end of the fuel line. Fuel should be discharged regularly and forcefully, and it should not contain bubbles. If the discharge is minimal, see D. and E. to find out whether the problem is in the pump or lines. If there are bubbles, see E.

The fuel collected in the glass should be carefully inspected for the presence of water and dirt. If very small water bubbles are present, the fuel in the tank may be treated with any of several products designed to make the water mix with the gas and thus be eliminated from the system. If a layer of water is formed on the bottom of the glass, the fuel system must be thoroughly cleaned as follows:

1. Drain the gas tank. Drains are provided on many tanks for removal of the water and dirt which tend to accumulate there. If no drain is provided, the fuel line will have to be disconnected, and the tank will have to be dismounted so the water and dirt can be drained out the filler pipe. The tank should be flushed with clean fuel before replacing the fittings and restoring it to service.

2. Check the condition of the fuel tank strainer, generally located in the pick-up and fuel gauge assembly, and replace it if it is damaged.

3. Blow out the tank-to-pump line and the pump-to-carburetor line with compressed air.

C. Check Pump Output Pressure

The pressure may be checked by removing the pump discharge line and connecting a pressure gauge to the pump outlet. There are many gauges on the market for testing fuel pump pressure, manifold vacuum, etc. These employ a connector of standard size which will fit into most fuel pump discharge openings.

A check of pump output pressure will determine the ability of the pump to force fuel to the carburetor, and also check its ability to draw fuel from the tank, and the ability of the tank-to-pump lines to supply it, provided a good discharge volume was noted in B. Most fuel pumps are rated at engine idle speed. If the engine will run, it is best to connect all fuel and ignition lines, start the engine, and allow it to run to fill the carburetor float bowl.

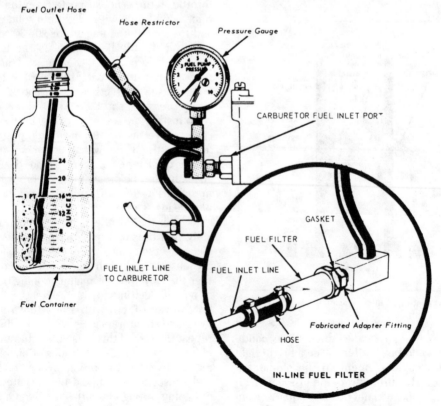

Pressure test equipment

Disconnect the fuel line at the pump, hook up the test gauge, and restart the engine, running it at slow idle on the fuel in the float bowl. If the engine will not run, pump operation at cranking speeds will give an indication of whether or not the pump will function well enough to permit the engine to start.

Fuel pump pressures generally range from three to seven pounds. Three pounds will at least supply the carburetor with adequate fuel for starting the engine. At idle speed, however, the pump pressure should be within the range specified by the manufacturer; either low or high pressures can cause operating problems.

If the fuel pump pressure is all right, be sure to check the pump-to-carburetor fuel line and carburetor strainer for clogging. Then go to F.

D. Check Pump Suction

A check of fuel pump suction will reveal whether or not the pump is faulty. Low output pressure can also result from a restriction or leak in the suction lines.

Disconnect *both* the pump discharge and inlet lines. The discharge is disconnected so there is no chance that a restriction in the line or carburetor strainer, or a normally functioning carburetor float, could restrict pump discharge and prevent the pump from developing its full suction power.

Connect a vacuum gauge to the pump, using an appropriate piece of rubber hose. Crank the engine until the gauge reaches a stable reading. It should be 15 in. or over. If not, the pump is faulty, and should be replaced.

A pump that will pull 15 in. of vacuum *can* be faulty. If checking and cleaning the strainers and lines as in E does not result in good fuel pump performance, replace the pump.

E. Check Strainers and Lines

If the fuel pump output pressure is inadequate, but the pump is capable of pulling a good vacuum, the fuel lines are most likely clogged or kinked, or the fuel system fittings are loose or cracked. A careful visual inspection of all accessible parts of the system should be made before the difficult-to-reach parts are checked out. The fitting at the fuel pump suction side should be very carefully inspected for cracks or deterioration. If a flexible hose is used here, the hose should be crack-free and firm in order to resist collapsing, and it must

be equipped with good clamps. Replace any doubtful parts. The entire length of the fuel lines along the frame to the fuel tank should be checked for the presence of kinks or dents that might have come from improper installation or road damage. The fuel line should then be removed from the tank and blown out with compressed air or replaced, as necessary. The fuel tank strainer should be inspected to ensure that it is clean and properly installed.

The fuel pump-to-carburetor line should also be checked for kinks, cracks, or bad fittings, and blown out with compressed air. The fuel strainer in the carburetor should be checked for cleanliness and cleaned or replaced as necessary. If the vehicle employs an inline fuel filter or strainer, be sure to check its condition and connections.

F. Check the Choke and Throttle Linkages

An inoperative throttle linkage could prevent starting by keeping the choke from closing during cranking or failing to supply adequate fuel/air mixture. Also, inadequate performance can frequently be traced to a linkage which does not open the throttle all the way. Have someone depress the accelerator pedal to the floor while you watch the throttle blade. It should reach a perfectly vertical position as the accelerator pedal reaches the floor. Adjustable linkages usually employ some sort of clamp or turnbuckle arrangement which is easily adjusted. Nonadjustable types that do not provide proper throttle operation usually perform improperly because of a bent bracket or a stretched cable.

Some four-barrel carburetors employ special air valves at the tops of their bores for controlling the metering of fuel. Check to see that the shafts which bear these valve flaps turn freely in their bores. Disassemble them and clean the shaft and the shaft bores if there is binding.

If a four-barrel carburetor uses vacuum diaphragm actuation of the secondary bores, the throttles must be observed with the engine running and air cleaner removed. At full-throttle position and high rpm, the secondary throttles should open fully. If they do not operate properly, check for binding or a leaky vacuum diaphragm.

An improperly functioning automatic choke is one of the most frequent causes of difficult starting. Because it operates through a delicate balance of carburetor air and thermostatic spring pressures, its tolerance to the accumulation of dirt is very low. Its delicate mechanism is also easily damaged.

An excellent indication of choke condition is its position when the engine is cold. Remove the air cleaner, open the throttle wide to release the choke mechanism from the fast idle cam, and observe what the choke does. It should close all the way if the engine is cold and the outside temperature is 70° or below. Under higher temperature conditions, the choke will generally be part-way closed until the engine thermostat opens (hot water is present in both radiator hoses). If the choke does not respond properly, it should be cleaned very carefully with solvent, and inspected for bent or broken linkage parts. The most effective procedure is to remove the screws that hold the choke flap to the choke (being *very* careful not to drop them down the carburetor throat), unfasten and remove the various parts of the linkage, usually simple metal clips, and pull the shaft and flap out of the carburetor throat. The shaft should be checked for bending, a very common cause of choke binding, and the shaft and the shaft bores in the carburetor very thoroughly cleaned of dirt and carbon deposits. If the choke uses a choke piston, located within the body of the carburetor, particular attention should be paid to determining that the piston and bore are clean, as this is another place binding can occur as a result of accumulated dirt.

During reassembly, all parts of the mechanism should be thoroughly checked to make sure no binding will occur due to bent parts. For example, if a U-shaped link is used in the mechanism, the center portion of the link should be straight, and the two ends should be parallel. There is a secondary air valve lock-out, on four-barrel carburetors, which rides along a pin located on the choke flap, parallel to the shaft. This can be bent during air cleaner installation and can cause binding of the choke. In either of these cases, the choke will malfunction even though all parts may be perfectly clean. The watchword is thoroughness. No part of the choke linkage should be above suspicion, and all parts should be carefully removed and inspected.

The same kind of care pays off in the cleaning process. Disassemble the linkage wherever one part turns on another. Treat the unit with solvent and wipe with a clean rag or paper towel to remove any grime loosened by the solvent.

After the mechanism is reassembled, several checks of choke operation should be made. These are best made with a factory manual or *Chilton's Auto Repair Manual.* These manuals contain specific instructions on the proper method of adjusting the various linkages and the proper specifications. Some cursory checks and adjustments can be made, however.

1. Choke coil operation. It would be wise to remove and inspect the choke coil. If the coil is housed in a circular chamber which is rotated to make the basic choke adjustment, mark the position of the chamber so it can be replaced in its original position. Remove the choke thermostatic coil housing and inspect the coil to make sure it is intact and clean. If there is evidence of corrosion, replace the choke heat tube or heat well so exhaust gases cannot continue to enter the coil housing. If the engine is hot, a rough check of choke coil adjustments can be made by placing the coil and housing in a cool spot until they have reached room temperature, and then quickly putting them in place on the carburetor, opening the throttle, and watching the choke. If the choke does not close fully, a slight twisting of an adjustable housing or a slight bend of the choke actuating rod, if the housing is not adjustable, will usually correct the problem. Move the choke flap to the wide open position to make sure the adjustment will not keep the choke from opening fully.

2. Choke vacuum break operation. The choke vacuum break is operated by the intake manifold vacuum created when the engine starts, and is placed on the carburetor to eliminate overly rich operation just after the engine has been started from cold. If the vehicle starts properly, but tends to run richly and smoke for the first few minutes of driving, the choke vacuum break may be at fault. The function of the vacuum diaphragm may be checked by starting the engine and allowing it to idle. Under these conditions, the vacuum diaphragm should recede into the housing and seat firmly. Check to see that this motion will pull the choke part-way open by forcing it toward the closed position until all the play in the linkage is removed and the diaphragm is keeping the choke from moving farther. To check this adjustment precisely, refer to a manual for instructions. These instructions will usually specify that the choke flap must be a certain distance from the front wall of the throttle bore with all the play in the linkage removed and the vacuum diaphragm firmly seated. The wire link between the vacuum di-

aphragm and the choke linkage is usually bent at the bottom of a U-shaped section to adjust the linkage. The vacuum diaphragm may be seated by running the engine, employing a vacuum pump on the end of the vacuum diaphragm hose, or by gently holding the diaphragm in the withdrawn position by hand. Using vacuum is preferable to handling the delicate mechanism, and guarantees that the diaphragm will be fully seated, if at least 15 in. of vacuum is employed.

If the vacuum diaphragm does not function, check for a cracked or loose hose, a plugged carburetor port, or binding in the linkage. If no problems are uncovered in these areas, replace the vacuum unit. Its diaphragm is probably ruptured.

3. Choke unloader operation. The choke unloader is operated by the throttle and is placed on the choke to permit the driver to relieve a flooding condition by cranking the engine with the throttle held to the floor. The choke unloader mechanism forces the choke part-way open mechanically, to provide a leaner mixture than is usually required when the engine is cold.

The mechanism usually consists of a tang which is mounted on the end of the throttle shaft near the fast idle cam. When the throttle is opened wide, the tang bears against one side of the fast idle cam. The fast idle cam is mounted on a shaft which protrudes from the side of the carburetor body. A linkage connects the cam and a lever mounted on the end of the choke shaft. The effect is that the unloader tang turns the cam slightly, which in turn, through its linkage, forces the choke valve part-way open regardless of the pressure of the thermostatic spring.

The tang is usually bent to adjust the opening of the unloader. A drill of specified size is inserted between the edge of the choke flap and the carburetor throttle bore wall, the choke is forced gently closed, and the throttle is held wide open. The adjustment is correct when the tang is bent so the unloader mechanism just allows the choke flap to be closed until it contacts the drill. If specific instructions and specifications are not available, an ineffective unloader mechanism can be made more effective by gently bending the tang so the choke will be opened somewhat more.

4. Fast idle adjustment. The fast idle mechanism uses the choke linkage to position a cam, which, under cold conditions, moves under the engine idle adjustment screw or an auxiliary screw provided for fast cold idle. Ei-

ther cold stalling or racing of the engine can usually be cured by bringing the fast idle adjustment to specifications. Fast idle is generally adjusted with the engine warm in order to standardize the conditions within the manifold and combustion chambers. The fast idle cam is manually turned to place the fast idle screw on the specified spot of the cam, for example, the highest point on the second step of the cam and the screw adjusted until the engine speed meets specifications (as measured by a tachometer).

Of course, adjustments can be made to cure either racing or cold stalling without the use of a tachometer and factory specs. However, such adjustments are frequently inadequate to cure the problem or else cause another problem, perhaps the opposite of the original. Specs and a tachometer allow a much more satisfactory adjustment.

G. Check for Carburetor Internal Problems

NOTE: *A carburetor is an extremely delicate, precision instrument. Carburetor disassembly and work should be attempted only by someone familiar with carburetion, or at least experienced with general mechanics. If possible, a* Chilton Auto Repair Manual *or factory manual should be consulted so that disassembly can be accomplished without damage. Also, it is recommended, for safety's sake, that gasoline not be used as a solvent because of its flammability. Other solvents are available at auto parts stores.*

In all cases, a carburetor gasket kit should be purchased before disassembly to permit replacement of all the gaskets that are disturbed in the process of disassembly. Gaskets, in general, *cannot* be expected to survive such an operation intact.

If the problem is a stuck float or other, relatively minor, malfunction, treat the carburetor with a carburetor cleaning solvent. If the only cause of malfunction is dirt accumulation, the problem can frequently be solved by such a treatment, thus saving the time and trouble of disassembly. Persistent problems are probably the result of mechanical wear and disassembly will, therefore, be required.

Disassembly is usually accomplished as follows:

1. Remove the carburetor linkages and fuel line, and then remove the nuts which hold the unit to the manifold. Place the unit on a clean bench.

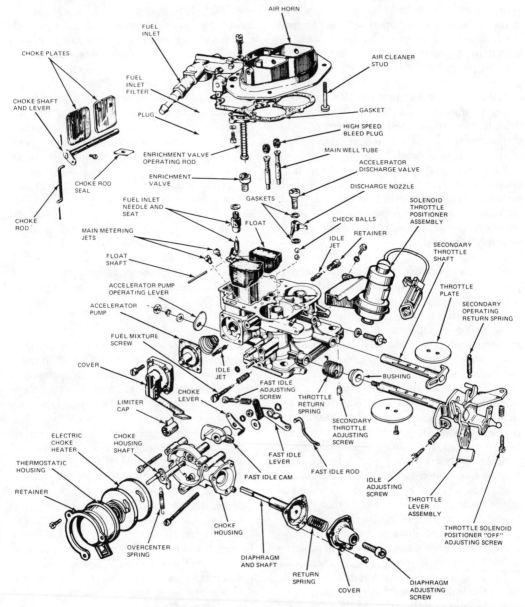

Exploded view—typical two-barrel carburetor

2. Remove all external linkages.

3. Remove the float bowl cover which is generally held on to the top of the carburetor with screws. The condition of the float, needle, and seat can usually be checked without further disassembly.

4. Remove the choke and float parts. Remove the power piston.

5. Remove the main jets, venturi cluster, and the throttle body from the bowl.

6. Disassemble the throttle body. Do not remove the idle mixture adjustment screws on late-model cars unless damage is evident.

Check the carburetor as outlined below:

a. Shake the float to make sure it is dry inside. If there is any evidence of fuel inside, replace the float. Inspect the needle and seat for wear. If there is evidence of a groove in the needle, replace the needle and seat. Upon reassembling the float mechanism, make sure the float is aligned properly (so its edge is parallel to the edge of the float bowl cover). Bend the float arm slightly if an adjustment is necessary. Adjust the float level and drop according to the manufacturer's specifications. Ensuring proper float, needle, and seat operation will cure many problems of rough running, hard starting, flooding, and poor fuel mileage.

b. Mounting of venturi cluster. If your carburetor is not dirty or badly worn, and full disassembly is not necessary, make sure that all of the venturi cluster mounting screws are snug. A leaky venturi cluster can cause rough idle, flat acceleration, and generally rough running.

c. Metering rod or power system valve adjustment and condition of parts. The metering valves and power system valves cannot be visually inspected. If the vehicle has been run for a long distance without a carburetor overhaul, replace the metering rod or power valve rods and jets, especially if high-speed performance is a problem. Make sure the power piston or metering rod vacuum piston and its bore are smooth and in good condition. Replace scored pistons. Inspect any springs, and replace them if they are distorted or broken. Adjustments should be made during reassembly. Specific procedures must be consulted. Curing power system and metering rod problems will help to eliminate many problems of poor fuel economy and sluggish performance.

d. The appearance of the fuel in the float bowl will indicate whether or not clean fuel is being supplied to the carburetor. If evidence of dirt or water in the bowl exists, clean the fuel system or clean or replace filters and strainers as necessary. The float bowl should be carefully checked for leakage while it is separated from the rest of the carburetor. This will be evidenced by a rapid drop in the level of fuel in the bowl.

e. Accelerator pump condition. Inspect all points in the mechanical linkages where wear may occur (e.g., shafts, bores, holes in shaft arms, etc.), and replace if necessary. Inspect all shaft arms for tightness on their shafts and replace any loose assemblies. Inspect any leather washers or diaphragms for cracks, turned edges, or damage, and replace as necessary. Inspect check balls for corrosion or other roughness, and replace a rough check ball or distorted retainer or spring. If the pump uses a check needle, replace it if it is bent or grooved. Blow through the pump jets to ensure cleanliness. Curing accelerator pump problems will aid throttle response and, in some cases, improve gas mileage and cure other performance complaints.

f. Inspect the condition of the throttle shafts and bores. About 0.005 in. clearance is normal. Excessively worn parts will cause air leakage and resultant dilution of the mixture. Throttle flaps should be perfectly flat and should have smooth edges. Replace excessively worn parts. Make sure the main jets (if not already checked under item c.) are clean. Use solvent and compressed air for cleaning, as forcing a thin gauge wire or other object through the jets will *invariably* damage them.

H. Check for Miscellaneous Fuel System Problems

POOR IDLE

A poor idle is most frequently caused by dirty idle jets or an improper idle mixture adjustment. In cars with emission control systems, though, especially where mixture screws are sealed, other problems should be suspected first. Check out the system as follows:

1. Inspect the manifold bolts, and the carburetor mounting bolts and screws for tightness. Look for cracks in the carburetor body or warping, which would be indicated by unevenness in the seams between the various sections of the carburetor. Manifold leaks can be detected by pouring oil on the joints between the manifold and engine block while the engine is idling. Improvement in idle indicates leaks. Intake manifold bolts should be tightened to specifications using a torque wrench. Consult a manual for the specified torque and tightening pattern.

2. If the vehicle has adjustable mixture screws, adjust them for the fastest possible idle speed. A tachometer or vacuum gauge can be used to indicate highest idle speed or manifold vacuum. Follow the instructions on the engine compartment sticker for idle mixture adjustments if the vehicle was built to meet emission standards. Where idle mixture screws are capped, all other possibilities should be exhausted before removing the caps and adjusting the mixture.

3. Make sure the engine is idling at the specified idle speed. Too slow an idle can cause rough running. Use a tachometer and consult the engine compartment sticker or owner's manual for idle speed specifications.

4. Check the PCV system. Replace the PCV valve if pinching the PCV hose near the valve does not cause idle speed to drop 40–80

rpm. Inspect all hoses for bad connections, cracks, or breaks.

5. Check the thermostatically controlled air cleaner. The air cleaner flap should cut off all engine compartment air and draw all air through the heat stove until the engine and compartment are warm. The flap should then remain closed enough to maintain a temperature of 85° F in the air horn. If the flap does not seem to function properly, the system may be tested by placing a small thermometer in the air horn with the air cleaner assembled and the engine operating. Check all hoses and connections, inspect the linkage between the diaphragm and flap, and test the flap by applying 9 in. of vacuum directly through the supply hose. Replace the diaphragm or repair the linkage as necessary. If the diaphragm tests out to be all right, replace the heat sensor. Supply air at less than 85° F will cause rough idle in cars using air preheat systems because of the very lean idle mixtures used.

6. Check the condition of the spark plugs, ignition timing and dwell, and look for leaks in the vacuum advance lines and diaphragms if fuel system problems are not uncovered. If the carburetor's idle mixture screws are capped, follow the manufacturer's specific instructions for the vehicle so the adjustment will not adversely affect exhaust emissions.

VAPOR LOCK

1. Check for unusual climatic conditions. If the weather is unusually warm for the time of year, vapor lock may occur because the fuel was formulated for easy starting in cooler weather, and thus contains an excessive amount of volatile hydrocarbons for the conditions.

2. Check the routing of the fuel lines to make sure the lines do not touch or run close to a hot engine part. Relocate the lines as necessary.

3. Check for any source of excess heat such as poor ignition timing and dwell, clogged cooling system, or slipping belts. Check to see that the manifold heat control valve operates freely; free it with solvent if necessary.

4. Check to see that fuel pump output and pressure meet specifications, and that the float system is in good condition and is properly adjusted.

5. If the problem persists in spite of the vehicle being in good mechanical condition, the manufacturer may provide a replacement fuel pump incorporating a vapor return line.

Installation of such a kit will usually alleviate the problem.

STALLING

1. Check fast idle and regular idle adjustments and bring them to specifications.

2. If the engine stalls when cold, check the function and adjustment of the choke mechanism as in subsection F.

3. If the engine stalls when warmed up, check the float level and the condition of the float needle and seat as in G. Check fuel pump pressure to make sure it is not too high. Check for worn or loose gaskets that might cause carburetor air or fuel leaks. If an anti-stall dashpot is used, check it for a faulty vacuum hose, ruptured diaphragm, or bent mounting bracket.

4. If the engine stalls only when very hot, check the hot idle compensator if the carburetor has one. This is a thermostatic valve that provides extra air to the carburetor when the engine is idling at higher-than-normal temperatures. It compensates for the abnormal amount of fuel vapor generated under these conditions. The valve draws its air from inside the air horn. Block off this port with the engine idling hot. If there is no reduction in idle speed, the carburetor will have to be disassembled and the compensator checked according to the manufacturer's instructions. The cooling system and manifold heat control valve should also be checked.

RUNNING ON

1. Bring idle speed to specifications. If necessary, set idle with the idle stop solenoid energized and also with it de-energized.

2. Make sure that the throttle linkage allows the throttle to close fully. If the carburetor uses a solenoid to control idle speed, make sure that when the ignition switch is turned off, the solenoid permits the throttle to close so that the slow idle screw becomes effective. Replace a faulty solenoid.

3. Check for any source of excess heat. Check ignition timing, and the condition of the cooling system and manifold heat control valve, and then correct any defects. Check spark plug heat range.

4. If the problem persists, the combustion chambers are probably severely carboned. In some cases, the carbon can be removed by slowly pouring a solvent manufactured for decarbonizing the engine into the carburetor while the engine is idling.

NOTE: *Do not try to correct the problem by*

removing or changing the cooling system thermostat to a lower temperature unit as this will accelerate engine wear and increase exhaust emissions. In some systems, the thermostat blocks the radiator bypass during heavy load conditions. In these systems, removal can cause overheating.

Emission Control Systems

There are very few simple statements one can make about emission control systems. To say that they tend to be complicated is at best a gross understatement. To give trouble-shooting procedures for all of the various emission control systems that are in existence would take several hundred pages. Since this book is intended to be general in scope, and nearly all emission control troubleshooting is specific to the piece being tested, only a broad overview is presented here. Where applicable, generalized tests and charts are presented.

EXHAUST GAS RECIRCULATION (EGR)

Exhaust gas recirculation is used primarily to lower peak combustion temperatures and control the formation of NO_x. NO_x emission at low combustion temperatures are not bad, but when the temperature goes over 2,500°F, the production of NO_x in the combustion chamber shoots way up. You can cut down on the peak combustion temperatures by retarding the spark or by introducing an inert gas to dilute the fuel air mixture. Introducing exhaust gases into the combustion chamber is a little like throwing water-soaked wood on a roaring fire. The water-soaked wood won't burn, so that the fire cools down and doesn't roar nearly as

much as it used to. Put a little exhaust gas in the combustion chamber and it takes the place of a certain amount of air fuel mixture. When the spark ignites the mixture, there isn't as much to burn so that the fire is not as hot. Also, the engine doesn't put out as much power.

Exhaust gas recirculation is kept to very low limits. The hole in the EGR valve is very small even when it is wide-open. It's surprising how little exhaust gas it takes to cool down the peak combustion temperatures.

Chrysler had one of the simplest exhaust recirculation systems with their floor jet under the carburetor. Holes were drilled in the bottom of the intake manifold and calibrated jets were screwed into the holes. The holes penetrated into the exhaust crossover passage and allowed the exhaust to come into the intake manifold at all times. The trouble with that system is that it allowed exhaust gas recirculation at idle, which wasn't necessary and didn't make for the smoothest idling engines. Chrysler engines now use a separate EGR valve the same as all the other manufacturers.

The EGR valve is mounted on the intake manifold so that when it opens, exhaust gases are allowed to go from the crossover passage into the throat under the carburetor. The EGR valve is vacuum-operated, sometimes by intake manifold vacuum and on some engines by ported vacuum. The ported vacuum systems are the simplest. At idle, the port is above the throttle blade, so that the EGR valve stays closed. When the throttle is opened, vacuum acts on the port and the EGR valve opens. At wide-open throttle, there is no intake manifold vacuum so that the EGR

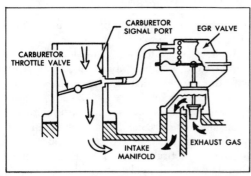

EGR system schematic

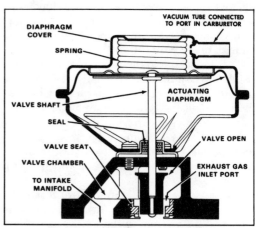

Cross-section of an EGR valve

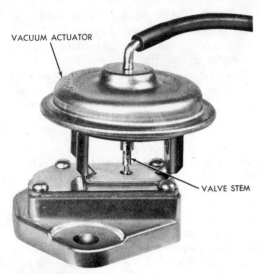

VACUUM ACTUATOR

VALVE STEM

EGR valve

valve closes to give the engine maximum power.

Some cars operate their EGR valve from intake manifold vacuum. They use an amplifier in the circuit to turn on the vacuum to the valve. The amplifier is controlled by venturi vacuum. A small hole in the carburetor venturi picks up vacuum when the airflow through the carburetor is high enough and sends the vacuum signal to the amplifier. The amplifier then opens to allow manifold vacuum to act on the EGR valve. The amplifier system is used to obtain precise control over when the EGR valve operates. Also, it means that exhaust recirculation does not start until the engine is considerably above idle.

Most of the EGR systems use a temperature control of some kind. This can be electric or strictly mechanical. American Motors used a unique system of two air bleeds called modulators. These were mounted behind the grille and on the firewall. At low temperatures, one of the modulators would open and at high temperatures the other opened, allowing air to bleed into the vacuum system to the EGR valve so that the vacuum was weakened and the valve did not open as much. Chrysler used a similar system with an air bleed that sensed temperature inside the cowl plenum chamber. These systems that were sensitive to outside air temperatures were discontinued after March 15, 1973 as a result of the EPA order.

Ford uses a temperature control that looks like a PVS valve, but only has two nozzles. It shuts off the vacuum to the EGR valve at low temperatures. When Chrysler dropped their

air temperature sensor in the plenum chamber, they went to a valve similar to Ford's, but mounted in the radiator. The valve has two nozzles with a hose connected to one and a foam filter to the other. At low temperatures, the valve opens which allows air to enter and weakens the vacuum so that the EGR valve stays closed.

Buick has changed their EGR temperature regulation considerably. In 1972, they didn't use any temperature control at all. In 1973, they had a temperature switch in the hose that shut off the vacuum to the EGR valve at low temperatures. This switch was sensitive to engine compartment temperature and was judged a defeat device by EPA, so that on March 15, 1973, Buick changed the switch to a coolant temperature switch working with a vacuum solenoid. At low temperatures, the coolant switch operated the solenoid to shut off the vacuum to the EGR valve. In 1974, Buick got rid of the electrics in the system and went to a straight coolant-vacuum switch that closed off the vacuum to the EGR valve at low temperatures.

Oldsmobile and Cadillac used a switch in the hose similar to Buick's first switch. After March 15, 1973, they enclosed the switch in a housing so that it was more sensitive to engine temperature rather than underhood temperature.

Pontiac probably has the most complicated system of all. Before March 15, 1973, the EGR system was tied in with the transmission control spark system. The two systems were hooked together so that when vacuum spark advance was allowed, there was no EGR. When EGR was allowed, there was no vacuum spark advance. This complicated system was eliminated on March 15, 1973 and from then on the EGR and the transmission control spark systems were separate.

OPEN POSITIVE CRANKCASE VENTILATION (PCV)

Positive crankcase ventilation uses intake manifold vacuum to draw the fumes out of the crankcase and into the manifold. They are burned in the combustion chamber and go out with the engine exhaust. The crankcase connection can be any place on the engine that has internal air passages connecting with the crankcase. The original systems were an add-on device connected at the same position as the old road draft tube. The hose ran from there up to the intake manifold. Later on, when the systems were designed into the

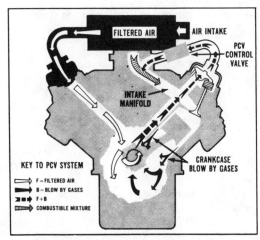

PCV system schematic

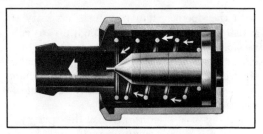

Cutaway view—PCV valve

engines, they found that they could connect to the crankcase at the rocker cover, at the valley cover, at either end of the block below the intake manifold or even at the fuel pump mounting flange. The crankcase connection should be where there is the least chance of picking up any oil, so it is usually made at the highest point, which is the rocker cover.

In 1971, Ford moved all of their crankcase connections from the rear of one rocker cover to the front of the opposite cover. This didn't affect the working of the system, but they found that they picked up less oil when the connection was at the front. For years, Pontiac has had their crankcase connection at the front of the valley cover, underneath the intake manifold.

From the crankcase connection most PCV systems use a hose or tube that runs to the intake manifold. But you can't just connect a big hose and let it go at that. There has to be some kind of restriction so that the engine doesn't pull more air out of the crankcase than it does through the carburetor. This restriction can be a plain orifice or a variable orifice, which is called the PCV valve. During the high vacuum at idle or deceleration, the plunger in the valve is pulled against a spring and seats against the end of the valve. In this position the amount of airflow through the valve is limited. At cruising speed, when intake manifold vacuum is a little bit less than it would be at idle, the spring pushes the valve off its seat, making the opening slightly bigger and allowing more airflow. At wide-open throttle, the spring pushes the valve completely off its seat, but because there is no vacuum at wide-open throttle there is no airflow through the valve at that time.

All PCV valves will close if there is an intake manifold explosion or intake backfire. When the intake manifold pops back through the carburetor, the pressure in the manifold increases and pushes the PCV valve plunger to the end, preventing this pressure from going down into the crankcase. The fixed orifice provides a similar amount of protection because the intake manifold explosion cannot get through the orifice fast enough to build up pressure in the crankcase. What is feared is that flame might travel along the hose and cause a crankcase explosion. This is impossible as long as the orifice or the PCV valve is in place.

Part of the positive crankcase ventilation system is the fresh air entry. There usually is an opening somewhere on the engine to allow fresh air to enter. Some car makers, particularly those who make import cars with small engines, have PCV systems without a fresh air entry. In that type of system the crankcase runs under vacuum at all times and there is very little flow through the PCV connection. They can get away with this because small engines do not have much blow-by. At wide-open throttle when there is no intake manifold vacuum to apply to the crankcase, the vapors are pushed into the intake manifold by crankcase pressure. This system obviously does not keep the crankcase purged of fumes as well as the type that has the fresh air entry.

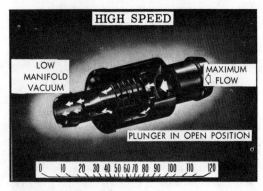

PCV valve—high speed position

In the open system the fresh air entry is usually the oil filler cap, although it can be a separate breather on the rocker cover. In that case, the oil filler cap is the solid type. Inside the fresh air breather cap or separate breather is a mesh type filter that keeps dirt from entering the crank case.

During wide-open throttle on the open system, there is no vacuum and the crankcase breathes from its own buildup of pressure, through the oil filler cap or breather. This system is not 100% perfect because at wide-open throttle it does allow crankcase vapors to escape into the atmosphere.

CLOSED POSITIVE CRANKCASE VENTILATION (PCV)

If you want a completely closed system with no leakage of crankcase fumes to the atmosphere, then you have to use what is known as closed positive crankcase ventilation. The PCV valve and the hose from the crankcase to the intake manifold are the same on both open and closed systems. The only difference in the closed system is the way that the fresh air entry is hooked up. Fresh air must enter from the air cleaner into a hose or other connection to the crankcase. Usually the system is set up so that fresh air enters a PCV filter inside the air cleaner, then goes through a hose to the rocker cover.

The advantage of a closed system is that it does not pass fumes from the crankcase into the atmosphere at wide-open throttle or if the PCV valve gets clogged. When the engine is running with intake manifold vacuum, the airflow through the fresh air hose is from the air cleaner to the rocker cover. When the engine is running without manifold vacuum such as at wide-open throttle or if the PCV valve should be plugged, then airflow is by crankcase pressure through the fresh air hose from the rocker cover back to the air cleaner. Once the fumes get inside the air cleaner they are sucked down into the engine, so that there is no way that the crankcase fumes can get outside the engine and into the atmosphere.

Some imported cars use a closed PCV system that does not have a valve. There is simply a hose connecting the crankcase to the air cleaner. A slight amount of suction in the air cleaner pulls the vapors out of the crankcase, but most of the flow is from crankcase pressure pushing out through the hose. In this system, as in all closed systems, the oil filler cap is the solid type.

Servicing Crankcase Ventilation Systems

Service on crankcase ventilation systems amounts mainly to cleaning the hoses, replacing the valve, and either cleaning or replacing the PCV filter. The car makers do not recommend that you attempt to clean the PCV valve because you cannot get it apart to find out if your cleaning was successful. Some of the older cars had valves that could be taken apart and it is alright to clean those types because you can see whether you've gotten them clean.

PCV systems give very little trouble, but there is one thing you must watch if you are replacing a PCV valve with a valve that is not original equipment. Some of the valves on the market are universal, made to fit just about any engine and can easily be installed backwards. A valve that is installed backwards will be closed all the time because intake manifold vacuum will suck the plunger against the end of the valve away from the spring.

If you use a non-standard PCV valve, make sure that it is specified for your particular engine. The amount of air flowing through the valve is determined by the size of the plunger and the holes inside. You can't get inside to measure it, so that you have to rely on the part number.

If you have an older car with so much blow-by that the original equipment PCV valve can't handle the smoke, a universal PCV valve may be the answer. Some of the universal valves pass so much air that you can actually run the engine on what comes up out of the crankcase with the carburetor mixture screws screwed all the way shut.

On an open system, a PCV valve that cannot handle the blow-by will show up in smoke and fumes coming out through the oil filler cap. On a closed system, you probably won't be able to see any fumes coming out of the air cleaner, but the air filter element will get dirty in a very short time because it is being forced to gulp oil fumes from the crankcase.

For many years Chrysler used a foam wrapper around their paper air cleaner elements to keep the oil off the element. A similar wrapper is now being used on other makes.

PCV Valve Troubleshooting

VALVE TEST

1. See if there are any deposits in the carburetor passages, the oil filler cap, or the hoses. Clean these as required.

PCV valves are generally, though not always, located in one of the valve covers. Just pull it out to test it.

2. Connect a tachometer to the engine.

3. With the engine idling, remove the PCV valve.

NOTE: *If the valve and the hoses are not clogged-up, there should be a hissing sound.*

4. Check the tachometer reading. Place a finger over the valve or hose opening (a suction should be felt).

5. Check the tachometer again. The engine speed should have dropped at least 50 rpm. It should return to normal when the finger is removed from the opening.

6. If the engine does not change speed or if the change is less than 50 rpm, the hose is clogged or the valve is defective. Check the hose first. If the hose is not clogged replace, do not attempt to repair, the PCV valve.

7. Test the new valve to make sure that it is operating properly.

NOTE: *There are several commercial PCV valve testers available. Be sure that the one used is suitable for the valve to be tested, as the testers are not universal.*

AIR PUMP EXHAUST CONTROLS

Air pump systems have a lot of plumbing, with hoses and lines running all over the engine which make them look very complicated, but actually, they are one of the simplest systems for emission control. The pump, driven by a belt at the front of the engine, pumps air under a pressure of only a few pounds into each exhaust port. The hydrocarbons and carbon monoxide that come out the port are very hot. The extra air mixed with them causes a fire in the exhaust manifold that oxidizes the carbon monoxide into harmless carbon dioxide and burns up the hydrocarbons into carbon dioxide and water. Stainless steel

Typical air pump

nozzles are used to direct the air into the port as close to the exhaust valve as possible. The stainless steel is necessary so that the nozzles will not burn away.

Between the nozzles and the pump is a check valve. The system can be set up so that there is one check valve per bank on a V8 engine or a single check valve for the whole system. The check valve keeps the hot exhaust gases from flowing back into the pump and hoses, and destroying them. The pump parts are made out of a special hard plastic. If you have ever smelled a pump that burned up because of a bad check valve, you'll never forget it.

During closed throttle deceleration, high intake manifold vacuum pulls a lot of extra fuel into the engine and out the exhaust system. If the pump continues pumping during deceleration you can get a lot of popping in the exhaust or even an exhaust explosion that can blow the mufflers apart. To prevent this, some way had to be found to shut off the pump during deceleration. The early systems used on most cars in 1966 and 1967 (and on some imported cars even later), used what was known as an anti-backfire valve or gulp valve. The gulp valve was connected between the pump and the intake manifold. A small sensing line or hose led from the valve diaphragm to the intake manifold. During the high vacuum of deceleration, the vacuum through the sensing line acted on the diaphragm, which pulled the valve open, allowing all of the air from the pump to flow directly into the intake manifold. The anti-backfire valve did not shut off the flow of air to the nozzles, but because it opened the system to the high intake manifold vacuum, almost all of the air from the pump flowed into the intake manifold with very little left to come out of the nozzles. Limiting the

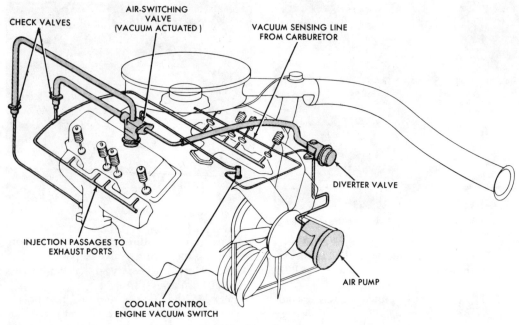

AIR system schematic

air going into the exhaust manifold prevented exhaust system explosions and the extra air entering the intake manifold leaned down the mixtures so that emissions were not so bad during deceleration. The disadvantage of the anti-backfire valve was that the engine kept on running during deceleration. In some cases backing off the throttle at 70 miles per hour would have no effect at all for a few seconds. It felt as if the throttle was stuck wide-open. This was quite a shock if you weren't expecting it, but even after you got used to it, it was still annoying to have a car feel like it was running away with you. Another disadvantage of the gulp valve was its tendency to open when the car first started. The gulp valves operate on a change in vacuum applied to the diaphragm. The change from no vacuum when the engine is not running to immediate vacuum when the engine starts was enough to open the valve for a few seconds. Many engines would shake because of the air entering the intake manifold immediately after they were started. Oldsmobile recognized the problem on V8 engines and provided an air bleed control valve that blocked off the air from the pump to the gulp valve until it built up to a high value. The gulp valve still opened when the engine started, but no air could enter the intake manifold because the control valve was closed.

The gulp valve was obviously not the way to go, so the next development became known as the dump valve, by-pass valve, or diverter

valve. It used a diaphragm operated from intake manifold vacuum, the same as the older gulp valve. However, air from the pump ran through the diverter valve at all times. During the high vacuum of deceleration, the diverter valve shut off the air to the nozzles and sent it to the air cleaner. The air entering the air cleaner has no effect on the operation of the car. It was sent to the air cleaner just to cut down on the noise. Later diverter valves, and the ones that are still used today, exhaust the air directly into the atmosphere through either a bronze or a cotton filter.

In both the gulp and the dump type of backfire suppressor valves, the diaphragm has a calibrated hole in it. This means that if you apply a sudden amount of vacuum to the sensing nozzle on the valve, the diaphragm will

Typical diverter valve

move against the spring to operate the valve. The hole in the diaphragm bleeds off the vacuum very quickly and the spring pushes the diaphragm back to the off position. Because of this bleed feature in the diaphragm, you can check the operation of the valve by disconnecting and reconnecting the hose or by simply pinching the hose and then letting it go. When you pinch the hose, you have to wait a few seconds for the vacuum to stabilize on each side of the diaphragm. When you reconnect the hose, the sudden surge of vacuum will make the valve operate. Of course, you can also check the valve by opening the throttle and allowing the engine to decelerate. In most cases, if you can reach the valve, or listen to the valve and work the throttle at the same time, making the engine decelerate is the easiest way to check the valve because you don't have any hoses or lines to disconnect.

Troubleshooting the Air Pump

Condition	Possible Cause	Correction
No air supply—accelerate engine to 1500 rpm and observe air flow from hoses. If the flow increases as the rpm's increase, the pump is functioning normally. If not, check possible cause.	1. Loose drive belt	1. Adjust belt tension.
	2. Leaks in supply hose	2. Locate leak and repair.
	3. Leak at fitting(s)	3. Tighten or replace clamps.
	4. Diverter valve leaking	4. If air is expelled through diverter muffler with vehicle at idle, replace diverter valve.
	5. Diverter valve inoperative	5. Usually accompanied by backfire during deceleration. Replace diverter valve.
	6. Check valve inoperative	6. Blow through hose toward air manifold, if air passes, function is normal. If air can be sucked from manifold, replace check valve.
Excessive pump noise, chirping, rumbling, or knocking	1. Leak in hose	1. Locate souce of leak using soap solution and correct.
	2. Loose hose	2. Reassemble and replace or tighten hose clamp.
	3. Hose touching other engine parts	3. Adjust hose position.
	4. Diverter valve inoperative	4. Replace diverter valve.
	5. Check valve inoperative	5. Replace check valve.
	6. Pump mounting fasteners loose	6. Tighten mounting screws.
	7. Pump failure	7. Replace pump.
Excessive belt noise	1. Loose belt	1. Adjust belt tension.
	2. Seized pump	2. Replace pump.
Excessive pump noise. Chirping	1. Insufficient break-in	1. Run vehicle 10–15 miles at turnpike speeds—recheck.
Centrifugal filter fan damaged or broken.	1. Mechanical damage	1. Replace centrifugal filter fan.
Exhaust tube bent or damaged.	1. Mechanical damage	1. Replace exhaust tube.
Poor idle or driveability.	1. A defective A.I.R. pump cannot cause poor idle or driveability.	1. Do not replace A.I.R. pump.

When the pumps first came out, a relief valve was pressed into the side of the pump. The relief valve would open under high rpm to prevent the buildup of excess pressure that might damage the hoses or the pump itself. On some later models, the relief valve is built into the diverter valve, so that the diverter valve actually has a dual function. It diverts and also relieves pressure. If anything goes wrong with the relief valve part of the diverter valve, the entire diverter valve has to be replaced.

All domestic cars use a pump that is manufactured by the Saginaw Division of General Motors. The only variation in the pumps is the location of the mounting ears and the air hose connections. The early pumps used in 1966 and 1967, and on some cars for a few years after that, were made with 3 vanes and rebuilding of them was encouraged. Saginaw furnished parts for the 3-vane pumps until 1970 and then the parts were discontinued. Many mechanics had a lot of trouble reassembling the pumps because of the eccentric arrangement of the vane. In most cases the pumps were being replaced anyway, so that the loss of the supply of parts affected very few shops.

The 3-vane pump was discontinued on most new cars in 1968 when Saginaw came out with a new 2-vane design. The 2-vane pump has never had any parts supply and it is factory-recommended procedure to replace the pump rather than attempt to repair it.

The 3-vane pumps took their fresh air supply from a separate air filter or from the clean side of the engine air cleaner. The most noticeable feature of the 2-vane pump was the elimination of any external air cleaner. The filter fan behind the front pulley of the pump acted as a centrifugal filter and kept dirt from getting into the inside of the pump. Cleaning of the filter fan is not recommended because it is too easy to get the dirt particles down inside of the pump. If the fan is so dirty that the air flow is restricted, then the pulley and filter fan should be removed and a new filter fan pressed on the hub.

It is a difficult job to get the filter fan off the hub without breaking it. Actually, it is designed so that you do have to break the fan to remove it. Anything that attaches to the outside of the 2-vane pump, such as a relief valve, a diverter valve, mounting brackets, the filter fan, the front pulley or any air nozzle connections, can be replaced if necessary and they are available if you order them from a dealer

parts department. The internal parts of the 2-vane pump are not available and it should not be taken apart.

The early pump systems used a lot of hoses and tubing, so many that in some cases that you couldn't even see the engine. Some car makers have stuck with the external lines and hoses, but others have built the air passages into the exhaust manifold, the intake manifold, or the cylinder head.

ENGINE MODIFICATION SYSTEMS

When exhaust emission controls were in the planning stage, every car maker except Chrysler Corporation felt that the only way to control exhaust emissions was with the air pump system. Chrysler was doing a lot of experimenting and running test fleets with engine modification systems. By running leaner fuel mixtures, retarded spark, higher idle speed and different combustion chambers, Chrysler thought that they could pass the emission tests without an air pump. When the 1966 California cars rolled off the end of the assembly line, every American manufacturer had an air pump on his engine except Chrysler. Their faith in the engine modification system paid off. One year later, other manufacturers also started to use the engine modification system and the air pump was on the way out.

Air pumps were used less and less by all manufacturers as they relied on the engine modification system until 1972. In that year, to meet the stricter requirements, Chrysler finally had to put its first air pump on California engines. As the requirements get stricter, it becomes more and more difficult to make an engine pass the emissions test without the pump, but the manufacturers are doing their best to lessen emissions with engine modifications only.

Chrysler's Clean Air Package (CAP) and Clean Air System (CAS)

Chrysler's system was originally called the Clean Air Package and later the name was changed to Clean Air System. The engine modifications in the system are really very simple. A normal, uncontrolled engine pollutes very badly at the idle because the mixture is so rich. The rich mixture is what causes unburned hydrocarbons and carbon monoxide to come out the tailpipe. If you run a very lean mixture the engine won't idle unless you open the throttle more to keep it running. With the throttle opened further the engine idles too

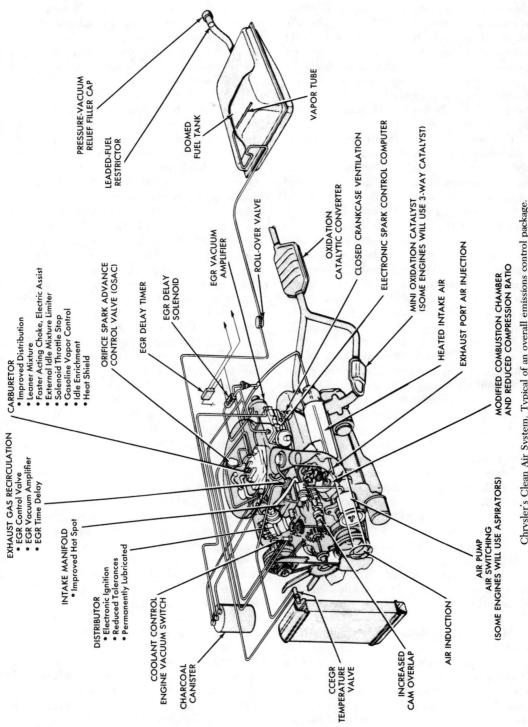

PRESSURE-VACUUM
RELIEF FILLER CAP

LEADED-FUEL
RESTRICTOR

VAPOR TUBE

DOMED
FUEL TANK

ROLL-OVER VALVE

OXIDATION
CATALYTIC CONVERTER

CLOSED CRANKCASE VENTILATION

ELECTRONIC SPARK CONTROL COMPUTER

MINI OXIDATION CATALYST
(SOME ENGINES WILL USE 3-WAY CATALYST)

HEATED INTAKE AIR

EXHAUST PORT AIR INJECTION

MODIFIED COMBUSTION CHAMBER
AND REDUCED COMPRESSION RATIO

EGR VACUUM
AMPLIFIER

ORIFICE SPARK ADVANCE
CONTROL VALVE (OSAC)

EGR DELAY TIMER

EGR DELAY
SOLENOID

CARBURETOR
• Improved Distribution
• Leaner Mixture
• Faster Acting Choke, Electric Assist
• External Idle Mixture Limiter
• Solenoid Throttle Stop
• Gasoline Vapor Control
• Idle Enrichment
• Heat Shield

EXHAUST GAS RECIRCULATION
• EGR Control Valve
• EGR Vacuum Amplifier
• EGR Time Delay

INTAKE MANIFOLD
• Improved Hot Spot

DISTRIBUTOR
• Electronic Ignition
• Reduced Tolerances
• Permanently Lubricated

COOLANT CONTROL
ENGINE VACUUM SWITCH

CHARCOAL
CANISTER

CCEGR
TEMPERATURE
VALVE

INCREASED
CAM OVERLAP

AIR INDUCTION

AIR PUMP
AIR SWITCHING
(SOME ENGINES WILL USE ASPIRATORS)

Chrysler's Clean Air System. Typical of an overall emissions control package.

fast. The easiest way to slow it down without affecting the throttle opening or the mixture is to retard the spark. This is the combination that is used at curb idle on all Chrysler engines with the Clean Air System. The idle mixture is lean, the throttle is opened further than it would be normally and the spark is retarded. The retarded spark, not only helps slow the engine down, but it also increases the temperature in the exhaust manifold which oxidizes the carbon monoxide and also burns up the hydrocarbons.

To ensure that the mixture will stay lean and not be affected by somebody fiddling with the idle mixture screws, Chrysler has used several different systems to limit the amount of fuel that you can get at idle. The cleverest one of these is an idle mixture limiter built into the carburetor. No matter how far out you unscrew the idle needle, the limiter prevents rich mixtures beyond a certain point. Some carburetors have a pinned needle. If you try to unscrew the mixture needle too far, the pin breaks the needle off and then you have the problem of either drilling it out and fixing the throttle body or replacing the carburetor.

The fuel mixture is also set very lean at acceleration and cruising so that the emissions will be as low as possible. It wasn't necessary to lean it out too much in the cruising range because engines normally do not pollute very much when they are cruising at part-throttle.

The lean mixtures and other changes mentioned so far resulted in, originally, over 50% reduction in hydrocarbon and carbon monoxide emissions during idle and acceleration, but further controls were necessary to control emissions during deceleration on manual transmission cars.

When an engine without emission controls decelerates, it pollutes very badly. The rich idle mixture is sucked into the engine under high vacuum. Very little air comes into the engine because the throttle is closed. Also, the high vacuum pulls the exhaust back through the open exhaust valves and makes a very bad mixture that doesn't burn up. The wider throttle setting used with the Clean Air Package helps to lower emissions on deceleration because it lets more air into the combustion chamber. This reduces the deceleration vacuum and there is less tendency for the exhaust to be pulled back through the open exhaust valves.

Cars with manual transmissions maintain the high vacuum of deceleration much longer than a car with an automatic. The automatic

gets an initial high vacuum when the driver takes his foot off the throttle, but this goes away pretty fast because of the slippage in the transmission. The automatic transmission CAP cars did not require any additional controls in most cases, but the manual transmission cars were still polluting heavily during deceleration. Chrysler engineers discovered that the best way to burn up those hydrocarbons on manual transmission cars during deceleration was to advance the spark. Normally the distributor vacuum diaphragm goes to the neutral or no advance position when the throttle is closed. If the engineers hooked up the vacuum diaphragm to the intake manifold, then they would get spark advance during deceleration but they would also have spark advance at idle when they definitely didn't want it. The solution to this problem was the Distributor Vacuum Control Valve or "Spark Valve". The ported vacuum line from the carburetor to the distributor ran through the spark valve. Another line was connected from the valve to intake manifold vacuum. During deceleration, the high intake manifold vacuum moved the valve so that the source of vacuum for the distributor was switched from the carburetor port to the intake manifold. The spark valve would stay in this position as long as the engine was decelerating with about 21½ in. Hg of vacuum or more. When the deceleration vacuum dropped off, the spark valve went back to its normal position and the distributor operated on ported carburetor vacuum the same as any other distributor.

Because you can't maintain deceleration vacuum on an engine that is sitting on the shop floor, the test for the spark valve is to see how many seconds it takes for it to switch back when you decelerate the engine without a load. Because the test is only for a few seconds, many people assume that the valve works that way on the engine, only opening for a few seconds when the driver takes his foot off the throttle. Actually, the valve goes to the intake manifold position as long as the engine is decelerating with more than about 21½ in. Hg of vacuum.

Other cars have also used the Chrysler spark valve. All of the spark valves, when used on Chrysler products or other cars, are adjustable by removing the end cap and turning the screw to increase or decrease the spring pressure. However, some car makers do not recommend adjustment.

One of the internal changes in the Clean Air Package was an increased quench height in the combustion chamber. On an overhead valve engine, the quench height is the distance from the top of the piston to the underside of the cylinder head where the smooth part of the head laps over the cylinder. If this space is made very small, the mixture squirts out of the space as the piston rises. This gives a swirling to the mixture which allows a much greater compression ratio without getting any detonation or ping. Without the ping you get the power of the higher compression ratio while using lower octane gas. The quench area is bad for emissions because sometimes the fuel in that little pocket does not burn. Also, it has a tendency to collect carbon, which makes the pocket even smaller increasing the problem. Opening up the quench area has a definite beneficial effect on emissions, but it forces the car maker to lower compression ratios.

A lot of other refinements have been made in carburetion to try to get better fuel distribution. Some of the CAP carburetors have a single idle mixture screw. This screw adjusts the mixture in both barrels of a two-barrel carburetor at the same time. Other carburetors have an adjustable idle air bleed which is adjusted at the factory.

Chrysler was one of the first to use a throttle dashpot which gave a slower closing throttle, on manual transmission cars. We normally think of the dashpot as being used to stop the engine from stalling when the driver takes his foot off the throttle on an automatic transmission car.

This dashpot was not to prevent stalling, but to stop the heavy emissions caused by the rich mixture from a closed throttle during deceleration.

Another clever design Chrysler has used is their solenoid retard vacuum advance. This solenoid is part of the vacuum advance unit and it is hooked up to a ground contact on the throttle stop screw. When the engine throttle is brought back to the curb idle position, the stop screw touches the contact, grounds the circuit, turns on the solenoid, and the spark is retarded by a small electromagnet in the vacuum advance that pulls the breaker plate to the retard position. The advantage of the solenoid retard is that it does not operate during cold start because the throttle stop screw is held off the contact by the fast idle cam. This gives an advanced spark for better cold starting. Another advantage is that the spark retard goes away immediately as soon as the throttle is opened. This allows the engine to run more normally above idle. In 1970, Chrysler finally had to add a heated air cleaner to their system

and it is now used on all of their engines.

When the Clean Air Package and Clean Air System first started, it was easy to lean over the engine compartment and point out the various components of the system. Now, so many other items have been added to the engine that it is hard to know where the Clean Air System ends and another system takes up. In 1972, Chrysler added air pumps to some California engines. They also added an NO_x spark control and exhaust gas recirculation. The old Clean Air Package is still there, but it's covered up by all the additional controls. When repairing Chrysler Corporation cars, it is much easier if you consider each individual system on its own, without thinking of the whole thing as one big Clean Air System.

American Motors Engine Modifications

After Chrysler proved that the engine modification system would work, the other manufacturers didn't waste any time in coming out with their own versions. American Motors brought out their Engine Mod system on the 232 6 cylinder engine in 1967. They used a composition cylinder head gasket which was thicker than the usual steel gasket and increased the quench height. The carburetor was set lean and the initial spark setting was retarded from 5 to 8 degrees.

In 1968, the Engine Mod system graduated to the American Motors V8s with automatic transmission. The heated air cleaner also appeared that year as the beginning of more and more units that had to be added to keep the emission levels down. In 1970, they reached the ultimate in gadgetry with a dual diaphragm vacuum advance and a deceleration valve similar to the one Chrysler was using. In 1971, transmission controlled spark took over from the dual diaphragm distributor and deceleration valve. American Motors has kept their system simple since then, sticking with transmission controlled spark on many of their cars. The reason that American Motors has not had to go to some of the complicated spark controls that other manufacturers have used, is that they were not afraid to drop an air pump on an engine when it looked as if the engine modification controls were getting out of hand. The air pump has always been the easiest solution to lowering emissions, although it is a costly one because there is so much hardware.

Late model American Motors cars seem to have just as many emission controls as most of the other cars do. Exhaust gas recirculation, transmission controlled spark, and even the air pump are still very much in the picture. Since American Motors uses the Ford carburetor they also have the Ford electric choke, which heats up the choke coil and gives a quicker choke opening. The term "Engine Mod," in reference to the American Motors engine modification system, has fallen by the wayside somewhat with the introduction of exhaust gas recirculation, transmission controlled spark, and the other systems. When working on an American Motors vehicle, it is better to consider each system individually than to try to consider the engine being controlled by one big Engine Mod system.

Ford's Improved Combustion (IMCO) System

Ford's IMCO system first appeared in the middle of 1967 on the 170 and 200 cubic inch 6 cylinder engines and on the 410 V8 in Mercury cars. None of the modifications that make up the IMCO system are visible when you lift the hood. Part of the system is the heated air cleaner, but the heated air cleaner is also used on other engines. The rest of the system consists of modifications to the carburetor, intake manifold, cylinder heads, combustion chamber, exhaust manifold, camshaft and distributor.

Modifications to the carburetor are mainly changes in the fuel flow to get leaner mixtures. Getting these leaner mixtures was not just a simple case of changing jet sizes, but involved relocating some of the components inside the carburetor such as the idle jet tube. The bowl vent designs were also changed to get better internal venting at all engine speeds.

Some Ford carburetors used an internal idle limiter needle. It was similar to the idle mixture screw, but was covered by a lead seal so that it couldn't be changed. The idle limiter needle was set to a maximum richness value so that no matter how far the idle mixture screw was unscrewed, the mixture would not richen beyond that point. Later models of Ford carburetors used idle limiter caps which are also used by most other manufacturers. Intake manifold changes were made to get better heat on the fuel passages and several of the passages were reshaped to give better distribution. Combustion chambers were changed so that they had the same volume, but less surface for unburned fuel to cling to. The exhaust manifolds were given a more free

flowing design and the camshaft was changed so that both intake and exhaust valves had less open time. Both the exhaust manifold and camshaft changes reduced back flow of the exhaust into the combustion chamber at idle, thereby, giving a better mixture that would burn more completely. Initial spark timing was retarded several degrees to get more complete burning of the fuel at idle and both vacuum and centrifugal spark advance curves were tailored to reduce emissions.

As soon as it was proved that the first IMCO system would work, Ford concentrated its efforts on eliminating air pumps from as many engines as possible. To eliminate the pump, they had to go to some of the most complicated systems in the industry. Many Ford engines use a dual diaphragm distributor which retards the spark at idle. Some six-cylinder engines also use a vacuum deceleration valve so that the spark will be advanced during deceleration.

In 1970, Ford started using electronic control of vacuum spark advance. This was their Electronic Distributor Modulator System, sometimes called the "Dist-O-Vac." Vacuum advance was shut off at low speeds and allowed at high speeds. In 1972, the Electronic Distributor Modulator system was changed slightly and given the new name of Electronic Spark Control. In 1973, exhaust gas recirculation, plus a change in the Federal test procedure resulted in the elimination of the electronic spark control from passenger car engines.

Ford has had more trouble with their six-cylinder engines than their V8s. Some of the six-cylinder engines have very complicated emission control systems. Many of these systems, such as Transmission Regulated Spark, Temperature Activated Vacuum, Delay Vacuum By-pass and the Spark Delay Valve, all are used to control distributor vacuum advance. A fair question is, why didn't Ford just eliminate the vacuum advance completely? The answer is that they had to keep it for better driveability, better gas mileage, and to help prevent engine overheating.

One important part of Ford's engine modification system is the fresh air tube, which they call a "zip tube." This tube connects from the grille at the front of the car to the air cleaner and supplies the engine with cool air from outside the engine compartment. The zip tube is used to cool the mixture down and help prevent detonation. The zip tube only affects engine operation on a very hot day when the outside air temperature is around 100° F. On that kind of a day, the temperature of the air inside the engine compartment can easily go to 200° F and that is much too hot to enable the engine to breathe without detonating, under a heavy load.

Ford still uses the term IMCO to describe their engine modification system, but IMCO itself is really not a specific system on the engine. All the term means is that the engine does not have an air pump. As with the other car makers, you should consider each emission control system individually and not try to think of IMCO as being one system, covering the whole engine.

General Motors Controlled Combustion System (CCS)

Because the only visual difference in an engine with the controlled combustion system is the heated air cleaner, it looks as if that is all there is to the system.

Actually, the heated air cleaner is only one of many modifications General Motors has made to their engines when they didn't use an air pump. The original CCS system, used in 1968 and 1969, consisted of only 4 modifications. The carburetor was specially calibrated for lean mixtures and the engine idle speed was increased. The distributor was calibrated for emissions and set with initial timing that was retarded. A high temperature thermostat was used to raise the engine operating temperature and a thermostatically controlled air cleaner heated the carburetor air intake. Most of these original modifications were designed to lower hydrocarbons and carbon monoxide, but they did not do much for NO_x.

In 1970, transmission controlled spark came in on some engines. In 1973, exhaust gas recirculation (EGR) was added to many engines. General Motors still uses the term CCS as applying to all their emission controlled engines, but CCS in itself is not a specific system.

The most confusing system on General Motors cars, especially Chevrolet, is their Transmission Controlled Spark. Each year changes were made to the TCS system, in some cases making it work exactly opposite to the year before. When you work on a General Motors car with Transmission Controlled Spark, you must use only the specifications and repair procedures for that particular year. A good example of the changes in the Chevrolet Transmission Controlled Spark system are the different vacuum solenoids used. In some years the vacuum solenoid shuts off vacuum

spark advance when it is energized. In other years, the solenoid is normally closed so that it shuts off the vacuum when it is not energized. You must be very careful to correctly identify the year of car you are working on, and determine that somebody has not substituted the wrong parts so that the system works backwards from the way it should.

SPARK CONTROLS

Transmission Controlled Spark (TCS)

Transmission Controlled Spark first came out in 1970 on General Motors cars, one year earlier than the law required. Transmission Controlled Spark is a system of shutting off the vacuum spark advance in the lower gears or at lower speeds. If the system is speed controlled, it is usually called speed controlled spark. However, American Motors calls their system Transmission Control Spark, although on cars equipped with automatic transmission, it is sensitive to car speed rather than gear position.

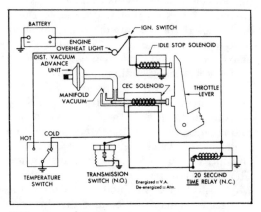

TCS system schematic

In all TCS systems, vacuum to the distributor is turned on and off by a vacuum solenoid. This solenoid receives current when the ignition switch is on and usually is fused in the car fuse block. The solenoid is grounded at the transmission in certain gears and ungrounded in others. The difficulty in checking out the system comes from the fact that their are two kinds of solenoids, normally open to vacuum or normally closed. The normally open solenoid allows vacuum to pass through it and act on the distributor when it is *not* energized. The normally closed solenoid allows vacuum to pass through the distributor only when it *is* energized. The early systems all used normally open solenoids. When the solenoid was energized, by the transmission being in the proper gear, it closed the vacuum passage and cut off the vacuum advance. This was a fail-safe system. If the fuse blew or anything happened to break the electrical circuit, then the solenoid would de-energize and you would have vacuum advance at all times.

Some manufacturers stayed with the normally open solenoid through all the years that they used transmission controlled spark. When using a normally open solenoid without a relay, the transmission switch in the solenoid ground circuit must be normally closed. In other words, if you turn the switch on with the engine not running, the transmission switch completes the circuit and the solenoid is energized. When the transmission goes into High gear, which is usually the gear in which vacuum advance is permitted, the transmission switch is opened. This de-energizes the vacuum soleoid and allows the vacuum to pass through it and act on the distributor vacuum advance.

The CEC or Combined Emission Control solenoid used on Chevrolet and also on the General Motors 6 cylinder engine, is a normally closed solenoid used with a normally open transmission switch. This means that when you turn on the ignition switch with the engine not running, nothing happens because the transmission switch is open, breaking the ground circuit. The CEC valve just sits there and does nothing until the transmission goes into High gear. At that time, the transmission switch closes, which energizes the CEC valve and turns on the vacuum to the distributor. The CEC valve has a dual function, which is why it is called a combined emission control. The same plunger in the valve that turns on the vacuum to the distributor also extends and pushes the throttle linkage open for a wider closed-throttle opening when the transmission is in High gear. When the throttle is held open, during deceleration, you don't get the high intake manifold vacuum that pulls so much fuel over from the idle circuit and makes such rich mixtures. This helps emission control.

The stem of the CEC valve is adjustable, but it is never used to set curb idle because at idle it doesn't even touch the throttle linkage. There is an rpm setting for the CEC valve, but it is only necessary to adjust it if the carburetor has been overhauled or somebody has been tampering with the adjustment. The CEC valve can always be recognized because there are vacuum hoses connected to it. The normal anti-dieseling solenoid that you find in the same position on many carburetors does not have vacuum hoses. It has only a single wire. Curb idle is always set with the anti-dieseling solenoid adjustment. Curb idle is never set with the stem of the CEC valve.

An additional control on many transmission controlled spark systems is an ambient temperature switch or a coolant temperature switch. Temperature switches usually provide a ground at low temperatures to turn the solenoid on, and open at high temperatures so that the system is not affected.

With a normally open vacuum solenoid, the solenoid is energized at all times, except in High gear. The temperature switch provides a ground at cold temperatures, but there isn't any way that this ground can be directly hooked up to turn the vacuum solenoid off and allow vacuum advance. To do this, a relay is inserted into the hot wire between the ignition switch and the vacuum solenoid. The temperature control switch provides a ground for the relay at low temperatures. This energizes the relay which then breaks the circuit between the battery and the vacuum solenoid, de-energizes the solenoid, and allows vacuum advance. The relay in this type of a system would be a normally closed relay. In other words, it is closed and allows current to flow to the vacuum solenoid, except when the temperature switch provides a ground to energize the relay.

Some temperature switches also provide a hot override. When the engine temperature gets up to the danger point, the hot override operates the solenoid, sometimes through a relay, to allow vacuum advance.

Additional controls are a time relay and a delay relay. The terminology on these two relays is confusing because they have both been called delay relays. In this book, the time relay is the one that allows vacuum advance for approximately 20 seconds after the ignition key is turned on and the engine started. The delay relay is the one that delays the application of vacuum to the distributor for 20 seconds after the transmission goes into High gear.

The time relay used on Chevrolet vehicles is always mounted on the firewall or somewhere in the engine compartment. The delay relay on Chevrolets is always mounted behind the instrument panel, so there is no chance of getting the two mixed up.

The Pontiac Transmission Controlled Spark used on 1973 models built before March 15th, is a completely different system from the Chevrolet and other General Motors systems. Some of the Pontiac spark controls also operate the exhaust gas recirculation valve. Mounted next to the Pontiac vacuum solenoid is a black delay relay, that delays the application of vacuum advance after the transmission goes into High gear. This delay relay is an innocent looking piece of equipment, but its cost is in the $20.00 range.

After March 15, 1973, Pontiac did away with the delay relay and used a start-up relay which is the same unit as the time relay used by Chevrolet.

CHRYSLER CORPORATION LEAN BURN SYSTEM

NOTE: *The 1978 Lean Burn System differs slightly from the earlier systems. 1978 information was not available at the time of printing.*

Introduced on the 400-4V engine in 1976, its availability was increased to the 318, 360, and 440 engines in 1977. This system, new for 1976, is based on the principle that lower NO_x emissions would occur if the air/fuel ratio inside the cylinder area was raised from its current point (15.5:1) to a much leaner point (18:1).

In order to make the engine workable, a solution to the problems of carburetion and timing had to be found since a lean running engine is not the most efficient in terms of driveability. Chrysler adapted a conventional Thermo-Quad carburetor to handle the added air coming in, but the real advance of the system is the Spark Control Computer mounted on the air cleaner.

Since a lean burning engine demands precise ignition timing, additional spark control was needed for the distributor. The computer supplies this control by providing an infinitely variable advance curve. Input data is fed instantaneously to the computer by a series of seven sensors located in the engine compartment which monitor timing, water temperature, air temperature, throttle position, idle/off-idle operation, and intake manifold vacuum. The program schedule module of the spark control computer receives the information from the sensors, processes it, and then directs the ignition control module to advance or retard the timing as necessary. This whole process is going on continuously as the engine is running, taking only a thousandth of a second to complete a circuit from sensor to distributor.

The components of the system are as follows: Modified Thermo-Quad carburetor; Spark Control Computer, consisting of two interacting modules: the Program Schedule Module which is responsible for translating input data, and the Ignition Control Module which transmits data to the distributor to advance or retard the timing; and the following sensors.

Start Pick-up Sensor, located inside the distributor, supplies a signal to the computer providing a fixed timing point which is only used for starting the car. It also has a back-up function of taking over engine timing in case the run pick-up fails. Since the timing in this pick-up is fixed at one point, the engine will be able to run, but not very well.

The Run Pick-up Sensor, also located in the distributor, provides timing data to the computer once the engine is running. It also monitors engine speed and helps the computer decide when the piston is reaching the top of its compression stroke.

Coolant Temperature Sensor, located on the water pump housing, informs the computer when the coolant temperature is below 150°.

Air Temperature Sensor, inside the computer itself, monitors the temperature of the air coming into the air cleaner.

Throttle Position Transducer, located on the carburetor, monitors the position and rate of change of the throttle plates. When the throttle plates start to open and as they continue to open toward full throttle, more and more spark advance is called for by the computer. If the throttle plates are opened quickly even more spark advance is given for about one second. The amount of maximum advance is determined by the temperature of the air coming into the air cleaner. Less advance under acceleration will be given if the air entering the air cleaner is hot, while more advance will be given if the air is cold.

Carburetor Switch Sensor, located on the end of the idle stop solenoid, tells the computer if the engine is at idle or off-idle.

Vacuum Transducer, located on the computer, monitors the amount of intake manifold vacuum present; the more vacuum, the more spark advance to the distributor. In order to obtain this spark advance in the distributor, the carburetor switch sensor has to remain open for a specified amount of time during which the advance will slowly build up to the

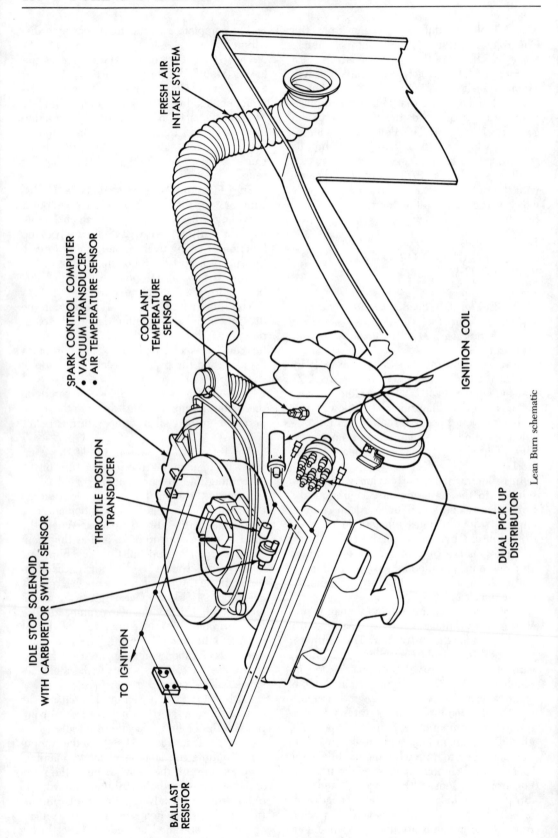

FRESH AIR
INTAKE SYSTEM

SPARK CONTROL COMPUTER
• VACUUM TRANSDUCER
• AIR TEMPERATURE SENSOR

COOLANT
TEMPERATURE
SENSOR

IGNITION COIL

THROTTLE POSITION
TRANSDUCER

IDLE STOP SOLENOID
WITH CARBURETOR SWITCH SENSOR

TO IGNITION

DUAL PICK UP
DISTRIBUTOR

BALLAST
RESISTOR

Lean Burn schematic

amount indicated as necessary by the vacuum transducer. If the carburetor switch should close during that time, the advance to the distributor will be cancelled. From here the computer will start with an advance countdown. If the carburetor switch is reopened within a certain amount of time, the advance will continue from a point where the computer decides it should. If the switch is reopened after the computer has counted down to "no advance," the vacuum advance process must start over again.

OPERATION

When you turn the ignition key on, the start pick-up sends its signal to the computer which relays back information for more spark advance during cranking. As soon as the engine starts, the run pick-up takes over and receives more advance for about one minute. This advance is slowly eliminated during the one minute warm-up period. While the engine is cold (coolant temperature below 150° as monitored by the coolant temperature sensor), no more advance will be given to the distributor until the engine reaches normal operating temperature, at which time normal operation of the system will begin.

In normal operation, the basic timing information is relayed by the run pick-up to the computer along with input signals from all the other sensors. From this data the computer determines the maximum allowable advance or retard to be sent to the distributor for any situation.

If either the run pick-up or the computer should fail, the back-up system of the start pick-up takes over. This supplies a fixed timing signal to the distributor which allows the car to be driven until it can be repaired. In this mode, very poor fuel economy and performance will be experienced. If the start pick-up or the ignition control module section of the computer should fail, the engine will not start or run.

Lean Burn System Testing and Service

Some of the procedures in this section refer to an adjustable timing light. This is also known as a spark advance tester, i.e., a device which will measure how much spark advance is present going from one point, a base figure, to another. Since precise timing is very important to the Lean Burn System, do not attempt to perform any engine tests calling for an adjustable timing light without one. In places where a regular timing light can be used, it will be noted in the text.

TROUBLESHOOTING

1. Remove the coil wire and hold it about ¼ in. away from an engine ground, then have someone crank the engine while you check for spark.

2. If you have a good spark, slowly move the coil wire away from the engine and check for arcing at the coil while cranking.

3. If you have good spark and it is not arcing at the coil, check the rest of the parts of the ignition system, if they are alright, the problem is not in the ignition system. Check the "Troubleshooting" section following Chapter 2.

Engine Not Running—Will Not Start

1. Check the battery specific gravity; it must be at least 1.220 to deliver the necessary voltage to fire the plugs.

2. Remove the terminal connector from the coolant switch and put a piece of paper or plastic between the curb idle adjusting screw and the carburetor switch. This is unnecessary if the screw and switch are not touching.

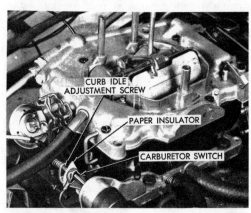

Preparing for power check

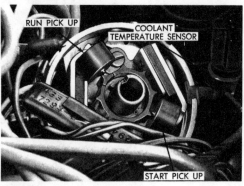

Engine sensors

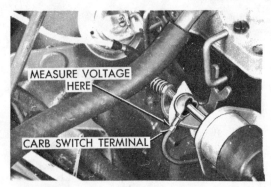

Power check

3. Connect the negative lead of a voltmeter to a good engine ground, turn the ignition switch to the "Run" position and measure the voltage at the carburetor switch terminal. If you receive a reading of more than five volts, go on to Step 7; if not, proceed to the next step.

4. Turn the ignition switch "Off" and disconnect the double terminal connector from the bottom of the Spark Control Computer. Turn the ignition switch back to the "Run" position and measure the voltage at terminal No. 4; if the voltage is not within 1 volt of the voltage you received in Step 3, check the wiring between terminal No. 3 and the ignition switch. If the voltage is correct, go on to the next step.

5. Turn the ignition switch "off" and disconnect the single connector from the bottom of the Spark Control Computer. Using an ohmmeter, check for continuity between terminal No. 11 and the carburetor switch terminal. There should be continuity present, if not, check the wiring.

Single connector power check

6. Check for continuity between terminal No. 2 (double connector) and ground. If there is continuity, replace the Spark Control Computer; if not, check the wiring. If the engine still will not start, proceed to the next step.

7. Turn the ignition switch to the "Run"

position and check for voltage at terminals Nos. 7 and 8 of the double connector. If you received voltage within 1 volt of that recorded in Step 3, proceed to the next step. If you did not on terminal No. 7, check the wiring between it and the ignition switch and check the 5 ohm side of the ballast resistor. If you did not on terminal No. 8, check the wiring, and the primary windings of the coil and the ½ ohm side of the ballast resistor.

Dual connectors

8. Turn the ignition switch "Off" and with an ohmmeter, measure resistance between terminals Nos. 5 and 6 of the dual connector. If you do not receive a reading of 150–900 ohms, disconnect the start pick-up leads at the distributor and measure the resistance going into the distributor. If you get a reading of 150–900 ohms here, the wiring between terminals Nos. 5 and 6 and the distributor is faulty. If you still do not get a reading between 150–900 ohms, replace the start pick-up. If you received the proper reading when you initially checked terminals Nos. 5 and 6, proceed to the next step.

9. Connect one lead of an ohmmeter to a good engine ground and with the other lead, check the continuity of both start pick-up leads going into the distributor. If there is not continuity, go on to the next step. If you do get a reading, replace the start pick-up.

10. Remove the distributor cap and check the air gap of the start pick-up coil. Adjust, if necessary, and proceed to the next step.

11. Replace the distributor cap, and start the engine; if it still will not start, replace the Spark Control Computer. If the engine still does not work, put the old one back and retrace your steps, paying close attention to any wiring which may be shorted.

Engine Running Badly (Run Pick-Up Tests)

1. Start the engine and let it run for a couple of minutes. Disconnect the start pick-up lead. If the engine still runs, leave this test and go on to the "Start Timer Advance Test." If the engine died, proceed to Step 2.

2. Reconnect the start pick-up, turn the ignition switch off, and disconnect the dual connector from the bottom of the spark control computer.

3. Using an ohmmeter, measure the resistance between terminals Nos. 3 and 5 of the dual connector. Resistance should be 150–900 ohms; if it is, proceed to the next step, if not, disconnect the run pick-up leads from the distributor. Measure the resistance going into the distributor. If the resistance is now between 150–900 ohms, there is bad wiring between terminals Nos. 3 and 5 of the double connector plug and the distributor connector terminal. If the resistance is still not within 150–900 ohms, replace the run pick-up, and try to start the engine. If the engine still fails to start, go on to Step 4.

4. Disconnect the run pick-up coil from the distributor. Use an ohmmeter to check for continuity at each of the leads going into the distributor. If there is continuity shown, replace the pick-up coil and repeat Step 1. If you do not get a reading of continuity, proceed to the next step.

Pickup coil connector identification

5. Remove the distributor cap, check the gap of the run pick-up and adjust it if necessary.

6. Reinstall the distributor cap, check the wiring, and try to start the engine. If it does not start, replace the computer and try again. If it still does not start, repeat the test paying close attention to all wiring connections.

Start Timer Advance Test

1. Hook up an *adjustable* timing light to the engine.

Checking run pickup at distributor leads

2. Have an assistant start the engine, place his foot firmly on the brake, then open and close the throttle, then place the transmission in Drive.

3. Locate the timing signal immediately after the transmission is put in Drive. The meter on the timing light should show about 5–9° advance. This advance should slowly decrease to the basic timing signal after about one minute. If it did not increase the 5–9° or return after one minute, replace the spark control computer. If it did operate properly, proceed to the next test.

Throttle Advance Test

Before performing this test, the throttle position transducer must be adjusted. The adjustments are as follows:

1. The air temperature sensor inside the spark control computer must be cool (below 135°). If the engine is at operating temperature, either turn it off and let it cool down or remove the top of the air cleaner and inject a spray coolant into the computer over the air temperature sensor for about 15 seconds. If Steps 2–5 take longer than 3–4 minutes, recool the sensor.

2. Start the engine and wait about 90 seconds, then connect a jumper wire between the carburetor switch terminal and ground.

3. Disconnect the electrical connector from the transducer and check the timing, adjusting if necessary. Reconnect the electrical connector to the transducer and recheck the timing.

4. If the timing is more than specified on the tune-up decal, loosen the transducer locknut and turn the transducer clockwise until it comes within limits, then turn it an additional ½ turn clockwise and tighten the locknut.

Checking for resistance at throttle transducer leads

5. If the timing is at the specified limits, loosen the locknut and turn the transducer counterclockwise until the timing just begins to advance. At that point, turn the transducer ½ turn clockwise and tighten the locknut. After this step you are ready to begin the throttle advance test.

6. Turn the ignition switch "Off" and disconnect the single connector from the bottom of the spark control computer.

7. With an ohmmeter, measure the resistance between terminals Nos. 9 and 10 of the single connector. The measured resistance should be between 50–90 ohms. If it is, go on to the next step, if not, remove the connector from the throttle position transducer and measure the resistance at the transducer terminals. If you now get a reading of 50–90 ohms, check the wiring between the computer terminals and the transducer terminal. If you do not get the 50–90 reading, replace the transducer and proceed to the next step.

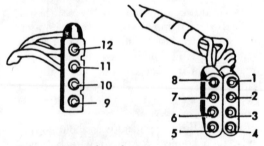

Connector terminal numbering

8. Reconnect the wiring and turn the switch to the "Run" position without starting the engine. Hook up a voltmeter, negative lead to an engine ground, and touch the positive lead to one terminal of the transducer while opening and closing the throttle all the way. Do the same thing to the other terminal of the transducer. Both terminals should show a 2 volt change when opening and closing the throttle. If not proceed to the next step.

Transducer Advance Specifications

Core Moved Out 1 in.	7–12° @ 75° F
	4–7° @ 104° F
Moved 5–6 Times	7–12°
	(One second duration each time)

Pick-Up Gaps

Start Pick-Up	(set to)	0.008 in.
	(check at)	0.010 in.
Run Pick-Up	(set to)	0.012 in.
	(check at)	0.014 in.

9. Position the throttle linkage on the fast idle cam and ground the carb switch with a jumper wire. Disconnect the wiring connector from the transducer and connect it to a transducer that you know is good.

10. Move the core of the transducer all the way in, start the engine, wait about 90 seconds, and then move the core out about an inch.

11. Adjust the timing light so that it registers the basic timing signal. The timing light should show the additional amount of advance as given in the "Transducer Advance Specifications" chart in this section. If it is within the specifications, move the core back into the transducer, and the timing should go back to the original position. If the timing did advance and return, go on to the next step. If it did not advance and/or return, replace the spark control computer and try this test over again. If it still fails, replace the transducer.

12. Reset the timing light meter, and have an assistant move the transducer core in and out 5–6 times quickly. The timing should advance 7–12° for about a second and then return to the base figure. If it did not, replace the spark control computer. If you did not get the 2 volt change in reading in Step 8, you should now replace the transducer since you have proved that the spark control computer is not causing it to check out faulty.

13. Remove the test transducer (from Step 9), and reconnect all wiring.

VACUUM ADVANCE TEST (VACUUM TRANSDUCER)

1. Hook up an adjustable timing light.

2. Turn the ignition switch to the "Run" position, but do not start the engine. Discon-

nect the idle stop solenoid wire and the wiring connector from the coolant switch. Push the solenoid plunger in all the way, and while holding the throttle linkage open, reconnect the solenoid wire. The solenoid plunger should pop out and when the throttle linkage is released, it should also hold the linkage in place. If it does not, replace the idle stop solenoid.

3. Start the engine and let it warm up; make sure that the transmission is in Neutral and the parking brake is on.

4. Place a small piece of plastic or paper between the carburetor switch and the curb idle adjusting screw; if the screw is not touching the switch, make sure that the fast idle cam is not on or binding; the linkage is not binding, or the throttle stop screw is not overadjusted. Adjust the timing light for the basic timing figure. The meter of the timing light should show 2–5° of advance with a minimum of 16 in. of vacuum at the vacuum transducer (checked with a vacuum gauge). If this advance is not present, replace the spark control computer and try the test again. If the advance is present, let the engine run for about 6–9 minutes, then go on to the next step.

5. After the 6–9 minute waiting period, adjust the timing light so that it registers the basic timing figure. The timing light meter should now register 32–35° of advance. If the advance is not shown, replace the spark control computer and repeat the test; if it is shown, proceed to Step 6.

6. Remove the insulator (paper or plastic) which was installed in Step 4; the timing should return to its base setting. If it does not, make sure that the curb idle adjusting screw is not touching the carburetor switch. If that is alright, turn the engine off and check the wire between terminal No. 11 of the single connector (from the bottom of the spark control computer), and the carburetor switch terminal for a bad connection. If it turns out alright, and the timing still will not return to its base setting, replace the spark control computer.

COOLANT SWITCH TEST

1. Connect one lead of the ohmmeter to a good engine ground, the other to the black wire with a tracer in it. Disregard the orange wire if there is one on the switch.

2. If the engine is cold (below 150°), there should be continuity present in the switch. With the thermostat open, and the engine warmed up, there should be no continuity. If either of the conditions in this step are not met, replace the switch.

LEAN BURN TIMING

This procedure is to set the basic timing signal as shown on the engine tune-up decal in the engine compartment.

1. Connect a jumper wire between the carburetor switch terminal and the ground. Connect a standard timing light to the No. 1 cylinder.

2. Block the wheels and set the parking brake. If the car has an automatic release type parking brake, remove and plug the vacuum line which controls it from the fitting on the rear of the engine.

3. Start and warm the engine up; raise engine speed above 1,500 rpm for a second, then drop the speed and let it idle for a minute or two.

4. With the engine idling at the point specified on the tune-up decal with the transmission in Drive, adjust the timing to the figure given on the tune-up decal.

IDLE SPEED AND MIXTURE

1. Follow the first three steps under "Lean Burn Timing," then insert an exhaust gas analyzer into the tailpipe.

2. Place the transmission in Drive, the air conditioning and headlights off. Adjust the idle speed to the specification shown on the tune-up decal by turning the idle solenoid speed screw.

3. Adjust the carbon monoxide level to 0.1% with the mixture screws while trying to keep hydrocarbons to a minimum and the idle speed to specification. Turn the screws alternately over their range to coordinate all three factors.

4. Place the transmission in Neutral; disconnect the wire at the idle stop solenoid and adjust the curb idle stop solenoid and adjust the curb idle speed screw to obtain 650 rpm. Reconnect the wire.

5. Remove the air cleaner cover and lift and support the air cleaner assembly high enough to gain access to the fast idle adjustment screw.

6. Place the fast idle speed screw on the highest step of the cam and adjust the idle speed to the specification shown on the tune-up decal.

7. Drop the idle back down to the curb idle position and turn the ignition switch off. Reconnect any hoses or electrical connections taken off in the procedure.

8. If the procedure has to be performed a second time, make sure that you start from the beginning or the readings will be inaccurate.

REMOVAL AND OVERHAUL

None of the components of the Lean Burn System (except the carburetor), are able to be disassembled and repaired. When one part is known to be defective, it is replaced.

The Spark Control Computer is secured by mounting screws inside the air cleaner. To remove the Throttle Position Transducer, loosen the locknut and unscrew it from the mounting bracket, then unsnap the core from the carburetor linkage.

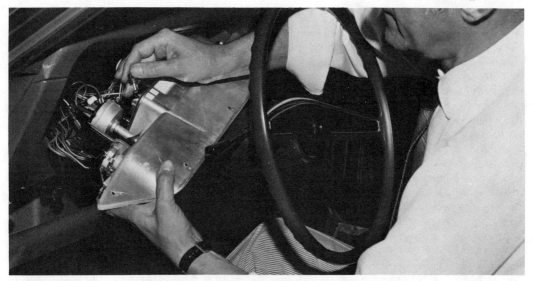

Chapter 5

Chassis Electrical

Understanding and Trouble-shooting Electrical Systems

For any electrical system to operate, it must make a complete circuit. This simply means that the power flow from the battery must make a complete circle. When an electrical component is operating, power flows from the battery to the component, passes through the component causing it to perform its function (lighting a light bulb), and then returns to the battery through the ground of the circuit. This ground is usually (but not always) the metal part of the car on which the electrical component is mounted.

Perhaps the easiest way to visualize this is to think of connecting a light bulb with two wires attached to it to your car battery. The battery in your car has two posts (negative and positive). If one of the two wires attached to the light bulb was attached to the negative post of the battery and the other wire was attached to the positive post of the battery, you would have a complete circuit. Current from the battery would flow out one post, through the wire attached to it and then to the light bulb, where it would pass through causing it to light. It would then leave the light bulb, travel through the other wire, and return to the other post of the battery.

The normal automotive circuit differs from this simple example in two ways. First, instead of having a return wire from the bulb to the battery, the light bulb returns the current to the battery through the chassis of the vehicle. Since the negative battery cable is attached to the chassis and the chassis is made of electrically conductive metal, the chassis of the vehicle can serve as a ground wire to complete the circuit. Secondly, most automotive circuits contain switches to turn components on and off as required.

There are many types of switches, but the most common simply serves to prevent the passage of current when it is turned off. Since the switch is a part of the circle necessary for a complete circuit, it operates to leave an opening in the circuit, and thus an incomplete or open circuit, when it is turned off.

Some electrical components which require a large amount of current to operate also have a relay in their circuit. Since these circuits carry a large amount of current, the thickness of the wire in the circuit (gauge size) is also greater. If this large wire were connected from the component to the control switch on the instrument panel, and then back to the component, a voltage drop would occur in the circuit. To prevent this potential drop in voltage, an electromagnetic switch (relay) is used. The large wires in the circuit are connected from the car battery to one side of the relay, and from the opposite side of the relay to the component. The relay is normally open, preventing current from passing through the circuit. An additional, smaller, wire is connected from the relay to the control switch for the circuit. When the control switch is turned on, it grounds the smaller wire from the relay and completes the circuit. This closes the relay and allows current to flow from the battery to the component. The horn, headlight, and starter circuits are three which use relays.

Did you ever notice how your instrument panel lights get brigher the faster your car goes? This happens because your alternator (which supplies the battery) puts out more current at speeds above idle. This is normal. However, it is possible for larger surges of current to pass through the electrical system of your car. If this surge of current were to reach an electrical component, it could burn it out. To prevent this from happening, fuses are connected into the current supply wires of most of the major electrical systems of your car. The fuse serves to head off the surge at the pass. When an electrical current of excessive power passes through the component's fuse, the fuse blows out and breaks the circuit, saving it from destruction.

The fuse also protects the component from damage if the power supply wire to the component is grounded before the current reaches the component.

Let us here interject another rule to the complete circle circuit. *Every complete circuit from a power source must include a component which is using the power from the power source.* If you were to disconnect the light bulb (from the previous example of a lightbulb being connected to the battery by two wires) from the wires and touch the two wires together (please take our word for this; don't try it), the result would be shocking. You probably haven't seen so many sparks since the Fourth of July. A similar thing happens (on a smaller scale) when the power supply wire to a component or the electrical component itself becomes grounded before the normal ground connection for the circuit. To prevent damage to the system, the fuse for the circuit blows to interrupt the circuit—protecting the components from damage. Because grounding a wire from a power source makes a complete circuit—less the required component to use the power—this phenomenon is called a short circuit. The most common causes of short circuits are: the rubber insulation on a wire breaking or rubbing through to expose the current carrying core of the wire to a metal part of the car, or a shorted switch.

Some electrical systems on the car are protected by a circuit breaker which is, basically, a self-repairing fuse. When either of the above-described events takes place in a system which is protected by a circuit breaker, the circuit breaker opens the circuit the same way a fuse does. However, when either the short is removed from the circuit or the surge subsides, the circuit breaker resets itself and does not have to be replaced as a fuse does.

The final protective device in the chassis electrical system is a fuse link. A fuse link is a wire that acts as a fuse. It is connected between the starter relay and the main wiring harness for the car. This connection is under the hood, very near a similar fuse link which protects the engine electrical system. Since the fuse link protects all the chassis electrical components, it is the probable cause of trouble when none of the electrical components function, unless the battery is disconnected or dead.

Electrical problems generally fall into one of three areas:

1. The component that is not functioning is not receiving current.

2. The component itself is not functioning.

3. The component is not properly grounded.

Problems that fall into the first category are by far the most complicated. It is the current supply system to the component which contains all the switches, relays, fuses, etc.

The electrical system can be checked with a test light and a jumper wire. A test light is a device that looks like a pointed screwdriver with a wire attached to it. It has a light bulb in its handle. A jumper wire is a piece of insulated wire with an alligator clip attached to each end.

If a light bulb is not working, you must follow a systematic plan to determine which of the three causes is the villain.

1. Turn on the switch that controls the inoperable bulb.

2. Disconnect the power supply wire from the bulb.

3. Attach the ground wire on the test light to a good metal ground.

4. Touch the probe end of the test light to the end of the power supply wire that was disconnected from the bulb. If the bulb is receiving current, the test light will go on.

NOTE: *If the bulb is one which works only when the ignition key is turned on (turn signal), make sure the key is turned on.*

If the test light does not go on, then the

problem is in the circuit between the battery and the bulb. As mentioned before, this includes all the switches, fuses, and relays in the system. Turn to the wiring diagram and find the bulb on the diagram. Follow the wire that runs back to the battery. The problem is an open circuit between the battery and the bulb. If the fuse is blown and, when replaced, immediately blows again, there is a short circuit in the system which must be located and repaired. If there is a switch in the system, bypass it with a jumper wire. This is done by connecting one end of the jumper wire to the power supply wire into the switch and the other end of the jumper wire to the wire coming out of the switch. Again, consult the wiring diagram. If the test light lights with the jumper wire installed, the switch or whatever was bypassed is defective.

NOTE: *Never substitute the jumper wire for the bulb, as the bulb is the component required to use the power from the power source.*

5. If the bulb in the test light goes on, then the current is getting to the bulb that is not working in the car. This eliminates the first of the three possible causes. Connect the power supply wire and connect a jumper wire from the bulb to a good metal ground. Do this with the switch which controls the bulb turned on, and also the ignition switch turned on if it is required for the light to work. If the bulb works with the jumper wire installed, then it has a bad ground. This is usually caused by the metal area on which the bulb mounts to the car being coated with some type of foreign matter.

6. If neither test located the source of the trouble, then the light bulb itself is defective.

The above test procedure can be applied to any of the components of the chassis electrical system by substituting the component that is not working for the light bulb. Remember that for any electrical system to work, all connections must be clean and tight.

Dash Gauges and Indicators

Dash gauges and indictors permit the driver to monitor the operating conditions of his engine and charging system, and the level of fuel in his fuel tank. Generally, the engine gauges monitor the oil pressure and the coolant temperature. Engine warning lights come on if oil pressure drops to a level that cannot ensure adequate protection of the engine's moving parts from heat and wear, or if coolant temperature rises to the point where coolant will be lost through boiling. Oil and coolant gauges are usually marked to indicate safe operating ranges.

The ammeter tells the driver whether current is flowing to or from the battery, and reports the amount. Charging system warning lights tell the driver whether or not the generator is operating. They do not give an indication of charging rate.

The fuel gauge reports the level of fuel in the tank, as measured by a tank float. Most such gauges are marked to indicate the level in increments of quarters of a tank.

While gauges indicate operating conditions over a wide range, warning lights are more easily noticed when trouble occurs suddenly.

Most gauge problems result from faulty wiring or connections, a faulty sensor, or a faulty gauge. In some cases a problem in several gauges at once is due to a malfunction in a special voltage regulator that supplies all the gauges. Because gauge parts are fairly inexpensive, troubleshooting in this area usually involves identifying the defective sensor, wiring, gauge, or gauge voltage regulator, and replacing the faulty unit. It should also be remembered that when many gauges malfunction at once, or repeated gauge problems occur, the voltage regulator in the charging system may be at fault.

GAUGE OPERATION

Bourdon Tube Gauges

This type of gauge is used to measure oil pressure or engine temperature. It responds to changes in pressure via a Bourdon tube which is a coil of tubing with a flattened side. As pressure rises inside the tubing, the flattened side tends to bow somewhat and

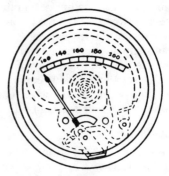

A bourdon tube type temp gauge

straighten the coil. The gauge needle is linked directly to the end of the tube.

When used as an oil pressure gauge, the unit responds directly to the pressure generated by the oil pump, although the gauge and the line to the oil system are kept full of air to make sure that pulsations from the oil pump are dampened out. If the gauge reads accurately but pulsates, the problem may be cured by draining the oil line and gauge and reconnecting all fittings more snugly. If there is evidence of leaks, replace the faulty parts. Reconnect the line at the gauge first, and then at the engine.

If the gauge fails to respond properly, remove the line at the gauge and place it over an empty container. Then start the engine. If oil does not flow from the line after expulsion of a few bubbles, blow out the line to allow pressure to reach the gauge.

If the gauge is still in question, the best procedure is to connect a guage of known accuracy into the system to determine that engine oil pressure is adequate and that the gauge line is clear. Replace the gauge if the good unit operates properly.

When this type of gauge is used to measure engine temperature, it responds to pressure generated by a volatile liquid sealed in a sensing bulb. The bulb is placed in or near the engine cooling water. The vapor pressure of the fluid varies directly with the temperature and the Bourdon tube and gauge are calibrated to reflect the temperature on the face of the gauge. This type of unit is entirely sealed. If the gauge simply does not move from the minimum reading, it may be assumed that the gauge, line, or sensing bulb has leaked, and the whole unit must be replaced. If readings are questionable, a unit of known accuracy may be substituted. If that unit performs accurately, the faulty unit should be replaced.

If the unit responds, but reads slightly low at all times, test the cooling system thermostat to make sure that it is operating properly. If that unit tests out, but the gauge reading has fallen substantially, the gauge unit is faulty.

Install the new unit carefully. Form a loop in the line somewhere between the engine and the gauge to minimize the effect of vibration on the gauge and sensing bulb.

Bimetal Gauges

These gauges employ a bimetallic strip to sense current flow. The two metals which make up this strip expand at different rates. As

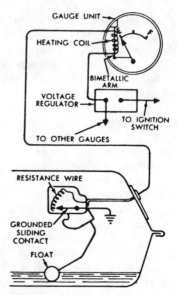

Fuel gauge circuit

the temperature of the strip changes, therefore, the two metals work against each other, making the strip bend back and forth. The free end of the strip operates the gauge needle through a simple linkage.

In the case of a fuel tank bimetal gauge, the sensing unit consists of a resistor and sliding contact. The position of the contact is determined by a float. As the sliding contact moves across the resistor, current is sent in varying amounts to the gauge or to ground. The current which flows to the gauge passes through a resistor which surrounds the bimetal strip, so the gauge indication varies with the position of the float in the tank.

When a bimetal gauge is used to sense

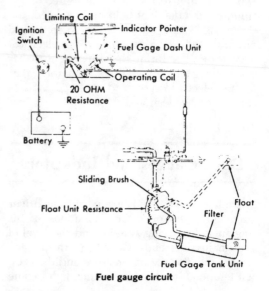

Fuel gauge circuit

engine temperature, the resistor and sliding contact are replaced by a resistor which changes its resistance with temperature. The resistor unit is immersed in the cooling water or placed in direct contact with the material of the engine block.

A bimetal gauge may also be used to measure oil pressure. In this application, the sending unit's linkage to the sliding contact is activated by a diaphragm, one side of which is exposed to engine oil pressure.

The bimetal gauge may be tested by removing it from the dash and applying voltage to it with flashlight batteries. If the gauge is the type that uses a constant voltage regulator, it operates at three volts (3 V). If other gauges are also malfunctioning, the constant voltage regulator is at fault.

To test a constant voltage type gauge, apply 3 V, using two flashlight cells in series and jumper wires. If the gauge operates at line voltage, use four batteries in series to provide 6 V. Under these conditions, the 3 V gauge will read full scale, while the 12 V unit will read half-scale. Replace the unit if it fails to read properly.

If the gauge checks out, or if replacing a faulty unit fails to correct the problem, the sending unit should be tested. Fuel gauge sending units should be removed from the tank and tested for continuity (with an ammeter) through the full range of float movement. If the unit shows zero resistance at any or all positions, it should be replaced. The float should also be checked for leaks. Check the mechanism for binding. Repair or replace the unit as necessary.

The only way to test oil pressure and temperature gauge sending units used with bimetal gauges is to substitute a good unit in place of the suspected one and operate the engine to check for normal response.

If the sending unit proves faulty, it must be replaced. If the problem does not lie in the sending unit, the wire between the sending unit and the gauge should be checked for continuity with an ohmmeter. Check also for bad connections. Clean and tighten connections or replace wiring as necessary.

Magnetic Gauges

The magnetic gauge employs two electromagnetic coils of different sizes to influence the position of the gauge pointer. The smaller coil, located on the left side of the gauge and known as the battery coil, pulls the needle toward the downscale side at all times. This

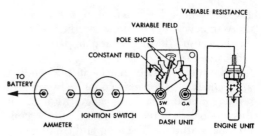

Water temperature gauge

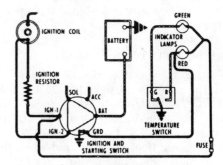

Temperature indicator circuit

coil receives a constant supply of current directly from the ignition switch. The larger coil, known as the ground coil, receives all of the current passing through the unit to ground when full scale readings are required. Under all other circumstances, varying amounts of the current are passed through the sending unit to ground. When less than full current passes through the ground coil, the battery coil pulls the pointer over toward the low side of the scale. The sending units for fuel and temperature gauges of this type work on the same principles that apply to the sending units used with bimetal fuel and temperature gauges. The two types of sending units resemble one another closely. However, units designed for one type of gauge cannot be used with the other. It is, therefore, necessary to use only the proper sending unit for the particular gauge.

TESTING GAUGES

Magnetic Fuel Gauges

To test the dash gauge, use a tank unit of known accuracy. Pull the wire from the tank unit and install it on the unit being used for the test. Ground the body of the unit being used for the test. Moving the float arm through its entire range should produce a consistent response from the gauge, with the needle moving from empty to full positions.

If the gauge reads properly, the problem is in the tank unit. Remove it and check for a gas-logged float, binding float, or lack of continuity somewhwere in the operating range of the float arm. Replace or repair parts of the unit as necessary.

If the problem does not lie in the sending unit, check all the connections between the sending unit and the dash gauge. Also, check the wire between the dash gauge and the tank unit for continuity. If wiring and connections are all right, or if rectifying problems in them does not give accurate readings, replace the dash gauge.

Magnetic Temperature Gauges

First, disconnect the wire at the sending unit. The gauge hand should be in the cold position. Ground the wire which goes to the sending unit. The gauge should move to the hot position.

If the gauge does not read cold when the wire to the sending unit is disconnected, either the gauge is defective or the wire is grounded somewhere. Disconnect the wire that goes to the sending unit at the gauge. If the gauge now reads cold, replace the wire. Otherwise, replace the gauge unit.

If the gauge reads to the cold side when the wire is disconnected, but does not move to the hot side when it is grounded, ground the sending unit terminal of the gauge. If this causes the gauge to read to the hot side, replace the wire that goes to the sending unit.

If there is no response from the gauge when the sending unit terminal is grounded, test for voltage with a voltmeter or test lamp at the ignition switch terminal of the gauge. If there is no voltage here, test for voltage at the ignition switch accessory terminal. If there is voltage at the ignition switch terminal, replace the wire between this terminal and the gauge. Otherwise, replace the ignition switch.

If this does not produce accurate readings, remove the engine thermostat and test it for proper operation as described in the cooling system troubleshooting section. If the thermostat is all right, or if replacing it does not rectify the problem, substitute a good sending unit for the one presently in the engine block. If this does not produce good readings, replace the dash gauge.

Warning Lights

Warning lights continuously receive voltage whenever the ignition switch is turned on. The circuit is completed to ground whenever the sending unit contacts close, allowing current to flow through the light.

Oil pressure warning light sending units consist of a diaphragm which responds to about five lbs oil pressure, opening the contacts when that pressure level is exceeded. Water temperature warning lights are energized when a bimetal element closes the contacts in the sending unit at a predetermined water temperature.

TESTING WARNING LIGHTS

Oil Pressure Warning Lights

If the oil light is on all the time, remove the connection at the sending unit. If the light is still on, the problem is a ground between the light and sending unit. Replace the wire between these two units.

If the light goes off when the wire is removed, connect a pressure gauge into the fitting where the oil pressure sending unit is normally installed. If the oil pressure exceeds five lbs, replace the sending unit. Otherwise, there is a mechanical problem causing low oil pressure.

If the light never operates, remove the wire from the sending unit and ground it. If this causes the light to come on, replace the sending unit. If there is no response, check for voltage at both terminals of the lamp socket and at the ignition switch accessory terminal. The faulty unit lies between a hot and a dead terminal. If the lamp socket is suspected, replace the lamp with one that is known to operate. If this produces no response, replace the socket.

Temperature Warning Lights

See the cooling system service section for procedures on testing this system. If the light does not operate in spite of coolant loss, the antifreeze strength, radiator cap, and cooling system pressure tests should be performed. If the light operates even though no coolant is lost, check the radiator cap and thermostat, and, if necessary, clean the system.

If these system tests do not uncover the problem, the light should be tested as outlined for the oil pressure light test above. If the system is known to operate properly, but the light comes on when it should not, or does not come on when overheating occurs, the sending unit should be replaced.

Troubleshooting Dash Gauges

All Gauges Pegged

Possible Cause	Correction
Loss of regulator case ground to vehicle.	1. Use ohmmeter to check for proper ground (zero resistance). 2. Use ohmmeter to check for cracked ground circuit in printed circuit.
Faulty instrument voltage regulator.	Use voltmeter or test light to check for pulsing instrument voltage regulator output.

All Gauges Do Not Indicate With Ignition Switch ON

Possible Cause	Correction
Open circuit in radio noise suppression choke.	Replace choke.
Faulty instrument voltage regulator.	Use voltmeter or test light to check for pulsing instrument voltage regulator output.
Open circuit in battery feed to instrument voltage regulator.	Use voltmeter or test light to locate open circuit in feed.
Open circuit in printed circuit	Use voltmeter or test light to locate open circuit in printed circuit.

Individual Fuel, Oil or Temperature Gauge Does not Indicate or Operate

Possible Cause	Correction
Associated sender not grounded.	Test sender ground with ohmmeter (zero resistance).
Open circuit in wiring harness or printed circuit.	Use voltmeter or test light to locate open circuit.
Open circuit winding in gauge or sender.	Test gauge and sending unit individually.

Individual Fuel, Oil or Temperature Gauge Pegged

Possible Cause	Correction
Harness or sender shorted to ground.	1. Bypass harness with jumper wire. 2. If still pegged, replace sender. 3. If operative, repair harness.

Erratic Operation of All Gauges

Possible Cause	Correction
Dirty contacts in instrument voltage regulator.	Replace instrument voltage regulator.

All Gauges Read Low

Possible Cause	Correction
Radio noise choke connected to output terminal.	Connect radio noise choke to IGN terminal.
Instrument voltage regulator out of calibration.	Check calibration.

Fuses, Circuit Breakers, and Fusible Links

Fuses are replaceable electrical conductors sealed in small glass cylinders for protection against dust and corrosion. The conducting portion ot the fuse is made of a metal with a low melting point. The fuse is designed so that if the amperage passing through it exceeds its rated capacity, the conducting material will melt and interrupt the flow of current through the circuit.

Circuit breakers are electrical switches that employ bimetallic elements to open the circuit whenever current exceeds a specified level. The heat from the passage of current through the unit bends the bimetallic arm to open the contacts of the switch. After a short period of cooling, the contacts close again.

Circuit breakers are usually used to protect heavy-duty electric motors that can be operated only intermittently. These motors power such auxiliaries as power windows, convertible tops, and tailgates.

Fusible links are sections of vehicle wiring designed to protect the wiring itself, as well as individual accessories. The links consist of wiring sections about four gauges smaller (larger numerically) than the regular wiring. If a severe overload occurs, the link will burn out entirely before the regular vehicle wiring is damaged.

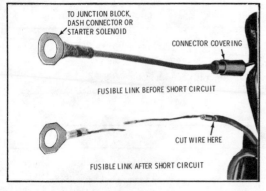

Fusible link before and after overload

Repair a burned out fusible link as follows:

A. Disconnect the battery. Cut out all remaining portions of the burned out link. Strip the main wiring insulation back about ½ in. on either end.

B. Solder in a 10 in. long link of wire that is four gauges smaller than the wire to be protected. Use resin core solder only.

C. Tape all exposed portions of the wire securely. Reconnect the battery.

Windshield Wiper Systems

Most windshield wipers are powered by small electric motors of either the permanent magnet or electromagnet type. Some systems are powered by hydraulic pressure from the power steering pump or by intake manifold vacuum.

The wiper systems usually provide two or three operating speeds. Speed is controlled by inserting a resistor into the circuit in the lower speed or speeds. The resistance element may either be located on the wiper switch or on the wiper motor itself. Most electrical system employ a circuit breaker which may be located on either the switch or the motor.

If the system does not operate at all, make sure that the blades are not frozen in place or adjusted so the motor cannot reach a park position. Pull the blades outward, then turn on the ignition and wiper switches and check the response. If the blades now move, adjust the blades so that when the motor is parked, they just reach the bottom of the windshield.

If the system does not operate at all, or does not park properly, an electrical check should be made to see if the problem is in the wiring, switch, or motor. If the motor operates but there is no response from the wipers, the gearbox on the motor is at fault.

Locate the wiper switch and test the terminal for the wire from the ignition switch for voltage. If there is no voltage, check for voltage at each connection between the wiper switch and the ignition switch and replace fuses or wiring as necessary.

If there is voltage to the switch but the system does not operate, remove the switch from the dash. Locate a factory manual for the vehicle. Perform a continuity test with an ohmmeter according to the instructions in the manual. This will involve testing for continuity between various terminals with the wiper switch in different positions. Replace the switch if continuity does not exist in one of the tests.

If the switch is good and the wipers still do not perform properly, check the wiring be-

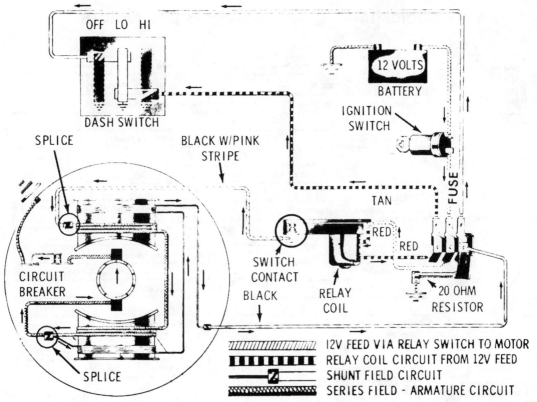

Typical windshield wiper schematic

tween the switch and the wiper motor. Each wire should be checked for continuity. If all wires are good, or if replacing any defective wire does not rectify the problem, the problem is a mechanical or electrical malfunction in the wiper motor.

Lighting, Turn Signals, and Warning Flashers

The first step in checking any lighting problem is to inspect all wiring and connectors. Make sure all insulation is sound and that all connectors in the circuits involved are securely connected. Also, make sure that the battery and charging systems are in good condition.

TROUBLESHOOTING

Headlamps

If a headlamp does not operate on one or both dimmer positions, substitute a lamp that is known to be good (perhaps the one from the other side of the car), or check for voltage at all terminals of the connector. All should have voltage in at least one of the dimmer positions. If all have voltage, replace the lamp.

If the connector at the lamp does not check out, check for voltage at the dimmer switch. Regardless of the type of switch, voltage should exist at all the terminals in at least one of the switch positions. If the dimmer switch is all right, replace wiring or correct loose connections between the switch and the headlight connector. If there is voltage anywhere in the switch, but one or more of the terminals has no voltage in either switch position, replace the switch.

If there is no voltage to the switch, check for voltage at each connection back to the battery. The faulty component is between a hot connection and a dead one. Replace wiring, fuses, or the headlight switch as necessary.

Direction Signals and Warning Flashers

If one of the direction signal lamps fails to operate, turn on the four-way flasher and check all lamps for operation. If the lamps operate with the flasher on, the defect is in the direction signal flasher or connections.

Troubleshooting Windshield Wiper Motors

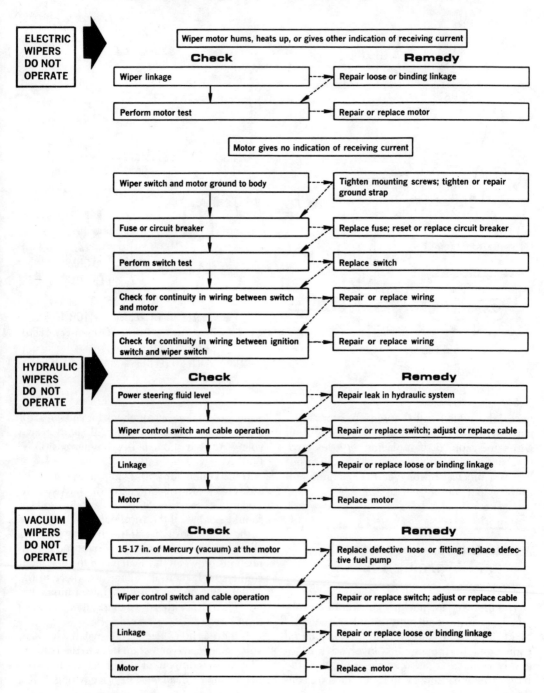

If the same lamp(s) fails to operate, substitute a lamp that is known to be good for the faulty lamp in each case. If this fails to correct the problem, check for voltage at each connection right back to the flasher. Also check for a corroded socket which might prevent proper grounding of the lamp, and clean up the socket as necessary. The faulty connector or wire is between a hot connection and a dead one. Replace wiring as necessary.

If all the lamps operate, and the direction signal or four-way flasher does not flash, replace the flasher unit. Remember that the unit flashes on and off by means of a bimetal strip that is heated by current flow. If any lamp is not getting current, the flasher will not operate properly.

If it is suspected that the flasher is faulty, it may be tested in either of two ways. If a replacement flasher is available, the wires may be removed from the one installed in the car and connected to the replacement flasher without removing the original unit. If this flasher works properly, replace the original one.

The flasher may also be tested for continuity by consulting a factory service manual for a table that lists which terminals should have continuity in the various switch positions.

If the flasher is not a fault, the wiring between the flasher and the battery or ignition switch should be tested for continuity. Replace wiring, fuses, or connectors as necessary.

The Air-Conditioning System

BASIC OPERATING PRINCIPLES

In order to understand how air conditioning works, it is necessary to understand several basic laws about the flow of heat. The refrigerant used in the system follows the same laws that apply to all other substances.

The law of entropy states that all things must eventually come to the same temperature. There will always be a flow of heat between objects which are at different temperatures. For example, when two objects at different temperatures are near each other, heat will flow from the warmer of the two objects to the cooler one. The rate at which heat is transferred from one object to another depends upon how great the difference is between their temperatures. If the temperature difference becomes greater, the transfer of heat will become greater, and if the temperature difference lessens, the transfer of heat will be reduced until both objects reach the same temperature. At that point, heat transfer stops altogether.

Because of entropy, the interior of an automobile will tend to remain at approximately the same temperature as the outside air. If we wish to cool an automobile interior, we must reverse the natural flow of heat no matter how thoroughly insulated the compartment might be. It will be necessary to continuously remove heat to make up for that which the body metal and glass absorb from the outside.

It is the refrigeration cycle of the air conditioning system that performs this job. The refrigeration cycle makes use of another law of heat flow. This might be called the theory of latent heat. This theory says that during a change of state, a material can absorb or reject heat without changing its temperature. A material is changing its state when it is freezing or thawing, or condensing or boiling. Thus, changes of state differ from ordinary heating and cooling in that they occur without the temperature of the substance changing, and cause a visible change in the form of the substance.

Many materials can exist in solid, liquid, or gas form. Water is a common material that can exist in all three states. Below 32°, it exists as solid ice. Above 212° at sea level air pressure, it exists as steam, a gas. Of course, at room temperature, it is in liquid form.

Since a change in state occurs at constant temperature, it follows that both liquid and gas can coexist at the same temperature without any exchange of heat between the two.

While the change from a solid to a liquid and vice versa always practically is the same for a given substance (32° F for water), the temperature at which a liquid will boil or condense depends upon the pressure conditions. For example, we know that water will boil at 212° F at sea level air pressure, and that its boiling point drops slightly at high altitudes, where the pressure of the surrounding air is lower. We also know that raising the pressure 15 lb. above normal air pressure in an enclosed automobile cooling system will keep the water from boiling until the temperature reaches 260°. Thus, the fact that the boiling point of a liquid varies with the surrounding pressure conditions is a familiar phenomenon.

One additional aspect of the behavior of a liquid at its boiling point must be clarified before we can understand how a refrigeration cycle works. Since liquid and gas can exist at the same temperature, either evaporation of liquid material or condensation of gaseous material can occur at the same temperature and pressure conditions. It's just a matter of whether the material is being heated or cooled.

When a pan of water is placed on top of a hot stove burner, the heat will tend to travel from the hot burner to the relatively cool pan and water. When the water reaches its boiling

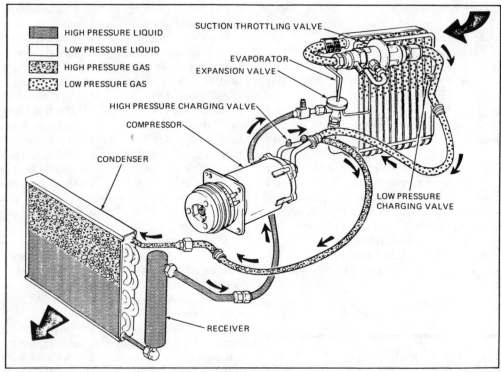

HIGH PRESSURE LIQUID
LOW PRESSURE LIQUID
HIGH PRESSURE GAS
LOW PRESSURE GAS

SUCTION THROTTLING VALVE
EVAPORATOR
EXPANSION VALVE
HIGH PRESSURE CHARGING VALVE
COMPRESSOR
CONDENSER
LOW PRESSURE
CHARGING VALVE
RECEIVER

Typical air-conditioning system

point, its temperature will stop rising and all the additional heat forced into it by the hot burner will be used to turn the liquid material into a gas. The gas thus contains more heat than the liquid material. If the top of the pan were now to be held a couple of inches above the boiling water, two things would happen. First, droplets of liquid would form on the lower surface. Secondly, the top would very quickly get hot. What is happening is that the heat originally used to turn the water to steam is being recovered. As the vapor comes in contact with the cooler surface of the metal, heat is removed from it and transferred to the metal. This heat is the heat that was originally required to change it into a vapor, and so it again becomes a liquid. Since water will boil only at 212° and above at sea level it follows that the steam must have been 212° when it reached the top and must have remained that hot until it became a liquid. The cooling effect of the top (which started out at room temperature) caused it to condense, but both the boiling and condensation took place at the same temperature.

In the example described above, heat flowed according to the natural flow described by the law of entropy—from a very hot electric coil or gas flame to relatively cool water,

and from relatively hot steam to a top that is near to room temperature. When cooling an automobile passenger compartment, we must make use of an external source of energy—the engine—to drive a mechanical compressor and cause pressure changes which will force the heat to flow from the cool compartment to the warmer outside air. To reiterate:

Refrigeration is the removal of heat from a confined space. The theory of refrigeration is based on three assumptions:

1. Heat will flow only from a relatively warm substance to a relatively cold substance.

2. A refrigerant exists as both a liquid and a gas at the same temperature, if it is at its "boiling point". A refrigerant at its boiling point will boil and absorb heat from its surroundings, if the surroundings are warmer than the refrigerant. A refrigerant at its boiling point will condense and become liquid, losing heat to its surroundings, if they are cooler than the refrigerant.

3. The boiling point of the refrigerant depends upon the pressure of the refrigerant, rising as the pressure rises, and falling as the pressure falls.

Explaining how the refrigeration cycle actually operates will illustrate how the cycle makes use of these three laws.

Refrigeration Cycle

All automobile air conditioning systems employ four basic parts. They are: a mechanical compressor, driven by the vehicle's engine; an expansion valve, which is a restriction the compressor pumps against; and two heat exchangers, the evaporator and the condenser. The refrigerant passes through the condenser on its way from the compressor outlet to the expansion valve. The condenser is located outside the passenger compartment, usually in front of the vehicle's radiator. The refrigerant passes from the expansion valve to the evaporator, and, after passing through the evaporator tubing, is returned to the compressor through its inlet. The evaporator is located inside the vehicle's passenger compartment.

When the compressor starts running, it pulls refrigerant from the evaporator coil and forces it into the condenser coil, thus lowering the evaporator pressure and increasing the condenser pressure. When proper operating pressures have been established, the expansion valve will open up and allow refrigerant to return to the evaporator as fast as the compressor is removing it. Under these conditions, the pressure at each point in the system will reach a constant level, but the condenser pressure will be much higher than the evaporator pressure. The pressure in the evaporator is low enough for the boiling point of the refrigerant to be well below the temperature of the vehicle's interior. Therefore, the liquid will boil and remove heat from the interior, and then pass from the evaporator as a gas. The heating effect produced by the work done on the refrigerant as it passes through the compressor keeps the gas from liquifying, and causes it to be discharged from the compressor at very high temperatures. This hot gas passes into the condenser. The pressure on this side of the system is high enough so that the boiling point of the refrigerant is well beyond the outside temperature. Therefore, the gas will cool until it reaches its boiling point, and then condense to a liquid as heat is absorbed by the outside air. The liquid refrigerant is then forced back through the expansion valve by the condenser pressure.

COMPONENT OPERATION

Refrigerant

Refrigerant 12 is used universally in automotive air conditioning systems. At normal temperatures it is a colorless, odorless gas,

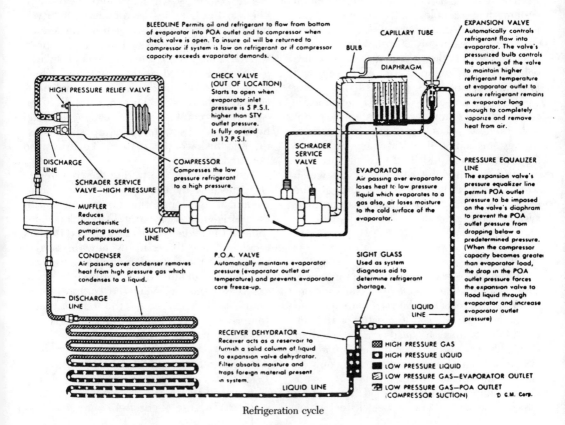

Refrigeration cycle

which is slightly heavier than air. Its boiling point at atmospheric pressure is −21.7° F. Whenever liquid R-12 is spilled in the open air, it can be seen for a brief period as a rapidly boiling, clear liquid.

When R-12 is stored in a closed container, its density is such that at least some liquid refrigerant will be present. Whenever liquid exists in a closed container, it will produce a pressure which can be predicted by knowing the surrounding temperature conditions. For example, at a moderate room temperature of 70°, the pressure inside a container of refrigerant will be just over 70 psi, while at 90°, the pressure will be nearly 100 psi. These same pressure conditions will exist in a refrigeration system that is idle. The tendency for the liquid R-12 to produce a pressure which depends on its temperature is by no means a property common only to refrigerant. Water behaves in exactly the same manner when it is above its atmospheric pressure boiling point. An automobile engine operating with a coolant temperature beyond 212° will produce a pressure which is exerted on the pressure cap. The only difference is that, with water, the pressure produced is lower at a given temperature.

There are some characteristics of refrigerant 12 that are particularly useful in a refrigeration system. For example, at the operating temperature of an evaporator coil, the refrigerant is under approximately 29 psi. Thus, if there are small leaks in the system, air and moisture will tend to be excluded, and refrigerant will force its way out. Also, pure refrigerant 12 is completely non-corrosive and chemically stable, so that, provided the system does not leak, there will be no corrosion of the parts of the system, and no chemical change in the refrigerant. Also, liquid R-12 mixes completely with oil, so that the compressor oil which works its way around the pistons and into the discharge gas can easily circulate around the system and be continuously returned to the crankcase.

Compressor

The compressor is a piston type pump, very similar to a gasoline engine in its construction, except in two respects: the valves are operated by the pressure differences created by the motion of the pistons; the heads are designed for negligible expansion space. The compressor operates like a gasoline engine having only an exhaust and intake stroke.

The compressor employs reed type valves, which are constructed of a special steel which will withstand being bent countless times before being permanently deformed. The intake valve is a flat sheet of metal which is mounted to the underside of the valve plate, and which tightly covers the intake port whenever the cylinder pressure is equal to or greater than the suction line pressure. The exhaust valve is similar, but is mounted to the top of the valve plate, so that it will seal the port whenever cylinder pressure is less than the pressure in the discharge line. The valves open when appropriate pressures force them to bend away from the ports.

The pistons are of cast iron and employ only annular grooves filled with oil for sealing, instead of piston rings. In most compressors, the connecting rods and crankshaft are similar to those which are used in a gasoline engine. In some systems, (GM, Toyota & Abacus) however, a special swash plate design is used. The swash plate is a disk which is integral with the compressor shaft, but which is not perpendicular with the center line of the shaft. It therefore wobbles as the shaft turns. This motion is imparted to three double acting pistons through ball bearings. These units, then, have five or six cylinders. Most other units employ either one or two.

The compressor is lubricated by oil supplied to the bearings by a crankshaft driven pump. The pump draws oil from the crankcase and supplies the bearings under pressure, and the pistons and cylinders by splash.

The oil is stored in the crankcase, which serves as an oil cooler. Heat from the oil is carried to the outside by the metal walls of the compressor crankcase. Also, cooling is aided by the flow of low temperature suction gas through the lower part of the unit on its way to the suction valves.

The problem of lubricating the compressor is aggravated by the fact that a significant amount of the lubricating oil circulates with the refrigerant because of the tendency for some of the oil to work its way around the pistons and leave the compressor with the discharge gas. A leak anywhere in the system will reduce the amount of oil returned to the crankcase, thus allowing the compressor to pump itself dry. It is for this reason that a compressor oil level check is an integral part of a leak repair.

The R-4 compressor is a newly designed radial, four cylinder unit intended to be used on 1975 GM cars equpped with six cylinder engines and 1976 GM cars with 4 & 6 cylinder engines. The use of the R-4 compressor was

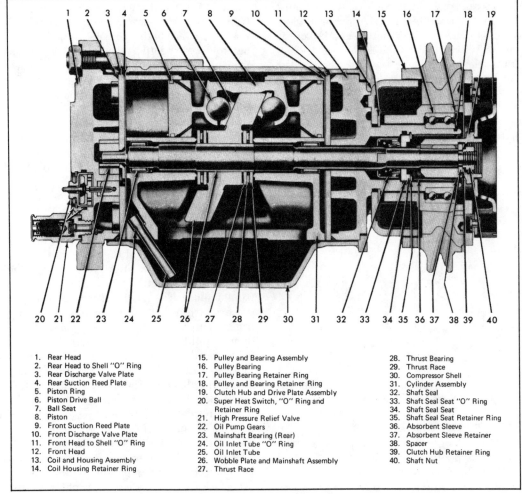

Cross-section of a typical compressor

1.	Rear Head	15.	Pulley and Bearing Assembly	28.	Thrust Bearing
2.	Rear Head to Shell "O" Ring	16.	Pulley Bearing	29.	Thrust Race
3.	Rear Discharge Valve Plate	17.	Pulley Bearing Retainer Ring	30.	Compressor Shell
4.	Rear Suction Reed Plate	18.	Pulley and Bearing Retainer Ring	31.	Cylinder Assembly
5.	Piston Ring	19.	Clutch Hub and Drive Plate Assembly	32.	Shaft Seal
6.	Piston Drive Ball	20.	Super Heat Switch, "O" Ring and	33.	Shaft Seal Seat "O" Ring
7.	Ball Seat		Retainer Ring	34.	Shaft Seal Seat
8.	Piston	21.	High Pressure Relief Valve	35.	Shaft Seal Seat Retainer Ring
9.	Front Suction Reed Plate	22.	Oil Pump Gears	36.	Absorbent Sleeve
10.	Front Discharge Valve Plate	23.	Mainshaft Bearing (Rear)	37.	Absorbent Sleeve Retainer
11.	Front Head to Shell "O" Ring	24.	Oil Inlet Tube "O" Ring	38.	Spacer
12.	Front Head	25.	Oil Inlet Tube	39.	Clutch Hub Retainer Ring
13.	Coil and Housing Assembly	26.	Wobble Plate and Mainshaft Assembly	40.	Shaft Nut
14.	Coil Housing Retainer Ring	27.	Thrust Race		

continued on 1977 and later GM models of 350 cubic inches or less. Less engine power is required to drive it as it is lighter in weight and more efficient than the six cylinder units used on other engines. The unit displaces 10.0 cubic inches and is protected by the low refrigerant protection system and superheat switch.

The basic compressor mechanism is a modified scotch yoke design with four cylinders located radially on the same horizontal plane. The pistons are pressed into a yoke which rides on a slider block located on the shaft eccentric. Shaft rotation provides piston motion without the use of connecting rods. The whole thing is balanced with counterweights. The shaft bearings and eccentric ride on needle bearings. The pistons, yokes, main cylinder housing and front cover are aluminum. The piston rings are made of teflon and the outer shell is a simple steel band which encloses a

large annular discharge muffler space. Seal between the shell and cylinder assembly is provided by two O-rings.

Refrigerant is drawn into the crankcase from the connector at the rear, through the reeds attached to the piston top during the suction stroke and is discharged through the discharge valve plate which is held in place at the top of the cylinder by a snap ring.

Magnetic Clutch

The compressor is equipped with a magnetic clutch, so that it may be left idle when it is not required. On thermostatically controlled systems, the compressor's capacity is controlled by cycling it on and off, using this clutch. A coil, which produces a magnetic field when it is energized, is mounted on the end of the compressor. When the coil is energized, the magnetic force draws a ring shaped armature, which is connected to the compressor shaft by flexible leaves, against the front surface of the compressor pulley, which is driven by the engine crankshaft via one or more belts. The resulting friction drives the compressor without slip, if the clutch is operating properly.

Compressor Cycle

Cycles of a typical refrigerant compressor are illustrated below.

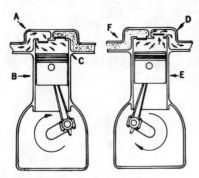

Compressor cycle of reciprocal compressor

A. Piston on downstroke creates vacuum in cylinder. Suction line pressure opens suction valve.

B. Piston downstroke.

C. Discharge valve held closed by pressure in discharge line.

D. Piston on upstroke creates pressure in cylinder. Gas enters discharge line.

E. Piston upstroke.

F. Suction valve held closed by cylinder pressure.

Refrigerant Oil

Refrigerant oil lubricates the moving parts of the compressor. Because of the low temperatures encountered in the system, it is extremely light as compared with motor oil. It is refined in a special manner to remove corrosive substances such as sulphur, substances that might solidify under the extreme cold (wax), and moisture. The oil has an anti-foaming agent, as does regular motor oil.

Since the compressor oil must have so many special qualities to perform adequately, it should be obvious that *no other lubricant* should ever be substituted for the recommended grade of refrigerant oil.

Condenser

Similar in construction to a conventional automobile radiator, the condenser is a sealed

unit that must withstand pressures exceeding 400 psi. High pressure refrigerant, laden with heat enters the condenser coils in the form of a gas and by giving up its heat to the air, the gas changes to a liquid. This is the heat that was transferred from the passenger compartment.

The efficiency of the condensing action is dependent on the motion of the vehicle to force air against the condenser fins combined with the cooling action of the belt driven radiator fan.

Care in keeping this unit free of obstructions, such as bugs and paper, will add to the efficiency of its function.

Receiver-Drier

The metal cylinder at the outlet of the condenser is called the drier, receiver, or the receiver-drier. It serves two purposes as the name implies. The receiver serves as a storage space which accepts any excess of liquid refrigerant to later insure a steady flow to the demands of the evaporator. The drier section is designed to retain any small amount of moisture in the system. There is also a screen in this unit that filters out foreign particles that might otherwise recirculate to obstruct the normal refrigerant flow. Most receivers incorporate a "window" or sight glass where the liquid refrigerant can be observed.

Some receiver-driers employ a pressure relief valve (sometimes on the bottom of the drier) which is designed to rupture in the event of excessively high pressure conditions within the system. Some of these relief valves are restricted with solder and repair of this type unit is not recommended. It is helpful, when searching for refrigerant leaks, to check this relief outlet for excessive compressor oil deposits.

Other A/C systems utilize similar relief valves which mechanically reset themselves after performing their function. These are also primary points in a search for refrigerant leakage.

It is imperative that receiver-drier units be sealed while in storage since they are so moisture-hungry. Installation should be done quickly so it is advisable to have all necessary tools and supplies close at hand for quick installation.

Expansion Valve

The expansion valve regulates the flow of refrigerant to the evaporator, ensuring that

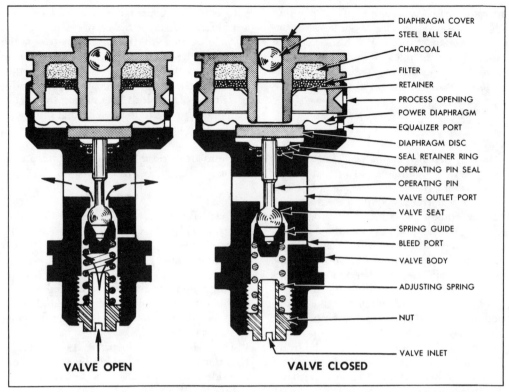

DIAPHRAGM COVER
STEEL BALL SEAL
CHARCOAL
FILTER
RETAINER
PROCESS OPENING
POWER DIAPHRAGM
EQUALIZER PORT
DIAPHRAGM DISC
SEAL RETAINER RING
OPERATING PIN SEAL
OPERATING PIN
VALVE OUTLET PORT
VALVE SEAT
SPRING GUIDE
BLEED PORT
VALVE BODY
ADJUSTING SPRING
NUT
VALVE INLET

VALVE OPEN   VALVE CLOSED

Expansion valve cutaway

the evaporator is as full of liquid refrigerant as possible, without allowing any liquid to pass into the compressor suction ine. The expansion valve ensures that liquid refrigerant boils completely, and then heats up to a temperature about ten degrees beyond its boiling point. This extra heating effect ensures that any droplets of liquid refrigerant that might be carried out of the evaporator by the escaping gaseous material will be evaporated before they reach the compressor.

A typical expansion valve consists of the following components: capillary tube and bulb, diaphragm, valve pin, and return spring. The bulb, which contains refrigerant, is fastened to the compressor suction line to act as a sensor. The spring serves to keep the valve entirely closed until the level of liquid refrigerant is somewhat below the top of the evaporator. As the level of the boiling liquid drops, the gas flowing toward the compressor has a greater and greater opportunity to pick up heat from the car's interior. The tension of the spring is such that when the bulb temperature (i.e. suction gas temperature) is about ten degrees above the evaporator temperature, the expansion valve will open and maintain the level of liquid refrigerant in the evaporator. It is the

pressure generated by the effect of heat on the feeler bulb which forces the diaphragm down to open the valve.

During normal operating conditions, the position of the expansion valve diaphragm is determined by the difference between evaporator pressure and the pressure generated by the feeler bulb. Since both pressures are directly proportional to the temperatures where they are generated, they serve as reliable indicators of the temperatures in the evaporator and suction line. The effect of the spring will be to ensure that suction gas temperature is higher than evaporator temperature.

In systems which use General Motors type Suction Throttling Valves, the expansion valve, via a pressure equalizer line, monitors the pressure of the suction gas passing to the compressor after it passes through the STV, rather than the actual pressure of the evaporator itself. Under heavy load conditions, the expansion valves in these systems operate normally. However, when the compressor capacity exceeds what is required, the STV valve will begin to throttle the refrigerant on its way to the compressor. This will cause the expansion valve to receive a falsely low reading, thus causing it to open up and flood the evaporator with refrigerant. This flooding poses no threat to the compressor because the throttling action of the STV valve lowers the pressure and evaporates all liquid in the suction gas. The evaporator is flooded at low loads to ensure better circulation of oil back to the compressor.

Evaporator

The evaporator, similar in design and construction to a conventional car heater, depends upon the difference between the temperatures of the boiling refrigerant and the car interior to perform its cooling job.

The evaporator blower fan draws air from the vehicle interior and forces it, at high velocity, across the evaporator coil. In addition to having the capacity to force sufficient air through the coil, the fan must be able to produce a high velocity in the discharge air ducts, in order to effectively circulate the conditioned air throughout the car's interior.

Most blowers have two or three operating speeds to allow most efficient use of the evaporator's cooling ability under various operating conditions. When the primary goal is to remove the greatest amount of heat from the car in the shortest possible time, the fan should be operated at the highest speed, as this will evaporate the refrigerant at the fastest possible rate and remove the most heat. However, when the car's interior has reached a comfortable temperature, the blower should be run at a slower speed. This will cause the air to linger on the evaporator coil longer, thus reducing the temperature of the discharge air, and removing more of its moisture.

Suction Throttling Valve

The function of the suction throttling valve is to maintain the evaporator pressure at a level high enough to avoid freezing of moisture on the evaporator core and at the same time provide maximum cooling efficiency. If pressure in the core were allowed to drop much below 29 psi, ice would form in the core and block air flow. The valve is connected in the refrigerant suction line between the evaporator outlet and the compressor inlet.

Under conditions of partial load, the valve supplies suction gas pressure rather than evaporator pressure to the expansion valve through the pressure equalizer line connected to it on the compressor side of the throttle. Under these conditions, the evaporator will flood with refrigerant, but the throttling effect of the STV will lower the boiling point and en-

sure complete evaporation of liquid refrigerant before it reaches the compressor.

An oil bleed line connected between the bottom of the evaporator and the outlet side of the Evaporator Pressure Regulator further aids circulation of oil to the compressor under conditions of part load by allowing the higher evaporator pressure to force oil that otherwise might hang up in the evaporator directly into the suction gas stream.

There are several types of suction throttling valves.

Valves-in-Receiver Unit (VIR)

The VIR is an assembly used on GM vehicles since 1973. It combines in one unit the thermostatic expansion valve, POA suction throttling valve, receiver-dehydrator, and sight glass.

Eliminated are the external equalizer line between the expansion valve and outlet of the POA valve, and the thermostatic capillary line and thermo-bulb.

The VIR assembly incorporates the old design units into one assembly by sealing them individually into capsule-type sections located within the VIR assembly.

The receiver-dehydrator portion of the unit is similar in function and flow design to the old style separate units.

The new capsule type expansion valve is made up of three separate pressure areas. The upper pressure area is basically suction pres-

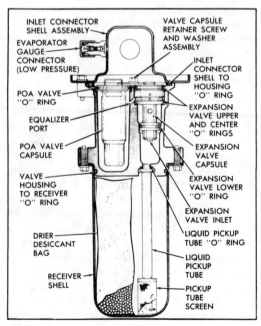

Valve-in-receiver unit

sure; the middle pressure area is basically evaporator pressure; the lower pressure area is basically discharge pressure. The pressure in the diaphragm is directly affected by the temperature of the refrigerant as it passes through the VIR to the POA. The diaphragm is partially filled with charcoal for filtering.

The new capsule type POA suction throttling valve is basically similar in design to the separate unit. Eliminated in the new unit are the inlet and outlet connections. The pressure in the piston spring and bellows is the same and is referred to in future notes as the "Bellows Cavity Pressure."

Note that in all units, all interconnecting, outside plumbing is eliminated. Also, no adjustment or repairs are possible to individual units. These units must be replaced when malfunctioning. Units, for this reason, are secured in place by means of O-rings.

AIR CONDITIONING SYSTEM TROUBLESHOOTING

Any in-depth troubleshooting of air-conditioner systems requires expensive equipment and specialized training. However, there are several general checks you can make without the aid of special tools.

WARNING: *Refrigerant gas is extremely harmful. It will freeze any surface, including your eyes, it comes in contact with. DO NOT attempt to work on any air-conditioning system without specialized tools and training.*

Air conditioners should be operated for a few minutes once a week, even in winter, to prevent oil from draining away from critical tolerance areas within the compressor. Before operating the compressor, if it has been idle for a few weeks, rotate the compressor several times by hand in the opposite direction to pump oil to the bearings. This will prevent galling and other bearing damage.

A. Check the Compressor Belts

Inspect the compressor belts for cracks or glazing. Cracks that will affect operation of the belt appear as a separation of a large portion of the lower section of the belt. Glazing is the result of slippage, and is indicated by an absolutely smooth appearance of the two belt surfaces that bear against the pulley grooves.

If the belt is cracked or glazed, replace it. Use only the belt specified for the application. Replace multiple belts with new, matched sets, even if one of the belts is still serviceable.

When replacing the belt:

1. Loosen the mounting bolts of the compressor and move the unit toward the fan so that the new belt can be installed without prying.

2. Tighten the belt by pulling the compressor away from the fan, prying it carefully with a breaker bar or, if the mount is provided with a square hole, by applying torque on the mount with the square end of a socket drive. Position the compressor and then tighten all the mounting bolts.

Belts should be tightened so that there is no slack and so they have a springy feel. Applying moderate thumb pressure should cause the belt to yield about ½–¾ in. for each 10 in. between the two pulleys. New belts should be slightly tighter to allow for tension loss during break-in.

Tighten all belts to these specifications, even if there is no evidence of wear. If the belt is noisy, the problem is usually slippage which can be cured by proper adjustment or replacement.

B. Make Sure the Compressor Is Turning

The front portion of the clutch remains stationary when the clutch is disengaged, even when the car's engine is operating. If that portion of the clutch turns with the pulley and belts, the compressor is operating.

If the compressor is not running, make sure that the air conditioning is turned on and that the controls are set for full cold. Also, the compressor of many units will not run if outside temperature is below 50° F. If all the switches are set properly and the weather is warm, the compressor should run at least intermittently. If there is no response, pull the wire from the connection on the clutch and test for voltage with a voltmeter. If voltage exists, the clutch is faulty and will have to be replaced. If there is no voltage, trace the wiring back toward the ignition switch. If the wire leads to a device mounted onto the receiver drier, or mounted on the firewall and electrically connected to the back of the compressor, the system has a low refrigerant protection system. If voltage exists on the ignition switch side of this unit but not on the clutch side, the system's refrigerant has leaked out. In this instance, repair by a professional air conditioning mechanic is required.

Otherwise, check each connection for voltage all the way back to the ignition switch. Lack of current can be caused by faulty wiring, bad connections, a blown fuse, or an inoperative thermostat (located right behind the temperature control). Fuses may be checked by removing them and checking for continuity with an ohmmeter. The faulty component lies between the last dead connection and the first to show voltage. Repair wiring, fuses, or switches as necessary.

C. Inspect the Condenser and Fan

Inspect the condenser for bent fins or foreign material. Straighten the fins and clean them, if necessary.

NOTE: *Be careful, when straightening fins, not to allow the tools being used to damage the condenser tubing.*

Check the fan for bent blades or improper operation caused by slipping belts or a faulty fan clutch. See the cooling system troubleshooting section. Any cooling system problem can contribute to inferior air conditioner performance.

D. Check for Leaks

Refrigerant system leaks show up as oily areas on the various components because the compressor oil is transported around the entire system along with the refrigerant. Look for oily spots on all the hoses and lines and at the hose and tubing connections, especially. If there are oily deposits, the system may have a leak and should be checked as in subsection E. A small area of oil on the front of the compressor is normal.

E. Check the Appearance of the Sightglass

NOTE: *Some late model cars no longer have sight glasses. If there is no sight glass, proceed to F.*

Start the engine and put the idle speed screw on one of the lower steps of the fast idle cam. Set the blower for high speed and set the thermostat for the lowest possible setting. Lo-

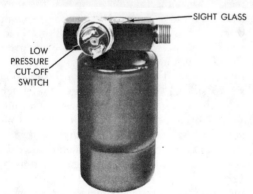

Typical sight glass location

cate the sightglass, remove any protective covers, and clean it with a rag. Have someone turn on the air conditioner while you watch the sightglass. The glass should foam and then become clear. After a few minutes of operation, the glass should be entirely clear unless outside temperature is below 70° F. A few bubbles will be present at cooler temperatures, even if the system is in perfect condition. If a few bubbles appear at warm temperatures, the system has probably leaked slightly and should be tested and recharged. If the glass shows severe bubbling or remains completely clear throughout the test, the refrigerant charge may be low, and unit operation should be discontinued immediately after making the test in F. If the sight glass foamed and then remained clear, go on to G.

F. Check the Temperature of the Lines

Feel along the small, liquid line that runs from the condenser to the expansion valve. This line should be warm along its entire length. If there is a sudden drop in temperature before reaching the expansion valve, the line is clogged at the point where the temperature changes. The line will have to be removed and cleaned by a professional refrigeration mechanic. If the temperature drop occurs at the receiver-drier, this unit will have to be replaced because of saturation with moisture or dirt.

While the liquid line between the condenser and the expansion valve is the most common location for clogging, a sudden drop in temperature in the condenser or in the compressor discharge line will also indicate clogging. Be careful when feeling either the line between the compressor and condenser, or the condenser itself, as the temperature may be very high.

If the compressor discharge and suction lines are at about the same temperature and the sight glass does not foam even at start up, the entire refrigerant charge has probably leaked out.

G. Check System Performance and Blower Operation

Operate the system with the blower at high speed and the temperature control set at the lowest setting. The engine should be operated at a fast idle (over 1,100 rpm).

The temperature at the discharge ducts varies with the weather and other conditions. However, most systems will maintain a comfortable temperature in all but the most extreme weather. If the temperature exceeds 90° F, a slight reduction in performance may be expected.

If system performance is inadequate, the problem may be in the blower, refrigeration system, or temperature control system.

If the blower operates on all speeds and changes its speed every time the blower speed switch is moved, it is probably operating properly. If it operates only on one or two of the positions, the blower resistor may be at fault.

This resistor is usually located in the engine compartment on the evaporator housing. Remove the resistor and check it for burned or shorted resistor coils. If there is any evidence of burning, separation, or bending of the coils, replace the resistor.

If the blower does not operate at all, run a jumper wire from the battery positive terminal to the blower motor terminal to see if the motor will operate. If it does not run, check the ground strap. If the ground is all right, replace the blower motor. If the blower oper-

Troubleshooting the Automotive Air Conditioning System

WARNING: Every automotive air conditioner refrigeration system contains fluid under high pressure—even when the system is at rest. Leakage can cause fracture of metal parts in a high pressure explosion. Such accidental explosions often result in the escape of liquid refrigerant that is at —26°F. At this temperature accidental contact with human skin can cause severe frostbite. NEVER ATTEMPT TO WORK ON AN AUTOMOTIVE AIR CONDITIONING SYSTEM WITHOUT THE PROPER TOOLS OR A THOROUGH KNOWLEDGE OF HOW THIS SYSTEM OPERATES. Any attempt to tighten a loose fitting can be dangerous unless the proper techniques, tools and safety precautions are used.

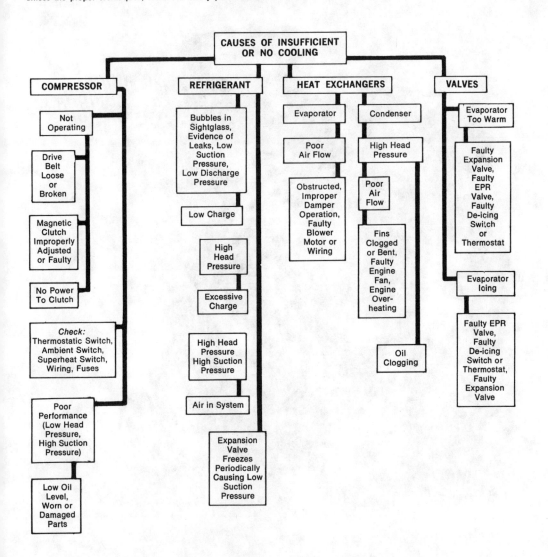

ates, check each connection between the motor and the air conditioning switch to isolate the faulty wire or connection.

If the system output is inadequate, even though the blower operates properly, the temperature control system may be at fault. Have someone move the temperature control lever back and forth while you look under the hood and dash for a moving control cable. The cable operates either an air mixing door or a water valve. If no cable movement is apparent and shifting the temperature control back and forth has a direct effect on the operation of the compressor, have the thermostatic switch checked by a professional air conditioning mechanic.

If the temperature control lever is moving a water valve or air door linkage, inspect the linkage to see that it is operating properly. The most common problem is an improper ad-

justment or slipping adjusting screw. The adjustment is usually made on the clamp which holds the cable in place. Adjust the cable's position so that the door or water valve will move to the fully closed or maximum cooling position just before the temperature control reaches the full cold setting. Where a vacuum-operated water valve is used to stop coolant flow through the heater core at maximum cooling only, check the vacuum line to the valve. If the vacuum line is not cracked and is tightly connected to the valve, have the valve checked by a professional. Otherwise, replace or tighten the line as necessary.

If the air conditioner performs satisfactorily for 20–40 minutes and then begins to perform less efficiently, the evaporator core is freezing. The suction throttling valve or de-icing switch is malfunctioning. Have a professional air conditioning man adjust or repair the unit.

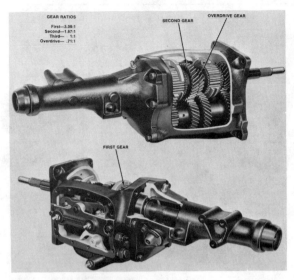

Chapter 6

GEAR RATIOS
First—3.09:1
Second—1.67:1
Third— 1:1
Overdrive— .71:1

SECOND GEAR
OVERDRIVE GEAR

FIRST GEAR

Transmissions and Clutch Assemblies

Manual Transmission and Clutch

BASIC OPERATING PRINCIPLES

Because of the way the gasoline engine breathes, it can produce torque, or twisting force, only within a narrow speed range. Most modern engines must turn at about 2,500 rpm to produce their peak torque. By 4,500 rpm they are producing so little torque that continued increases in engine speed produce no power increases.

The transmission and clutch are employed to vary the relationship between engine speed and the speed of the wheels so that adequate engine power can be produced under all circumstances. The clutch allows engine torque to be applied to the transmission input shaft gradually, due to mechanical slippage. The car can, consequently, be started smoothly from a full stop.

The transmission changes the ratio between the rotating speeds of the engine and the wheels by the use of gears. Three-speed or four-speed transmissions are most common. The lower gears allow full engine power to be

applied to the rear wheels during acceleration at low speeds.

The clutch driven plate is a thin disc, the center of which is splined to the transmission input shaft. Both sides of the disc are covered with a layer of material which is similar to brake lining and which is capable of allowing slippage without roughness or excessive noise.

The clutch cover is bolted to the engine flywheel and incorporates a diaphragm spring which provides the pressure to engage the clutch. The cover also houses the pressure plate. The driven disc is sandwiched between the pressure plate and the smooth surface of the flywheel when the clutch pedal is released, thus forcing it to turn at the same speed as the engine crankshaft.

The transmission contains a mainshaft which passes all the way through the transmission, from the clutch to the driveshaft. This shaft is separated at one point, so that front and rear portions can turn at different speeds.

Power is transmitted by a countershaft in the lower gears and reverse. The gears of the countershaft mesh with gears on the mainshaft, allowing power to be carried from one to the other. All the countershaft gears are integral with that shaft, while several of the main-

159

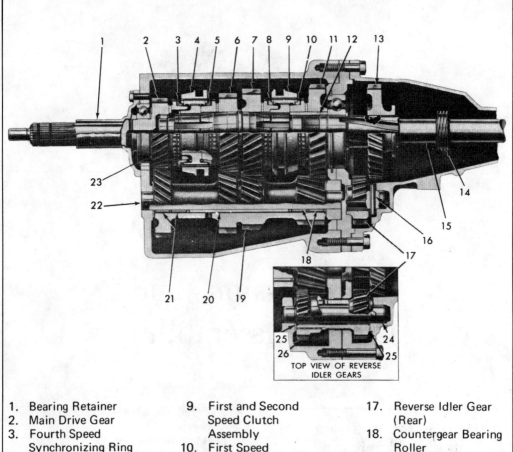

1. Bearing Retainer
2. Main Drive Gear
3. Fourth Speed
    Synchronizing Ring
4. Third and Fourth
    Speed Clutch
    Assembly
5. Third Speed
    Synchronizing Ring
6. Third Speed Gear
7. Second Speed Gear
8. Second Speed
    Synchronizing Ring
9. First and Second
    Speed Clutch
    Assembly
10. First Speed
    Synchronizing Ring
11. First Speed Gear
12. First Speed Gear
    Sleeve
13. Reverse Gear
14. Speedometer Drive
    Gear
15. Mainshaft
16. Reverse Idler Shaft
    Roll Pin
17. Reverse Idler Gear
    (Rear)
18. Countergear Bearing
    Roller
19. Countergear
20. Countershaft Bearing
    Roller Spacer
21. Countershaft Bearing
    Roller
22. Countergear Shaft
23. Oil Slinger
24. Reverse Idler Shaft
25. Thrust Washer
26. Reverse Idler Gear
    (Front)

Four-speed transmission—typical

shaft gears can either rotate independently of the shaft or be locked to it. Shifting from one gear to the next causes one of the gears to be freed from rotating with the shaft, and locks another to it. Gears are locked and unlocked by internal dog clutches which slide between the center of the gear and the shaft. The forward gears usually employ synchronizers: friction members which smoothly bring gear and shaft to the same speed before the toothed dog clutches are engaged.

The clutch is operating properly if:

1. It will stall the engine when released with the vehicle held stationary.

2. The shift lever can be moved freely between first and reverse gears when the vehicle is stationary and the clutch disengaged.

A clutch pedal free-play adjustment is in-

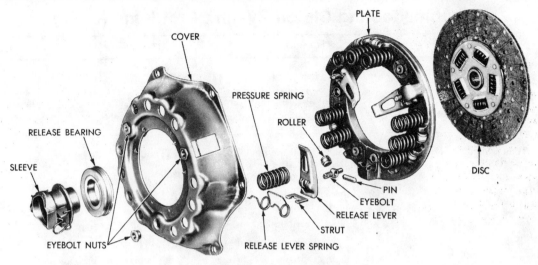

PLATE

COVER

PRESSURE SPRING

ROLLER

RELEASE BEARING

SLEEVE

DISC

PIN
EYEBOLT
RELEASE LEVER
STRUT
EYEBOLT NUTS
RELEASE LEVER SPRING

Exploded view—clutch assembly

corporated in the linkage. If there is about 1–2 in. of motion before the pedal begins to release the clutch, it is adjusted properly. Inadequate free-play wears all parts of the clutch releasing mechanisms and may cause slippage. Excessive free-play may cause inadequate release and hard shifting of gears.

Some clutches use a hydraulic system in place of mechanical linkage. If the clutch fails to release, fill the clutch master cylinder with fluid to the proper level and pump the clutch pedal to fill the system with fluid. Bleed the system in the same way as a brake system. If leaks are located, tighten loose connections or overhaul the master or slave cylinder as necessary.

Troubleshooting Clutch System Problems

The Condition	The Possible Cause	The Corrective Action
Clutch Chatter	(1) Grease on driven plate (disc) facing	(1) Replace drive plate
	(2) Binding clutch linkage	(2) Check for worn, bent, broken parts. Replace as required. Lube linkage.
	(3) Loose, damaged facings on driven plate (disc)	(3) Replace driven plate
	(4) Engine mounts loose	(4) Tighten mounts. Replace if damaged
	(5) Incorrect height adjustment of pressure plate release levers	(5) Adjust release lever height
	(6) Clutch housing or housing to transmission adapter misalignment	(6) Check bore and face run out. Correct as required
	(7) Loose driven plate hub	(7) Replace driven plate
Clutch Grabbing	(1) Oil, grease on driven plate (disc) facing	(1) Replace driven plate

Troubleshooting Clutch System Problems (cont.)

The Condition	The Possible Cause	The Corrective Action
Clutch Grabbing	(2) Broken pressure plate	(2) Replace pressure plate
	(3) Warped or binding driven plate. Driven plate binding on clutch shaft	(3) Replace warped driven plate. Replace clutch shaft if defective, scored, worn
Clutch Slips	(1) Lack of lubrication in clutch linkage (linkage binds, causes incomplete engagement).	(1) Lubricate linkage
	(2) Incorrect pedal, or linkage adjustment	(2) Adjust as required
	(3) Broken pressure plate springs	(3) Replace pressure plate
	(4) Weak pressure plate springs	(4) Replace pressure plate
	(5) Grease on driven plate facing (disc)	(5) Replace driven plate
Incomplete Clutch Release	(1) Incorrect pedal or linkage adjustment on linkage binding	(1) Adjust as required. Lubrication linkage
	(2) Incorrect height adjustment on pressure plate release levers	(2) Adjust release lever height
	(3) Loose, broken facing on driven plate (disc)	(3) Replace driven plate
	(4) Bent, dished, warped driven plate caused by overheating	(4) Replace driven plate
Grinding, Whirring Grating Noise When Pedal Is Depressed	(1) Worn or defective throwout bearing	(1) Replace throwout bearing
	(2) Starter drive teeth contacting flywheel ring gear teeth	(2) Look for milled or polished teeth on ring gear. Align clutch housing, replace starter driven or drive spring as required
Squeal, Howl, Trumpeting Noise When Pedal Is Being Released (Occurs During First Inch to Inch and One Half of Pedal Travel)	(1) Pilot bushing worn or lack of lubricant	(1) Replace worn bushing. If bushing appears OK, polish bushing with emery, soak lube wick in oil, lube bushing withoil, apply film of chassis grease to clutch shaft pilot hub, reassemble. NOTE: *Bushing wear may be due to housing or housing to transmission adapter*
Vibration or Clutch Pedal Pulsation with Clutch Disengaged (Pedal Fully Depressed)	(1) Worn or defective engine transmission mounts	(1) Inspect and replace as required
	(2) Flywheel run out, or damaged or defective clutch components	(2) Replace components as required. (Flywheel run out at face not to exceed 0.005″)

MANUAL TRANSMISSION POWER FLOW

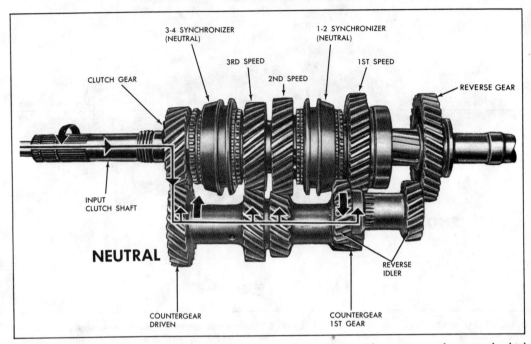

In neutral, with the clutch engaged, the main drive gear turns the countergear. The countergear then turns the third, second, first, and reverse idler gears. But, because the third and fourth and first and second speed clutch sleeves are neutrally positioned, and the reverse gear is positioned at the rear, away from the reverse idler gear, power will not flow through the mainshaft.

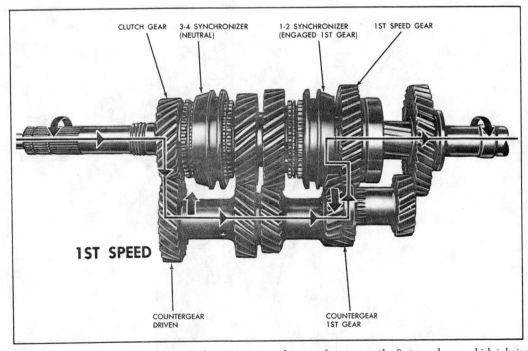

In first gear, the first and second speed clutch (sleeve) is moved rearwards to engage the first speed gear, which is being turned by the countergear. Because the first and second speed clutch (hub) is splined to the mainshaft, torque is imparted to the mainshaft from the first speed gear through the clutch assembly.

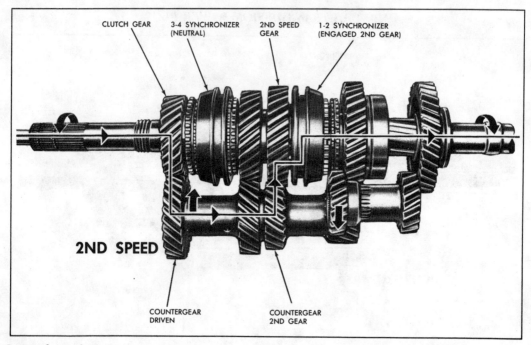

In second gear, the first and second speed clutch (sleeve) is moved forward to engage the second speed gear, which is being turned by the countergear. The engagement of the clutch (sleeve) with the second speed gear imparts torque to the mainshaft because the first and second speed clutch (hub) is splined to the mainshaft.

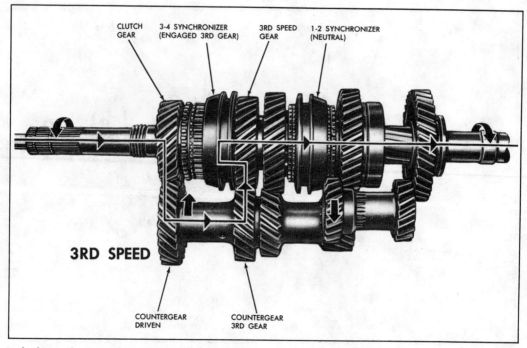

In third gear, the first and second speed clutch assumes a neutral position. The third and fourth speed clutch (sleeve) moves rearward to engage the third speed gear, which is being turned by the countergear. Because the third and fourth speed clutch (hub) is splined to the mainshaft, torque is imparted to the mainshaft from the third speed gear through the clutch assembly.

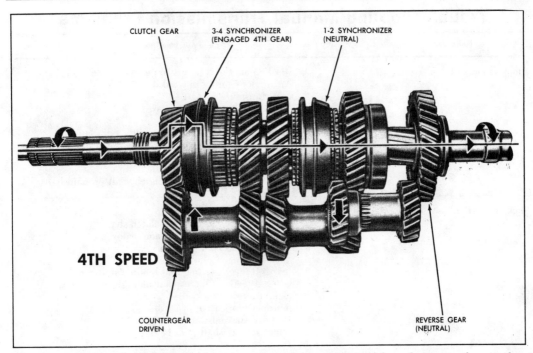

In fourth gear (or direct drive) the third and fourth speed clutch (sleeve) is moved forward to engage the main drive gear, and the first and second speed clutch remains in a neutral position. This engagement of the main drive gear with the third and fourth speed clutch assembly imparts torque directly to the mainshaft.

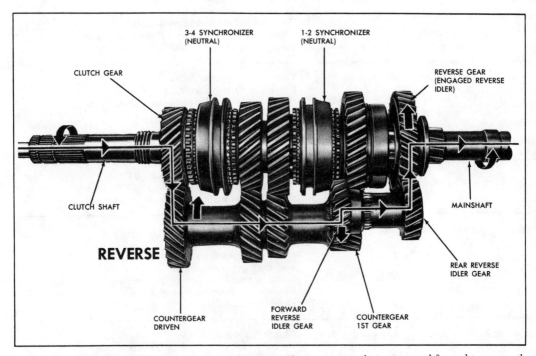

In reverse, both clutch assemblies assume a neutral position. The reverse speed gear is moved forward to engage the rear reverse idler gear, which is being turned by the countergear. Because reverse is splined to the mainshaft, this engagement causes the mainshaft to turn: however, because power flows from the main drive gear to the countergear and then through the reverse idler gear to the reverse speed gear, the direction of rotation will be opposite that of the engine.

Troubleshooting Manual Transmission Problems

The Condition	*The Probable Cause*
Jumping out of High Gear	1. Misalignment of transmission case or clutch housing. 2. Worn pilot bearing in crankshaft. 3. Bent transmission shaft. 4. Worn high speed sliding gear. 5. Worn teeth in clutch shaft. 6. Insufficient spring tension on shifter rail plunger. 7. Bent or loose shifter fork. 8. End-play in clutch shaft. 9. Gears not engaging completely. 10. Loose or worn bearings on clutch shaft or mainshaft.
Sticking in High Gear	1. Clutch not releasing fully. 2. Burred or battered teeth on clutch shaft. 3. Burred or battered transmission mainshaft. 4. Frozen synchronizing clutch. 5. Stuck shifter rail plunger. 6. Gearshift lever twisting and binding shifter rail. 7. Battered teeth on high speed sliding gear or on sleeve. 8. Lack of lubrication. 9. Improper lubrication. 10. Corroded transmission parts. 11. Defective mainshaft pilot bearing.
Jumping out of Second Gear	1. Insufficient spring tension on shifter rail plunger. 2. Bent or loose shifter fork. 3. Gears not engaging completely. 4. End-play in transmission mainshaft. 5. Loose transmission gear bearing. 6. Defective mainshaft pilot bearing. 7. Bent transmission shaft. 8. Worn teeth on second speed sliding gear or sleeve. 9. Loose or worn bearings on transmission mainshaft. 10. End-play in countershaft.
Sticking in Second Gear	1. Clutch not releasing fully. 2. Burred or battered teeth on sliding sleeve. 3. Burred or battered transmission main-shaft. 4. Frozen synchronizing clutch. 5. Stuck shifter rail plunger. 6. Gearshift lever twisting and binding shifter rail. 7. Lack of lubrication. 8. Second speed transmission gear bearings locked will give same effect as gears stuck in second. 9. Improper lubrication. 10. Corroded transmission parts.
Jumping out of Low Gear	1. Gears not engaging completely. 2. Bent or loose shifter fork. 3. End-play in transmission mainshaft. 4. End-play in countershaft. 5. Loose or worn bearings on transmission mainshaft. 6. Loose or worn bearings in countershaft. 7. Defective mainshaft pilot bearing.
Sticking in Low Gear	1. Clutch not releasing fully. 2. Burred or battered transmission mainshaft. 3. Stuck shifter rail plunger. 4. Gearshift lever twisting and binding shifter rail. 5. Lack of lubrication. 6. Improper lubrication. 7. Corroded transmission parts.

Troubleshooting Manual Transmission Problems (cont.)

The Condition	*The Probable Cause*
Jumping out of Reverse Gear	1. Insufficient spring tension on shifter rail plunger. 2. Bent or loose shifter fork. 3. Badly worn gear teeth. 4. Gears not engaging completely. 5. End-play in transmission mainshaft. 6. Idler gear bushing loose or worn. 7. Loose or worn bearings on transmission mainshaft. 8. Defective mainshaft pilot bearing.
Sticking in Reverse Gear	1. Clutch not releasing fully. 2. Burred or battered transmission mainshaft. 3. Stuck shifter rail plunger. 4. Gearshift lever twisting and binding shifter rail. 5. Lack of lubrication. 6. Improper lubrication. 7. Corroded transmission parts.
Failure of Gears to Synchronize	1. Binding pilot bearing on mainshaft, will synchronize in high gear only. 2. Clutch not releasing fully. 3. Detent spring weak or broken. 4. Weak or broken springs under balls in sliding gear sleeve. 5. Binding bearing on clutch shaft. 6. Binding countershaft. 7. Binding pilot bearing in crankshaft. 8. Badly worn gear teeth. 9. Scored or worn cones. 10. Improper lubrication. 11. Constant mesh gear not turning freely on transmission mainshaft. Will synchronize in that gear only.
Gears Spinning When Shifting into Gear from Neutral	1. Clutch not releasing fully. 2. In some cases an extremely light lubricant in transmission will cause gears to continue to spin for a short time after clutch is released. 3. Binding pilot bearing in crankshaft.
Noisy in All Gears	1. Insufficient lubricant. 2. Worn countergear bearings. 3. Worn or damaged main drive gear or countergear. 4. Damaged main drive gear or mainshaft bearings. 5. Worn or damaged countergear anti-lash plate.
Noisy in High Gear	1. Damaged main drive gear bearing. 2. Damaged mainshaft bearing. 3. Damaged high speed gear synchronizer.
Noisy in Neutral	1. Damaged main drive gear bearing. 2. Damaged or loose mainshaft pilot bearing. 3. Worn or damaged countergear anti-lash plate. 4. Worn countergear bearings.
Noisy in All Reduction Gears	1. Insufficient lubricant. 2. Worn or damaged drive gear or countergear.
Noisy in Second Only	1. Damaged or worn second gear constant mesh gears. 2. Worn or damaged countergear rear bearings. 3. Damaged or worn second gear synchronizer.

Troubleshooting Manual Transmission Problems (cont.)

The Condition	*The Possible Cause*
Noisy in Third Only (Four Speed)	1. Damaged or worn third gear constant mesh gears. 2. Worn or damaged countergear bearings.
Noisy in Reverse Only	1. Worn or damaged reverse idler gear or idler bushing. 2. Worn or damaged mainshaft reverse gear. 3. Worn or damaged reverse countergear. 4. Damaged shift mechanism.
Excessive Backlash in All Reduction Gears	1. Worn countergear bearings. 2. Excessive end play in countergear.

Automatic Transmissions

BASIC OPERATING PRINCIPLES

The automatic transmission allows engine torque and power to be transmitted to the rear wheels within a narrow range of engine operating speeds. The transmission will allow the engine to turn fast enough to produce plenty of power and torque at very low speeds, while keeping it at a sensible rpm at high vehicle speeds. The transmission performs this job entirely without driver assistance. The transmission uses a light fluid as the medium for the transmission of power. This fluid also works in the operation of various hydraulic control circuits and as a lubricant. Because the transmission fluid performs all of these three functions, trouble within the unit can easily travel from one part to another. For this reason, and because of the complexity and unusual operating principles of the transmission, a very sound understanding of the basic principles of operation will simplify troubleshooting.

The Torque Converter

The torque converter replaces the conventional clutch. It has three functions:

1. It allows the engine to idle with the vehicle at a standstill—even with the transmission in gear.

2. It allows the transmission to shift from range to range smoothly, without requiring that the driver close the throttle during the shift.

3. It multiplies engine torque to an increasing extent as vehicle speed drops and throttle opening is increased. This has the effect of making the transmission more responsive and reduces the amount of shifting required.

The torque converter is a metal case which is shaped like a sphere that has been flattened on opposite sides. It is bolted to the rear end of the engine's crankshaft. Generally, the entire metal case rotates at engine speed and serves as the engine's flywheel.

The case contains three sets of blades. One set is attached directly to the case. This set forms the torus or pump. Another set is directly connected to the output shaft, and forms the turbine. The third set is mounted on a hub which, in turn, is mounted on a stationary shaft through a one-way clutch. This third set is known as the stator.

A pump, which is driven by the converter hub at engine speed, keeps the torque converter full of transmission fluid at all times. Fluid flows continuously through the unit to provide cooling.

Under low-speed acceleration, the torque converter functions as follows:

The torus is turning faster than the turbine. It picks up fluid at the center of the converter and, through centrifugal force, slings it outward. Since the outer edge of the converter moves faster than the portions at the center, the fluid picks up speed.

The fluid then enters the outer edge of the turbine blades. It then travels back toward the center of the converter case along the turbine blades. In impinging upon the turbine blades, the fluid loses the energy picked up in the torus.

If the fluid were now to immediately be returned directly into the torus, both halves of the converter would have to turn at approximately the same speed at all times, and torque input and output would both be the same.

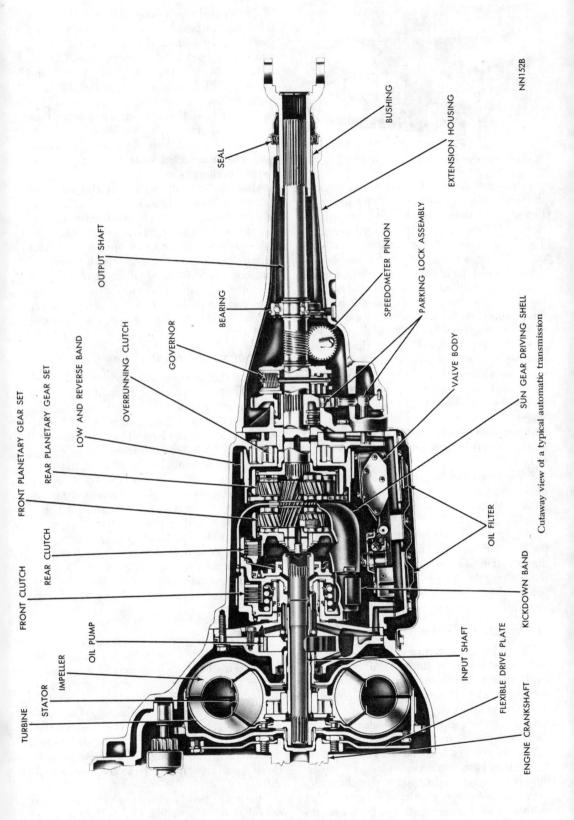

NN152B

TURBINE

STATOR

IMPELLER

OIL PUMP

FRONT CLUTCH

REAR CLUTCH

FRONT PLANETARY GEAR SET

REAR PLANETARY GEAR SET

LOW AND REVERSE BAND

OVERRUNNING CLUTCH

GOVERNOR

BEARING

OUTPUT SHAFT

SEAL

BUSHING

EXTENSION HOUSING

SPEEDOMETER PINION

PARKING LOCK ASSEMBLY

VALVE BODY

SUN GEAR DRIVING SHELL

OIL FILTER

KICKDOWN BAND

FLEXIBLE DRIVE PLATE

INPUT SHAFT

ENGINE CRANKSHAFT

Cutaway view of a typical automatic transmission

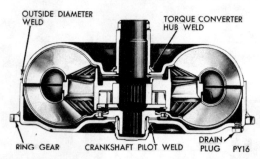

Torque converter cross-section

In flowing through the torus and turbine, the fluid picks up two types of flow, or flow in two separate directions. It flows through the turbine blades, and it spins with the engine. The stator, whose blades are stationary when the vehicle is being accelerated at low speeds, converts one type of flow into another. Instead of allowing the fluid to flow straight back into the torus, the stator's curved blades turn the fluid almost 90° toward the direction of rotation of the engine. Thus the fluid does not flow as fast toward the torus, but is already spinning when the torus picks it up. This has the effect of allowing the torus to turns much faster than the turbine. This difference in speed may be compared to the difference in speed between the smaller and larger gears in any gear train. The result is that engine power output is higher, and engine torque is multiplied.

As the speed of the turbine increases, the fluid spins faster and faster in the direction of engine rotation. As a result, the ability of the stator to redirect the fluid flow is reduced. Under cruising conditions, the stator is eventually forced to rotate on its one-way clutch in the direction of engine rotation. Under these conditions, the torque converter begins to behave almost like a solid shaft, with the torus and turbine speeds being almost equal.

The Planetary Gearbox

The ability of the torque converter to multiply engine torque is limited. Also, the unit tends to be more efficient when the turbine is rotating at relatively high speeds. Therefore, a planetary gearbox is used to carry the power output the turbine to the driveshaft to make the most efficient use of the converter.

Planetary gears function very similarly to conventional transmission gears. However, their construction is different in that three elements make up one gear system, and in that all three elements are different from one another. The three elements are: an outer gear

that is shaped like a hoop, with teeth cut into the inner surface; a sun gear, mounted on a shaft and located at the very center of the outer gear; and a set of three planet gears, held by pins in a ring-like planet carrier and meshing with both the sun gear and the outer gear. Either the outer gear or the sun gear may be held stationary, providing more than one possible torque multiplication factor for each set of gears. Also, if all three gears are forced to rotate at the same speed, the gearset forms, in effect, a solid shaft.

Most modern automatics use the planetary gears to provide either a single reduction ratio of about 1.8:1, or two reduction gears: a low of about 2.5:1, and an intermediate of about 1.5:1. Bands and clutches are used to hold various portions of the gearsets to the transmission case or to the shaft on which they are mounted. Shifting is accomplished, then, by changing the portion of each planetary gearset which is held to the transmission case or to the shaft.

The Servos and Accumulators

The servos are hydraulic pistons and cylinders. They resemble the hydraulic actuators used on many familiar machines, such as bulldozers. Hydraulic fluid enters the cylinder, under pressure, and forces the piston to move to engage the band or clutches.

The accumulators are used to cushion the engagement of the servos. The transmission fluid must pass through the accumulator on the way to the servo. The accumulator housing contains a thin piston which is sprung away from the discharge passage of the accumulator. When fluid passes through the accumulator on the way to the servo, it must move the piston against spring pressure, and this action smooths out the action of the servo.

The Hydraulic Control System

The hydraulic pressure used to operate the servos comes from the main transmission oil pump. This fluid is channeled to the various servos through the shift valves. There is generally a manual shift valve which is operated by the transmission selector lever and an automatic shift valve for each automatic upshift the transmission provides: i.e., two-speed automatics have a low-high shift valve, while three-speeds will have a 1–2 valve, and a 2–3 valve.

There are two pressures which effect the operation of these valves. One is the governor pressure which is affected by vehicle speed.

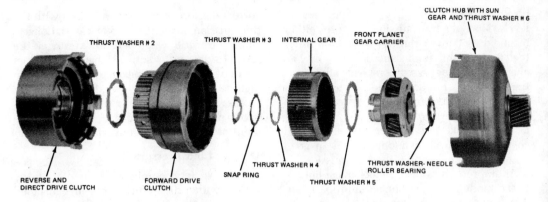

Exploded view of a planetary gearset

The other is the modulator pressure which is affected by intake manifold vacuum or throttle position. Governor pressure rises with an increase in vehicle speed, and modulator pressure rises as the throttle is opened wider. By responding to these two pressures, the shift valves cause the upshift points to be delayed with increased throttle opening to make the best use of the engine's power output.

Most transmissions also make use of an auxiliary circuit for downshifting. This circuit may be actuated by the throttle linkage or the vacuum line which actuates the modulator, or by a cable or solenoid. It applies pressure to a special downshift surface on the shift valve or valves.

The transmission modulator also governs the line pressure, used to actuate the servos. In this way, the clutches and bands will be actuated with a force matching the torque output of the engine.

AUTOMATIC TRANSMISSION TROUBLESHOOTING

A. Check the Transmission Fluid Level

The transmission fluid level should always be checked first when troubleshooting for transmission slippage or failure to engage either forward or reverse gears. Loss of only a small amount of fluid can cause air to be drawn into the transmission oil pump pick-up. The resultant foaming of the oil prevents proper engagement of the clutches and bands.

Check the fluid as follows:

1. Operate the vehicle for 15 miles or so to bring the transmission to normal operating temperature. If the transmission gears will not engage, add at least enough oil to produce a measurement on the dipstick.

2. Place the selector lever in each of the positions, and then place it in Park.

3. Check the fluid level by removing the dipstick, wiping it, reinserting it, and then removing it for a reading. Make sure the dipstick is all the way in during the final insertion into the transmission. Bring the fluid up to the full mark. If the fluid level is too high, drain fluid from the pan until it is within the proper range. Excess fluid will cause foaming within the transmission. The gears will pick up the fluid and throw it around inside the housing.

If the transmission leaks fluid, the leak should be repaired. Leaks should be detected as follows:

1. Operate the vehicle until the transmission fluid is at operating temperature.

2. Thoroughly remove all oil and grease from the bottom of the transmission.

3. Look for the leak with the engine operating.

4. If no leak is detected with the engine in operation, check again with the engine stopped, after fluid has had a chance to drain back into the transmission sump.

Leaks occur at the seam between the oil pan and transmission case because of improperly torqued pan bolts, a faulty pan gasket, or a gasket mounting face that is rough. The front and rear seals, and all seals where shafts, cables, and filler pipes pass through the case should be checked.

In some cases, leaks are caused by porosity of the transmission case. These leaks may frequently be repaired with epoxy cement.

B. Check the Engine Condition and Linkage Adjustments.

If the transmission shifts are consistently late (at too high a speed) and rough or harsh, and performance is sluggish, the engine may be at fault. An engine which is out of tune, or has mechanical problems such as low compression will suffer reduced torque at high throttle openings and low manifold vacuum levels. Since the transmission measures either manifold vacuum or throttle position in order to determine shift points and line pressure, an abnormal engine condition will affect the transmission. Also, an engine which performs poorly will prevent the torque converter from working at its best, resulting in very poor performance. Make sure that the engine has good compression on all cylinders and is in good tune before condemning the transmission.

An improperly adjusted mechanical linkage to the modulator valve, or an improperly adjusted vacuum modulator can cause late and harsh shifts, or early, sluggish shifts. Vacuum leaks in the manifold or in the line to the vacuum modulator valve can also cause problems.

Factory manuals provide adjustment specifications for mechanical linkages. However, if these specifications are not readily available, the linkage may be adjusted to see if the problem is merely improper adjustment at assembly or last overhaul. Adjust as follows:

1. Examine the linkage to see which way it moves as the engine throttle is opened.

2. Remove the cotter pin or other locking device.

3. Turn the adjustment so that the transmission linkage will move farther in the direction of open throttle for later, harsher shifts, or toward closed throttle for earlier, smoother shifts.

4. Replace the locking device.

Vacuum modulators are adjustable if an adjusting screw protrudes from the cover. Turn the screw inward (clockwise) for earlier, smoother shifts, and outward for later, harsher shifts.

It would be wise to consult the specifications tables provided by the factory regarding proper shift points. Early, smooth shifts can cause premature clutch wear.

C. Check the Torque Converter

Torque converter problems are usually characterized by either of the following:

1. Low engine rpm at lower speeds, and sluggish acceleration until cruising speeds are reached.

2. Normal performance until cruising conditions are reached, at which time the engine races, and fuel economy is very poor.

The first problem is caused by a slipping stator clutch, while the second results if the clutch is frozen. The first symptom may be checked further by running a stall test according to the manufacturer's instructions. This in-

volves measuring engine revolutions with the transmission in gear, the vehicle stationary, and the throttle wide open. Make sure, if the second symptom is noticed, that the problem is not failure of the transmission to shift into high gear.

Improper stall speed or other torque converter problems can be cured only by replacement of the complete converter unit.

D. The Line Pressure Test.

This test is accomplished by operating the vehicle with a 200 lbs pressure gauge installed in a special fitting in the side of the transmission. A long hose is used with the gauge so it may be read while the mechanic is riding inside the passenger compartment of the car. Most factory manuals have a line pressure chart which lists proper pressure under various operating conditions. Finding whether the line pressure is normal, low, or high helps considerably in troubleshooting internal transmission problems.

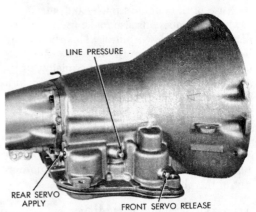

LINE PRESSURE

REAR SERVO APPLY

FRONT SERVO RELEASE

Typical pressure test locations

Consult the chart below to locate various transmission problems.

FAILURE TO UPSHIFT

Low fluid level
Incorrect linkage adjustment
Faulty or sticking governor
Leaking valve body
Leak in vacuum lines to vacuum modulator
Faulty modulator
Stuck shift valve, detent cable, or downshift solenoid
Faulty clutches, servos, or oil pump

FAILURE TO DOWNSHIFT (KICK-DOWN)

Improperly adjusted throttle linkage
Sticking downshift linkage or cable

Faulty modulator
Stuck shift valve
Faulty downshift solenoid or wiring
Faulty detent valve
Faulty clutches or servos

High Line Pressure

Vacuum leak or modulator leak or malfunction

Faulty Pressure Regulator

Improper pressure regulator adjustment
Faulty valve body

Low Line Pressure

Low fluid level
Faulty modulator
Faulty oil pump

Clogged strainer
Faulty seals in accumulators or clutches
Faulty transmission case

Slippage

Low oil level
Low line pressure (see above)
Faulty accumulator seals
Faulty servo piston seals
Clutch plates worn or burned
Incorrect shift linkage adjustment

Noise

Low oil level
Clogged strainer
Faulty oil pump
Water in oil
Valve body malfunction (buzzing)

Chapter 7

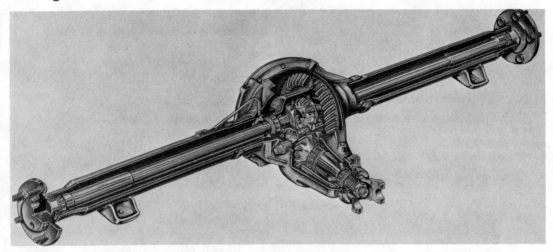

Drive Train and Rear Axle

Driveshaft and U-Joints

BASIC OPERATING PRINCIPLES

The driveshaft is the means by which the power from the engine and transmission (in a front-engine, rear wheel drive car) is transferred to the differential and rear axles, and finally to the rear wheels.

The driveshaft assembly incorporates two universal joints, one at each end, and a slip yoke at the front end of the assembly, which fits into the back of the transmission.

All driveshafts are balanced when installed in a car. Therefore, when removing a driveshaft, mark it so that it may be reassembled in the proper position. In addition, some driveshafts incorporate a third U-joint in the middle of the driveshaft.

DIAGNOSING DRIVESHAFT AND UNIVERSAL JOINT NOISES

Install a tachometer on the vehicle and operate it at the speed at which vibration oc-

curs. Then slow the vehicle and shift it to a lower gear. Operate the vehicle at the same engine speed at which the vibration occurs in high gear.

If the vibration recurs, it is in the transmission or engine. If it does not appear, or is at a much lower frequency, it is in the drive line.

Driveshaft and Universal Joint Troubleshooting Chart

VIBRATION

Undercoating on driveshaft
Missing balance weights
Loose U-joint flange bolts
Worn U-joints
Excessive U-joint bolt torque
Excessively tight U-joints
Damaged companion flange
Drive shaft or companion flange unbalanced
Incorrect rear joint angle due to improper riding height or other rear suspension defects

NOISES

Worn U-joints
Loose companion flange
Loose control arm bushing (coil type rear springs)

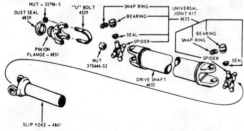

Exploded view—driveshaft and universal joints

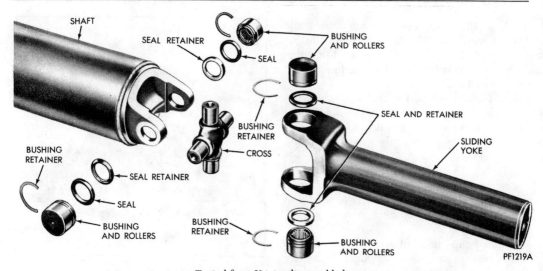

Typical front U-joint disassembled

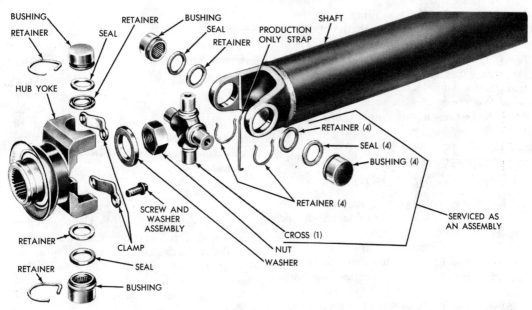

Typical rear U-joint disassembled

The Rear Axle

BASIC OPERATING PRINCIPLES

The rear axle is a special type of transmission that reduces the speed of the drive from the engine and transmission and divides the power to the rear wheels. Power enters the rear axle from the driveshaft via the companion flange. The flange is mounted on the drive pinion shaft. The drive pinion shaft and gear which carry the power into the differential turn at engine speed. The gear on the end of the pinion shaft drives a large ring gear the axis of rotation of which is 90° away from that of the pinion. The pinion and gear reduce the speed and multiply the power by the gear ratio of the axle, and change the direction of rotation to turn the axle shafts which drive both wheels. The rear axle gear ratio is found by dividing the number of pinion gear teeth into the number of ring gear teeth.

The ring gear drives the differential case. The case provides the two mounting points for the ends of a pinion shaft on which are mounted two pinion gears. The pinion gears drive the two side gears, one of which is located on the inner end of each axle shaft.

By driving the axle shafts through this ar-rangement, the differential allows the outer drive wheel to turn faster than the inner drive wheel in a turn.

The main drive pinion and the side bear-ings, which bear the weight of the differential case, are shimmed to provide proper bearing preload, and to position the pinion and ring gears properly.

NOTE: *The proper adjustment of the rela-tionship of the ring and pinion gears is criti-cal. It should be attempted only by those with extensive equipment and/or experi-ence.*

Limited-slip differentials include clutches which tend to link each axle shaft to the dif-ferential case. Clutches may be engaged ei-ther by spring action or by pressure produced by the torque on the axles during a turn. Dur-ing turning on a dry pavement, the effects of the clutches are overcome, and each wheel turns at the required speed. When slippage occurs at either wheel, however, the clutches will transmit some of the power to the wheel which has the greater amount of traction. Be-cause of the presence of clutches, limited-slip units require a special lubricant. Consult a Chilton Manual or factory information for unit identification and lubricant recommendations.

DIFFERENTIAL DIAGNOSIS

The most essential part of rear axle service is proper diagnosis of the problem. Bent or broken axle shafts or broken gears pose little problem, but isolating an axle noise and cor-rectly interpreting the problem can be ex-tremely difficult, even for an experienced me-chanic.

Any gear driven unit will produce a certain amount of noise, therefore, a specific diag-nosis for each individual unit is the best prac-tice. Acceptable or normal noise can be clas-sified as a slight noise heard only at certain speeds or under unusual conditions. This noise tends to reach a peak at 40–60 mph, depending on the road condition, load, gear ratio and tire size. Frequently, other noises are mistakenly diagnosed as coming from the rear axle. Vehicle noises from tires, transmis-sion, driveshaft, U-joints and front and rear wheel bearings will often be mistaken as ema-nating from the rear axle. Raising the tire pressure to eliminate tire noise (although this will not silence mud or snow treads), listening for noise at varying speeds and road conditions and listening for noise at drive and coast con-

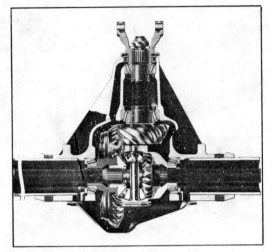

Typical rear axle assembly

ditions will aid in diagnosing alleged rear axle noises.

External Noise Elimination

It is advisable to make a thorough road test to determine whether the noise originates in the rear axle or whether it originates from the tires, engine transmission, wheel bearings or road surface. Noise originating from other places cannot be corrected by servicing the rear axle.

ROAD NOISE

Brick roads or rough surfaced concrete, may cause a noise which can be mistaken as coming from the rear axle. Driving on a different type of road, (smooth asphalt or dirt) will deter-mine whether the road is the cause of the noise. Road noise is usually the same on drive or coast conditions.

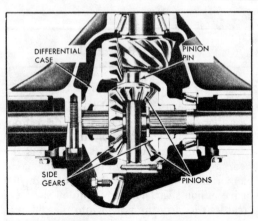

Rear axle components

TIRE NOISE

Tire noise can be mistaken as rear axle noises, even though the tires on the front are at fault. Snow tread and mud tread tires or tires worn unevenly will frequently cause vibrations which seem to originate elsewhere; *temporarily, and for test purposes only,* inflate the tires to 40–50 lbs. This will significantly alter the noise produced by the tires, but will not alter noise from the rear axle. Noises from the rear axle will normally cease at speeds below 30 mph on coast, while tire noise will continue at lower tone as car speed is decreased. The rear axle noise will usually change from drive conditions to coast conditions, while tire noise will not. Do not forget to lower the tire pressure to normal after the test is complete.

ENGINE AND TRANSMISSION NOISE

Engine and transmission noises also seem to originate in the rear axle. Road test the vehicle and determine at which speeds the noise is most pronounced. Stop the car in a quiet place to avoid interfering noises. With the transmission in neutral, run the engine slowly through the engine speeds corresponding to the car speed at which the noise was most noticeable. If a similar noise was produced with the car standing still, the noise is not in the rear axle, but somewhere in the engine or transmission.

FRONT WHEEL BEARING NOISE

Front wheel bearing noises, sometimes confused with rear axle noises, will not change when comparing drive and coast conditions. While holding the car speed steady, lightly apply the footbrake. This will often cause wheel bearing noise to lessen, as some of the weight is taken off the bearing. Front wheel bearings are easily checked by jacking up the wheels and spinning the wheels. Shaking the wheels will also determine if the wheel bearings are excessively loose.

Rear Axle Noises

If a logical test of the vehicle shows that the noise is not caused by external items, it can be assumed that the noise originates from the rear axle. The rear axle should be tested on a smooth level road to avoid road noise. It is not advisable to test the axle by jacking up the rear wheels and running the car.

True rear axle noises generally fall into two classes; gear noise and bearing noises, and can be caused by a faulty driveshaft, faulty wheel bearings, worn differential or pinion shaft bearings, U-joint misalignment, worn differential side gears and pinions, or mismatched, improperly adjusted, or scored ring and pinion gears.

REAR WHEEL BEARING NOISE

A rough rear wheel bearing causes a vibration or growl which will continue with the car coasting or in neutral. A brinelled rear wheel bearing will also cause a knock or click approximately every two revolutions of the rear wheel, due to the fact that the bearing rollers to not travel at the same speed as the rear wheel and axle. Jack up the rear wheels and spin the wheel slowly, listening for signs of a rough or brinelled wheel bearing.

DIFFERENCIAL SIDE GEAR AND PINION NOISE

Differential side gears and pinions seldom cause noise, since their movement is relatively slight on straight ahead driving. Noise produced by these gears will be more noticeable on turns.

PINION BEARING NOISE

Pinion bearing failures can be distinguished by their speed of rotation, which is higher than side bearings or axle bearings. Rough or brinelled pinion bearings cause a continuous low pitch whirring or scraping noise beginning at low speeds.

SIDE BEARING NOISE

Side bearings produce a constant rough noise, which is slower than the pinion bearing noise. Side bearing noise may also fluctuate in the above rear wheel bearing test.

GEAR NOISE

Two basic types of gear noise exist. First, is the type produced by bent or broken gear teeth which have been forcibly damaged. The noise from this type of damage is audible over the entire speed range. Scoring or damage to the hypoid gear teeth generally results from insufficient lubricant, improper lubricant, improper breakin, insufficient gear backlash, improper ring and pinion gear alignment or loss of torque on the drive pinion nut. If not corrected, the scoring will lead to eventual erosion or fracture of the gear teeth. Hypoid gear tooth fracture can also be caused by extended overloading of the gear set (fatigue fracture) or by shock overloading (sudden failure). Differential and side gears rarely give trouble, but common causes of differential failure are shock loading, extended overloading and differential pinion seizure at the cross-shaft, resulting from excessive wheel spin and consequent lubricant breakdown.

The second type of gear noise pertains to the mesh pattern between the ring and pinion gears. This type of abnormal gear noise can be recognized as a cycling pitch or whine audible in either drive, float or coast conditions. Gear noises can be recognized as they tend to peak out in a narrow speed range and remain constant in pitch, whereas bearing noises tend to vary in pitch with vehicle speeds. Noises produced by the ring and pinion gears will generally follow the pattern below.

A. Drive Noise: Produced under vehicle acceleration.

B. Coast Noise: Produced while the car coasts with a closed throttle.

C. Float Noise: Occurs while maintaining constant car speed (just enough to keep speed constant) on a level road.

D. Drive, Coast and Float Noise: These noises will vary in tone with speed and be very rough or irregular if the differential or pinion shaft bearings are worn.

Drive Axle Noise Diagnosis

The Problem	The Probable Cause
1. Identical noise in Drive or Coast conditions	1. Road noise. Tire noise. Front wheel bearing noise
2. Noise changes on a different type of road	2. Road noise. Tire noise
3. Noise tone lowers as car speed is lowered	3. Tire noise
4. Similar noise is produced with car standing and driving	4. Engine noise. Transmission noise
5. Vibration	5. Rough rear wheel bearing. Unbalanced or damaged driveshaft. Unbalanced tire. Worn universal joint in driveshaft. Misaligned drive shaft at companion flange. Excessive companion flange runout
6. A knock or click approximately every two revolutions of rear wheel	6. Brinelled rear wheel bearing
7. Noise most pronounced on turns	7. Differential side gear and pinion wear or damage
8. A continuous low pitch whirring or scraping noise starting at relatively low speed	8. Damaged or worn pinion bearing
9. Drive noise, coast noise or float noise	9. Damaged or worn ring and pinion gear
10. Clunk on acceleration or deceleration	10. Worn differential cross-shaft in case
11. Clunk on stops	11. Insufficient grease in driveshaft slip yoke
12. Groan in Forward or Reverse	12. Improper differential lubricant
13. Chatter on turns	13. Improper differential lubricant. Worn clutch plates
14. Clunk or knock during operation on rough roads.	14. Excessive end-play of axle shafts to differential cross-shaft.

Troubleshooting Drive Axle Problems

The Condition	The Possible Cause	The Correction
Rear Wheel Noise	(a) Loose wheel.	(a) Tighten loose wheel nuts.
	(b) Spalled wheel bearing cup or cone.	(b) Check rear wheel bearings. If spalled or worn, replace.

Troubleshooting Drive Axle Problems (cont.)

The Condition	*The Possible Cause*	*The Correction*
Rear Wheel Noise	(c) Defective or brinelled wheel bearing.	(c) Defective or brinelled bearings must be replaced. Check rear axle shaft end play.
	(d) Excessive axle shaft endplay.	(d) Readjust axle shaft end play.
	(e) Bent or sprung axle shaft flange.	(e) Replace bent or sprung axle shaft.
Scoring of Differential Gears and Pinions	(a) Insufficient lubrication.	(a) Replace scored gears. Scoring marks on the pressure face of gear teeth or in the bore are caused by instantaneous fusing of the mating surfaces. Scored gears should be replaced. Fill rear axle to required capacity with proper lubricant.
	(b) Improper grade of lubricant.	(b) Replace scored gears. Inspect all gears and bearings for possible damage. Clean and refill axle to required capacity with proper lubricant.
	(c) Excessive spinning of one wheel.	(c) Replace scored gears. Inspect all gears, pinion bores and shaft for scoring, or bearings for possible damage.
Tooth Breakage (Ring Gear and Pinion)	(a) Overloading.	(a) Replace gear. Examine other gears and bearings for possible damage. Avoid future overloading.
	(b) Erratic clutch operation.	(b) Replace gear, and examine remaining parts for possible damage. Avoid erratic clutch operation.
	(c) Ice-spotted pavements.	(c) Replace gears. Examine remaining parts for possible damage. Replace parts as required.
	(d) Improper adjustments.	(d) Replace gears. Examine other parts for possible damage. Be sure ring gear and pinion backlash is correct.
Rear Axle Noise	(a) Insufficient lubricant.	(a) Refill rear axle with correct amount of the proper lubricant. Also check for leaks and correct as necessary.
	(b) Improper ring gear and pinion adjustment.	(b) Check ring gear and pinion tooth contact.
	(c) Unmatched ring gear and pinion.	(c) Remove unmatched ring gear and pinion. Replace with a new matched gear and pinion set.
	(d) Worn teeth on ring gear or pinion.	(d) Check teeth on ring gear and pinion for contact. If necessary, replace with new matched set.
	(e) End-play in drive pinion bearings.	(e) Adjust drive pinion bearing preload.
	(f) Side play in differential bearings.	(f) Adjust differential bearing preload.

Troubleshooting Drive Axle Problems (cont.)

The Condition	The Possible Cause	The Correction
Rear Axle Noise	(g) Incorrect drive gearlash.	(g) Correct drive gear lash.
	(h) Limited-slip differential—moan and chatter.	(h) Drain and flush lubricant. Refill with proper lubricant.
Loss of Lubricant	(a) Lubricant level too high.	(a) Drain excess lubricant.
	(b) Worn axle shaft oil seals.	(b) Replace worn oil seals with new ones. Prepare new seals before replacement.
	(c) Cracked rear axle housing.	(c) Repair or replace housing as required.
	(d) Worn drive pinion oil seal.	(d) Replace worn drive pinion oil seal with a new one.
	(e) Scored and worn companion flange.	(e) Replace worn or scored companion flange and oil seal.
	(f) Clogged vent.	(f) Remove obstructions.
	(g) Loose carrier housing bolts or housing cover screws.	(g) Tighten bolts or cover screws to specifications and fill to correct level with proper lubricant.
Overheating of Unit	(a) Lubricant level too low.	(a) Refill rear axle.
	(b) Incorrect grade of lubricant.	(b) Drain, flush and refill rear axle with correct amount of the proper lubricant.
	(c) Bearing adjusted too tightly.	(c) Readjust bearings.
	(d) Excessive wear in gears.	(d) Check gears for excessive wear or scoring. Replace as necessary.
	(e) Insufficient ring gear-to-pinion clearance.	(e) Readjust ring gear and pinion backlash and check gears for possible scoring.

Bearing Failure Chart

General Wear

Cause	Serviceability
Wear on races and rollers caused by fine abrasives	Clean all parts and check seals. Install new bearing if old one is rough or noisy.

Normal wear pattern. (© Chevrolet Div. G.M. Corp.)   Step wear. (© Chevrolet Div. G.M. Corp.)

Step Wear

Cause	Serviceability
Wear pattern on roller ends caused by fine abrasives	Clean all parts and check seals. Install new bearings if old one is rough or noisy.

Indentations

Cause	Serviceability
Surface depressions on races and rollers caused by hard foreign particles	Clean all parts and check seals. Install new bearing if old one is rough or noisy.

Indentations. (© Chevrolet Div. G.M. Corp.)

Galling. (© Chevrolet Div. G.M. Corp.)

Galling

Cause	Serviceability
Metal smears on roller ends due to overheating from improper lubricant or overloading	Install a new bearing. Check seals and use proper lubricant.

Etching

Cause	Serviceability
Bearing surfaces appear gray or gray-black with related etching	Install new bearing and check seals. Use proper lubricant.

Etching. (© Chevrolet Div. G.M. Corp.)

Cage wear. (© Chevrolet Div. G.M. Corp.)

Bearing Failure Chart (cont.)

Cage Wear

Cause	Serviceability
Wear around outside diameter of cage and rollers caused by foreign material and poor lubrication	Clean all parts, check seals, and install new bearing.

Fatigue Spalling

Cause	Serviceability
Flaking of surface metal due to fatigue	Clean all parts and install new bearing.

Fatigue spalling. (© Chevrolet Div. G.M. Corp.)

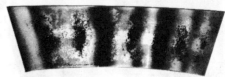

Heat discoloration. (© Chevrolet Div. G.M. Corp.)

Heat Discoloration

Cause	Serviceability
Discoloration from faint yellow to dark blue due to overload or lubricant breakdown. Softening of races or rollers also	Check for softening of parts by drawing a file over suspected area. The file will glide easily over hard metal, but will cut soft metal. If overheating is evident, install new bearings. Check seals and other parts.

Stain Discoloration

Cause	Serviceability
Stain discoloration ranging from light brown to black, caused by lubricant breakdown or moisture	Reuse bearings if stains can be removed by light polishing and no overheating exists. Check seals.

Stain discoloration. (© Chevrolet Div. G.M. Corp.)

Brinelling. (© Chevrolet Div. G.M. Corp.)

Brinelling

Cause	Serviceability
Surface indentations in race caused by rollers under impact load or vibration while the bearing is not rotating	If the old bearing is rough or noisy, install a new bearing.

Bent Cage

Cause	Serviceability
Improper handling	Install a new bearing.

Bent cage. (© Chevrolet Div. G.M. Corp.)   Bent cage. (© Chevrolet Div. G.M. Corp.)

Misalignment

Cause	Serviceability
Outer race misaligned as shown	Install a new bearing and be sure races and bearing are properly seated.

Misalignment. (© Chevrolet Div. G.M. Corp.)   Cracked inner race. (© Chevrolet Div. G.M. Corp.)

Cracked Inner Race

Cause	Serviceability
Crack due to improper fit, cocked bearing, or poor bearing seats	Install a new bearing and be sure it is seated properly.

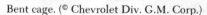

Bearing Failure Chart (cont.)

Frettage

Cause	Serviceability
Corrosion due to small movement of parts with no lubrication	Clean parts and check seals. Install a new bearing and be sure of proper lubrication.

Frettage. (© Chevrolet Div. G.M. Corp.)

Smears. (© Chevrolet Div. G.M. Corp.)

Smears

Cause	Serviceability
Metal smears due to slippage caused by poor fit, improper lubrication, overloading, or handling damage	Clean parts, install new bearing, and check for proper fit and lubrication.

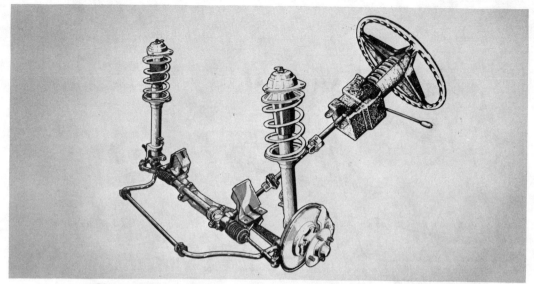

Chapter 8

Suspension and Steering

Front Suspension

BASIC OPERATING PRINCIPLES

The two most common types of front suspension in use today are the unequal length A-arm type and the McPherson strut type.

In the unequal length A-arm type, there are a pair of upper and lower control arms which are attached to the chassis or frame rails. On General Motors and Ford cars, a coil spring and shock absorber assembly are used for rebound control. The location of the coil spring varies. On some cars, it is located between the two control arms. On others, it is located on top of the upper arm. The shock absorber is generally located inside the coil spring. On Chrysler Corporation cars, a torsion bar is used instead of a coil spring to control wheel action. Basically, a torsion bar is a coil spring stretched out straight. They are attached to the chassis at one end and to the upper or lower control arm at the other. As the control arm moves up or down in response to road surface, it twists the torsion bar, which resists this twisting force and thereby returns the control arm to the normal position.

The outer ends of the control arms are kept an equal distance apart by spindles or steering knuckles. These steering knuckles are held in place by ball joints at the top and the bottom. The ball joints permit the upward and downward motion of the steering knuckles and the turning motion required for cornering, while keeping them vertical.

McPherson strut front suspension differs considerably from unequal length A-arm suspension. This type of suspension is found most frequently on compact and sub-compact cars, both domestic and imported. In this type of suspension, the steering knuckles are suspended by a lower control arm at the bottom and a combined coil spring/shock absorber unit at the top. There is, of course, no upper ball joint, only a lower one. On McPherson strut suspensions, the only front end alignment procedure possible is toe-in adjustment, since caster and camber are fixed.

WHEEL ALIGNMENT

Basic Operating Principles

Front wheel alignment (also known as front end geometry) is the position of the front wheels relative to each other and to the vehicle. Correct alignment must be maintained to provide safe, accurate steering, vehicle stability, and minimum tire wear. The factors which determine wheel alignment are interdependent. Therefore, when one of the factors is adjusted, the others must be adjusted to compensate.

Caster Angle

Caster angle is the number of degrees that a line, drawn through the center of the upper and lower ball joints and viewed from the

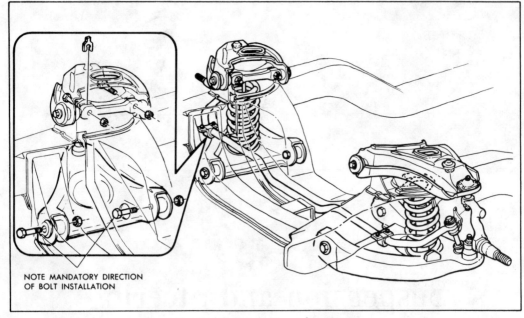

NOTE MANDATORY DIRECTION
OF BOLT INSTALLATION

Front suspension—spring on lower arm

side, can be tilted forward or backward. Positive caster means that the top of the upper ball joint is tilted toward the rear of the car, and negative caster means that it is tilted toward the front. A car with a slightly positive caster setting will have its lower ball joint pivot slightly ahead of the tire's center. This will assist the directional stability of the car by causing a drag at the bottom center of the wheel when it turns, thereby resisting the turn and tending to hold the wheel steady in whatever direction the car is pointed. Therefore, the car is less susceptible to crosswinds and road surface deviations. A car with too much (positive) caster will be hard to steer and shimmy at low speeds. A car with insufficient (negative) caster may tend to be unstable at high speeds and may respond erratically when the brakes are applied.

Camber Angle

Camber angle is the number of degrees that the wheel itself is tilted from a vertical line, when viewed from the front. Positive camber means that the top of the wheel is slanted away from the car, while negative camber means that it is tilted toward the car. Ordinarily, a car will have a slight positive camber when unloaded. Then, when the car is loaded and rolling down the road, the wheels will just about be vertical. If you started with no camber at all, then loading the car would produce a negative camber. Excessive camber (either positive or negative) will produce rapid

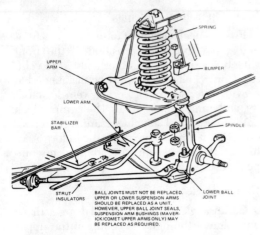

Front suspension—spring on upper arm

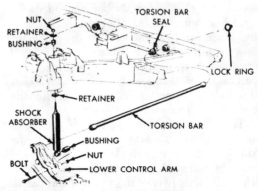

Front suspension—longitudinal torsion bar

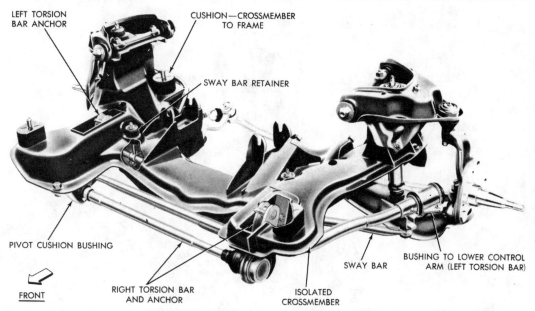

LEFT TORSION BAR ANCHOR

CUSHION—CROSSMEMBER TO FRAME

SWAY BAR RETAINER

PIVOT CUSHION BUSHING

FRONT

RIGHT TORSION BAR AND ANCHOR

ISOLATED CROSSMEMBER

SWAY BAR

BUSHING TO LOWER CONTROL ARM (LEFT TORSION BAR)

Front suspension—transverse torsion torsion bars

tire wear, since one side of the tire will be more heavily loaded than the other side.

Steering Axis Inclination

Steering axis inclination is the number of degrees that a line drawn through the upper and lower ball joints and viewed from the front, is tilted to the left or the right. This, in combination with caster, is responsible for the directional stability and self-centering of the steering. As the steering knuckle swings from lock to lock, the spindle generates an arc, causing the car to be raised when it is turned from the straight-ahead position. The reason the car body must rise is straightforward: since

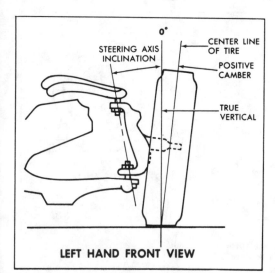

0°

STEERING AXIS INCLINATION

CENTER LINE OF TIRE

POSITIVE CAMBER

TRUE VERTICAL

LEFT HAND FRONT VIEW

Steering axis inclination

the wheel is in contact with the ground, it cannot move down. However, when it is swung away from the straight-ahead position, it must move either up or down (due to the arc generated by the steering knuckle). Not being able to move down, it must move up. Then, the weight of the car acts against this lift, and attempts to return the spindle to the straight-ahead position when the steering wheel is released.

Toe-In

Toe-in is the difference (in inches) between the front and the rear of the front tires. On a car with toe-in, the distance between the front wheels is less at the front than at the rear. Toe-in is normally only a few fractions of an inch, and is necessary to ensure parallel rolling of the front wheels and to prevent excessive tire wear. As the car is driven at increasingly faster speeds, the steering linkage has a tendency to expand slightly, thereby allowing the front wheels to turn out and away from each other. Therefore, initially setting the front wheels so that they are pointing slightly inward (toe-in), allows them to turn straight ahead when the car is underway.

Included Angle

The included angle is the sum of the steering axix inclination and the camber angle. Included angle determines the point of intersection of the wheel and the steering axis center lines. This is important because this determines, in turn, whether the wheel will toe out

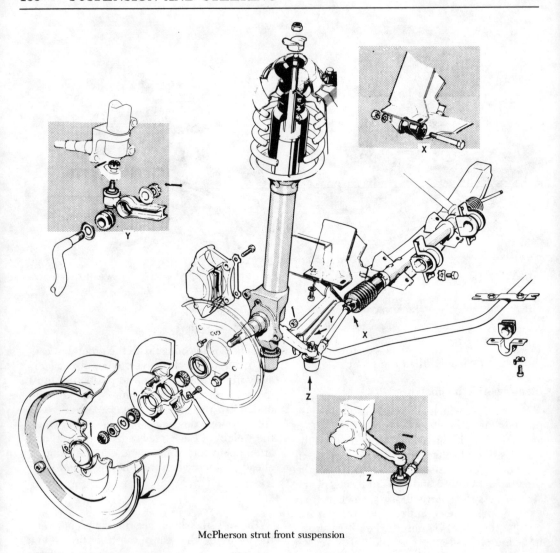

McPherson strut front suspension

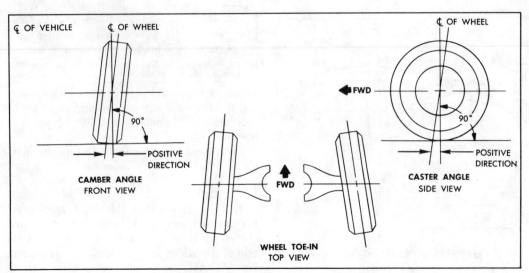

Caster, camber, and toe-in

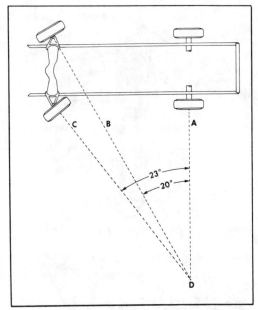

Toe-out during turns

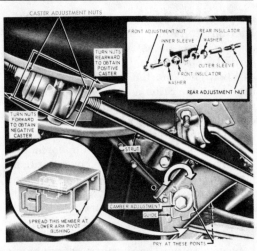

Typical caster and camber adjustments

or toe in. When the point of intersection is below the road surface, the wheel will toe out. When the intersection point is above the road surface, the wheel tends to toe in.

Toe-Out (During Turns)

The steering is designed so that the inner wheel turns more sharply toward the center of the turn than the outer wheel turns. This compensates for the fact that the inner wheel actually travels a shorter distance during the turn. Designing the steering in this manner avoids having the front wheels fight each other, thus improving tire life and aiding stability. Where toe-out is to be checked, angles are given for the inner and outer wheel relative to travel in

a straight line. Thus, in a left-hand turn, the left (inner) wheel might be 24° from straight ahead, and the right (outer) wheel 20° from straight ahead. For a right turn, the figures would be reversed.

Checking and Adjusting Front End Alignment

NOTE: *Front end alignment can only be checked through the use of sophisticated equipment. These procedures are given for informational purposes only.*

Before making any front end adjustments, all components which affect steering geometry should be inspected. These include worn or loose tie rod ends, steering linkage joints, ball joints, control arm bushings, and improperly adjusted or worn wheel bearings. Any defective components must be replaced prior to any front end alignment. Also note that the follow-

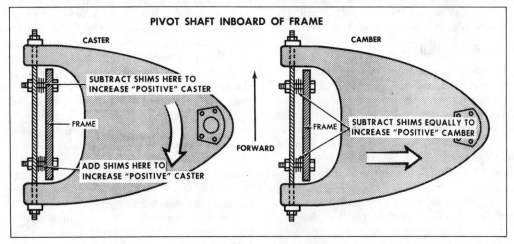

Typical caster and camber adjustments

ing procedures do not apply to cars with Mc-Pherson strut front suspension. Caster and camber angles are not adjustable on this type of front suspension, although toe-in is.

When checking the front end alignment, first check the caster and camber, then check the toe-in. (There are exceptions to this general rule on Vegas, for instance, camber is adjusted before caster). Caster is first adjusted to specifications by moving the upper control arm. This may be accomplished by repositioning shims, changing the length of a strut with adjusting nuts, or by repositioning the mounting point of a strut on the frame. Camber adjustment is then accomplished by pulling the entire control arm toward the frame or forcing it further away. This involves repositioning shims equally at the front and rear of the control arm, turning adjusting nuts an equal amount, or repositioning a strut. Toe-in is adjusted after caster and camber have been set by turning the adjusting sleeves on the tie rods. These sleeves should be turned in equal amounts in opposite directions in order to keep the steering wheel centered.

When caster, camber, and toe-in have been adjusted, steering axis inclination and toe-out figures should be correct. If not, a worn ball joint or bent suspension or steering part is at fault.

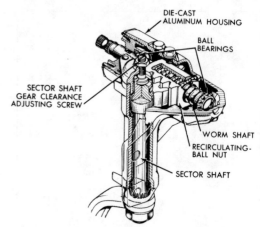

Cutaway view of a recirculating ball steering box

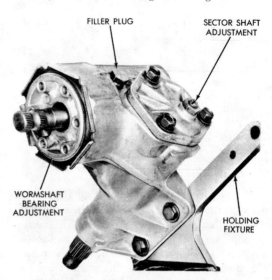

Typical adjustment points

Manual Steering

BASIC OPERATING PRINCIPLES

There are two types of manual steering in genral use today. They are worm and sector steering, also known as recirculating ball, and rack and pinion steering.

Recirculating Ball Steering

In this type of steering, the end of the steering input shaft, called the wormshaft, is machined with a continuous spiral groove in which ball bearings ride. These ball bearings move a ball nut assembly up or down the wormshaft in response to steering input. Tubes connect the lock nut/sleeve unit and allow the balls to constantly recirculate, distributing wear evenly among them. The wormshaft is supported by ball bearing assemblies at either end of the steering box housing. These bearings are usually adjustable to compensate for wear.

Since the wormshaft is coupled directly to the steering column shaft, turning the steering wheel causes the wormshaft to turn in the same direction. This action moves the ball nut assembly along its length. The balls circulate in one direction for a right-hand turn and in the other direction for a left-hand turn. Teeth on the ball nut assembly then engage teeth on the sector shaft (also called the Pitman shaft since it is connected to the Pitman arm) causing the Pitman or sector shaft to move the Pitman arm, thereby converting the rotating force of the steering wheel into the slower, higher torque rotation of the Pitman arm. The Pitman arm in turn transmits the desired directional movement to the front wheels through the steering linkage.

There are generally two adjustments possible on a recirculating ball steering box. There is the previously mentioned worm bearing adjustment, of which there are two kinds. In some designs, an adjusting screw is employed, while in others shims may be used to provide the proper bearing preload. Generally, preload is measured with a spring scale, although there are various methods.

An adjusting screw is also provided for positioning the cross-shaft for proper meshing of the worm or ball nut and the sector gear. After worm bearing preload is adjusted, play is removed from the unit with the cross-shaft adjusting screw, and a recheck of turning effort is made. The adjusting screw must then be backed off slightly if too great a steering wheel turning torque is required. Consult the manufacturer's instructions to make these adjustments because of variations in actual procedures and torque specifications.

Rack and Pinion Steering

This steering design uses a steering gear connected to the steering column shaft by a flexible coupling. This gear, similar in design to the pinion gear used in a differential, is cut on an angle and meshed on one side with a steel bar or rack which also has teeth cut in it. This rack is contained in the steering gearbox, which is positioned between the tie rods in the steering linkage. When the steering wheel is turned, the pinion gear operates directly on the rack, causing it to move from side to side and transmitting motion to the front wheels. This type of steering gear avoids the use of a Pitman arm and is a more direct and precise type of steering, although those used to recirculating ball steering occasionally find its directness disconcerting.

Before beginning to troubleshoot manual

steering problems, check the condition and pressure of the tires, and the lubrication of the steering gear and suspension components. If there is uneven tire wear, it might be wise to align the front end before trying to track down steering malfunctions.

Power Steering

BASIC-OPERATING PRINCIPLES

Power steering units are mechanical steering gear units incorporating a power assist. A worm shaft, which is rotated by the shaft coming down from the steering wheel via a flexible coupling, causes a rack piston nut to slide up

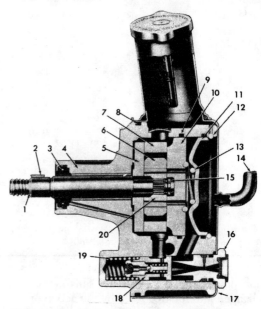

Cutaway view of a typical power steering pump

1. Shaft
2. Woodruff key
3. Shaft seal
4. Pump housing
5. Thrust plate
6. Vanes
7. Pump ring
8. Reservoir "O" ring seal
9. Pressure plate "O" ring
10. Pressure plate
11. End plate
12. End plate retaining ring
13. Pressure plate spring
14. Pump inlet tube
15. Rotor-to-drive shaft retaining ring
16. Pump outlet union
17. Reservoir
18. Flow control valve
19. Flow control valve spring
20. Rotor

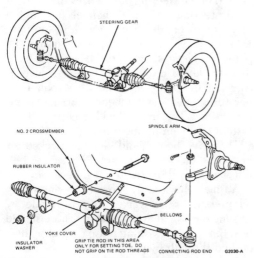

Rack and pinion steering

Troubleshooting Manual Steering Systems

The Condition	The Possible Cause	The Corrective Action
Hard Steering	(a) Low or uneven tire pressure	(a) Inflate tires to recommended pressures
	(b) Insufficient lubricant in the steering gear housing or in steering linkage	(b) Lubricate as necessary
	(c) Steering gear shaft adjusted too tight	(c) Adjust according to instructions
	(d) Front wheels out of line	(d) Align the wheels. See the appropriate Front Suspension System Section
	(e) Steering column misaligned	(e) See the appropriate Car Section for alignment procedures
Excessive Play or Looseness in the Steering Wheel	(a) Steering gear shaft adjust too loose or badly worn	(a) Replace worn parts and adjust according to instructions
	(b) Steering linkage loose or worn	(b) Replace worn parts. See the appropriate Front Suspension Section
	(c) Front wheel bearings improperly adjusted	(c) Adjust according to instructions
	(d) Steering arm loose on steering gear shaft	(d) Inspect for damage to the gear shaft and steering arm, replace parts as necessary
	(e) Steering gear housing attaching bolts loose	(e) Tighten attaching bolts to specifications
	(f) Steering arms loose at steering knuckles	(f) Tighten according to specifications
	(g) Worn ball joints	(g) Replace the ball joints as necessary. See the appropriate Front Suspension System Section
	(h) Worm shaft bearing adjustment too loose	(h) Adjust worm bearing preload according to instructions

and down inside the housing. This motion is changed into rotating force by the action of an output shaft sector gear. The rack piston nut is forced up and down inside the housing by the rotation of the worm gear, which forces the nut to move through the action of recirculating balls. The nut fits tightly inside the housing, and is sealed against the sides of the housing by a ring type seal. Power assist is provided by forcing hydraulic fluid into the housing on one side or the other of the rack piston nut.

The hydraulic pressure is supplied by a rotary vane pump, driven by the engine via V belts. The pump incorporates a flow control valve that bypasses the right amount of fluid for the proper operating pressure. The pump contains a fluid reservoir, located above the main body of the pump. The same fluid lubricates all parts of the power steering unit.

A rotary valve, spool valve, or pivot lever, located in the steering box, senses the rotation of the steering wheel and channels fluid to the upper or lower surface of the rack piston nut.

When power steering problems occur, the pump fluid level should first be checked. Note that two levels are given. The lower level is correct if the pump and fluid are at room temperature, after having been inoperative for some time. The upper level is correct if the system has been in operation (about 175°).

The drive belt should also be checked for looseness, cracks, or glazing. Replace the belt if it is damaged, or tighten it if necessary.

A quick check of the power steering pump oil pressure relief valves may be made by turning the wheel to either stop. There should be a buzzing or swishing noise caused by flow of fluid through by-pass valves.

If steering is difficult, the power steering

pump pressure may be tested. A special set of valves and gauges is required. Perform the test as follows:

1. With the engine off, remove the two hoses at the pump and install the gauges and valves.

2. Open both valves, and then start the engine and operate it at idle. The fluid must be brought up to 165–170° F. Closing valve B to build up 350 lbs pressure will speed the process.

3. When the fluid is fully warmed, close valve B. The pressure should be 620 psi or more, or else the pump is faulty.

4. Close both valve A and valve B. *Do not keep valves closed for more than five seconds.* This should raise the pressure level to the manufacturer's specifications for this type of test.

This test measures the ability of the pump to produce pressure. It does not test the pump's pressure regulating valve, a malfunction of which can also cause lack of steering assist.

Troubleshooting Power Steering Systems

The Condition	The Possible Cause	The Corrective Action
Hard Steering	(a) Improper tire pressure	(a) Inflate tires to recommended pressures
	(b) Loose pump drive belt	(b) Tighten or replace belt
	(c) Low or incorrect fluid	(c) Refill reservoir with proper fluid; check for leaks
	(d) Loose, bent or poorly lubricated front end parts	(d) Tighten or replace parts; lubricate at all fittings
	(e) Improper front end alignment	(e) Align front end
	(f) Bind in steering column or linkage	(f) Disassemble and inspect component parts. Repair or replace as necessary.
	(g) Air in hydraulic system	(g) Bleed system, refill and check for leaks.
	(h) Low pump output or leaks in system	(h) Disassemble pump, check for worn or damaged parts. Check for leaks in the system.
	(i) Obstruction in lines	(i) Clean or replace lines
	(j) Pump valves sticking or out of adjustment	(j) Replace or adjust valves
Loose Steering	(a) Loose wheel bearings	(a) Adjust wheel bearings
	(b) Faulty shocks	(b) Replace shocks
	(c) Worn linkage components	(c) Replace worn components
	(d) Loose steering gear mounting or linkage points	(d) Tighten mountings or linkage
	(e) Steering mechanism worn or improperly adjusted	(e) Replace and/or adjust mechanism
	(f) Valve spool improperly adjusted	(f) Adjust valve spool
Veer or Wander	(a) Improper tire pressure	(a) Inflate tires to recommended pressures
	(b) Improper front end alignment	(b) Align front end
	(c) Dragging brakes	(c) Inspect, replace and/or adjust brakes
	(d) Bent frame	(d) Straighten frame
	(e) Improper rear end alignment	(e) Inspect shocks and control arm torque. Replace and/or adjust as necessary

Troubleshooting Power Steering Systems (cont.)

The Condition	The Possible Cause	The Corrective Action
Veer or Wander	(f) Faulty shocks or springs	(f) Replace as necessary
	(g) Loose or bent front end components	(g) Replace as necessary
	(f) Play in Pitman arm	(f) Inspect bushings and arm. Replace as necessary
	(g) Loose wheel bearings	(g) Adjust to specifications
	(h) Binding Pitman arm	(h) Replace arm
	(i) Spool valve sticking or improperly adjusted	(i) Adjust or replace as necessary
Wheel Oscillation	(a) Improper tire pressure	(a) Inflate tires to recommended pressures
	(b) Loose wheel bearings	(b) Adjust to specifications
	(c) Improper front end alignment	(c) Align front end
	(d) Bent spindle	(d) Replace spindle
	(e) Worn, bent or broken front end components	(e) Inspect, repair or replace as necessary
	(f) Tires out of round or out of balance	(f) Replace or balance tires
	(g) Excessive lateral runout in disc brake rotor	(g) Reface or replace rotor
Noises	(a) Loose belts	(a) Replace and/or adjust belts
	(b) Low fluid, air in system	(b) Refill and check for leaks
	(c) Foreign matter in system	(c) Disassemble and clean system
	(d) Improper lubrication	(d) Lubricate all fittings
	(e) Interference or chafing in linkage	(e) Disassemble, inspect, replace or adjust components
	(f) Steering gear mountings loose	(f) Tighten mountings
	(g) Incorrect adjustment or wear in gear box	(g) Dissamble, inspect, repair, replace and/or adjust parts
	(h) Faulty valves or wear in pump	(h) Replace parts as necessary

Tires

BIAS PLY

Bias ply tires are the most basic and simple design available. The plies of fabric cord which strengthen the tire are applied in a criss-cross fashion for strength. The plies run from rim-edge to rim-edge to help increase the tire's resistance to bruises, and to the forces of braking and cornering.

BELTED BIAS

These tires are constructed very similarly to the bias-ply tires—with the plies applied in a criss-cross fashion. However, circumferential belts are applied just under the tread to strengthen it and keep it as flat as possible. Thus, the life and performance of the tire are improved. Because the construction is somewhat more complex than that of bias ply tires, belted bias tires are slightly more expensive.

RADIAL

Radial tires are the most expensive and best tires made. They offer both improved cornering and improved tread life over belted bias and bias ply tires. The body plies run from rim to rim in a hoop fashion, and the tire employs circumferential belts. The result is that the tread is kept still more perfectly flat and open than with belted bias tires.

There is a relationship between a tire's cornering ability and its ability to provide long tread wear. A tread that remains flat and does not squirm or close up when under heavy load wears more evenly and suffers less from scuffing. Therefore, most manufacturers recommend that the tire buyer consider purchase of a belted bias or radial tire, claiming that the cost per mile will be lower.

Of course, if the buyer does not plan to keep his car until the new rubber is fully worn out, a less expensive tire should be considered. However, if long mileage is desired, especially under rough cornering or heavy loading conditions, the more expensive designs may prove to be more economical.

If good cornering is desired, the radial is the obvious choice. The cornering characteristics of these tires are so significantly superior to those of other types that mixing radials and other types of tires on the same vehicle is not recommended. The differences in traction between the types can cause undesirable cornering characteristics.

Tire Troubleshooting Chart

TIRE WORN IN CENTER OF TREAD

Overinflation: Excess pressure causes the center of the tread to contact the road, while the edges ride free.

TIRE WORN ON OUTER EDGES ONLY

Underinflation: Underinflation causes the tread to bow, lifting the center off the road. This also increases flexing and heat, and may result in weakening of the tire cords. Note, however, that it is normal for the two sections of tread just one section from the outer edges to wear more than the others on bias belted tires.

TIRES WORN ON ONE SIDE ONLY

1. Improper toe-in adjustment: This is the problem if both outer edges or both inner edges are worn.
2. Improper camber adjustment.
3. Hard cornering: In addition to wearing the outer edges more than the center, this will round off the edges.

TIRES WORN IN SEVERAL SPOTS AROUND THE CIRCUMFERENCE OF THE TREAD

1. Underinflation combined with improper toe-in adjustment.
2. Improperly balanced tires and wheels.
3. Worn shock absorbers.
4. Worn suspension components.
5. Out-of-round brake drums.

NOISES

1. Irregular wear.
2. Low pressure.
3. Bulges due to faulty construction or structural damage.

NOTE: *Inflating tires to 50 pounds pressure for test purposes tends to stop noises. Driving the car on a very smooth road and inflating the tires to a very high pressure, one at a time, will isolate the noisy tire.*

TIRE CARE

Because the tire employs air under pressure as part of its structure, it is designed around the supporting strength of a gas at a specified pressure. For this reason, running a tire with either too high or too low a pressure actually undermines its structural strength, and, in effect, makes its shape improper for the job to be done.

Not only will improper inflation pressure keep the tread from properly laying on the road, it will reduce the tire's ability to resist damage from road shock. It can also increase operating temperatures.

Tire pressures should, therefore, be carefully checked *at least* once a month. A hand tire gauge of good quality should be used.

In almost all cases, the manufacturer's recommendations for pressures should be followed. While manufacturers tended to recommend low pressures several years ago, in order to achieve good ride characteristics, their recommendations from about 1968 are generally quite accurate. Remember that the differential between pressures at front and rear is of particular importance in maintaining stability on the road. The recommended differential should be maintained, and where higher pressures are recommended for high speeds or heavy loads, pressures should be tailored to the operating conditions. Check the tires when they are cold in order to ensure accurate pressure measurement. Do not bleed air out of hot tires to maintain the recommended pressure level. Remember to use

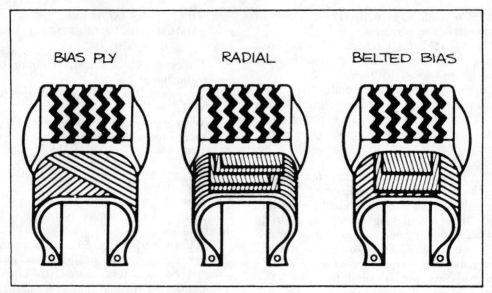

BIAS PLY   RADIAL   BELTED BIAS

Different types of tire construction

TIRE WEAR PATTERNS

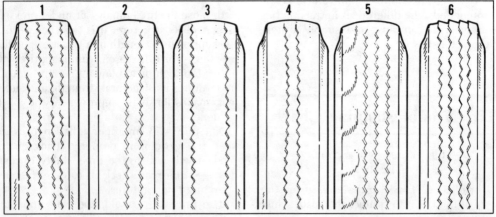

1   2   3   4   5   6

1. Tread Wear Bars. These appear when your tires are ready for replacement due to normal wear. The indicators are molded into the bottoms of the tread grooves. When bands appear in two or more adjacent grooves, replace the tire.

2. Incorrect Camber. When one side of the tire wears more rapidly than the other, suspect incorrect camber. If that side is worn smoothly, it means that a front end alignment is needed. Take the car to a specialist.

3. Overinflation. If your tires look as if only the center treads are wearing, you have been overinflating them. Find the proper inflation pressure in the Tire Inflation Chart. Check the tires with gauge of known accuracy and adjust pressure as necessary.

4. Underinflation. If the outer edges of your tires are wearing more

than the center treads, you probably have them underinflated. Inflate the tires to the correst pressure as shown in the chart. Consider purchasing a tire pressure gauge which you can use to maintain correct pressure.

5. Cupping. This wear pattern can be caused by a number of problems. Misalignment resulting fom bent steering linkage can cause this condition. A wheel/tire assembly that is out of balance can also cause this wear pattern.

6. Feathering. Saw-toothed wear patterns are caused by incorrect toe-in. Your font wheels must be turned inward slightly at the front. If this "toe-in" is excessive, however, the tires will wear in the pattern shown above. Have the front end alignment checked.

valve caps to keep dirt out of the valve core.

Tires should be rotated about every 6,000 miles. This will even out wear that might otherwise destroy a small segment of the tread prematurely, thereby wasting the remainder. The spare tire should be included in the rotation, as inactivity is harmful to a tire.

The tires should be statically and dynamically balanced at the first sign of ride roughness. Static balance means that the tire would remain in any selected position without turn-

ing itself on the wheel bearings with the vehicle on a lift. Dynamic balance refers to distribution of weight from side to side of the tire. Static balance is performed with the tire at rest; dynamic balance is done with the tire in motion.

TIRE SELECTION

Higher-priced tires do not necessarily increase cost per operating mile. Radial tires offer the longest mileage, and belted bias tires

TIRE CHECKS

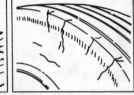

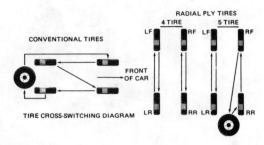

Radial tires will appear under-inflated compared to standard tires. Check pressure with gauge.

Safe tread depth is at least 1/16 inch.

Remove stones or glass chips embedded in tread.

Check for sidewall cracks or abrasion.

Tire rotation diagram

last longer than bias ply designs. The increased manufacturing cost is not usually as great as the gain in mileage.

If possible, all four tires on an automobile should be of the same type. If mixing is necessary, make sure that tires on one axle are not of different designs.

These precautions are particularly important with radial tires, which have vastly different cornering characteristics. If radials and another design *must* be mixed, put the radials on the rear axle.

Rims are generally 5–5½ in. wide, with some optional rims, as on station wagons, going as wide as 6 in. Super wide tires sometimes use rims up to 7 in. wide. Generally, it is permissible to go one range wider than original equipment without changing the rims. In other words, an E78 or E70 tire may use a 5½ in. rim with good results. In going to E60 tires, however, wider (7–8 in.) rims are recommended. Tire dealers have charts showing recommended rim widths for various tire sizes.

It should be remembered that, when wider rims and tires are used, wheel bearing wear may be increased due to the increased load on the bottom of the outer bearing and the top of the inner bearing.

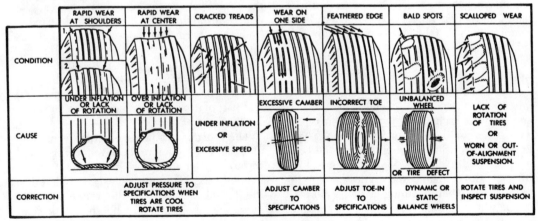

	RAPID WEAR AT SHOULDERS	RAPID WEAR AT CENTER	CRACKED TREADS	WEAR ON ONE SIDE	FEATHERED EDGE	BALD SPOTS	SCALLOPED WEAR
CONDITION							
CAUSE	UNDER INFLATION OR LACK OF ROTATION	OVER INFLATION OR LACK OF ROTATION	UNDER INFLATION OR EXCESSIVE SPEED	EXCESSIVE CAMBER	INCORRECT TOE	UNBALANCED WHEEL ... OR TIRE DEFECT	LACK OF ROTATION OF TIRES OR WORN OR OUT-OF-ALIGNMENT SUSPENSION.
CORRECTION	ADJUST PRESSURE TO SPECIFICATIONS WHEN TIRES ARE COOL ROTATE TIRES			ADJUST CAMBER TO SPECIFICATIONS	ADJUST TOE-IN TO SPECIFICATIONS	DYNAMIC OR STATIC BALANCE WHEELS	ROTATE TIRES AND INSPECT SUSPENSION

Troubleshooting tire wear problems

Chapter 9

The Cooling System

Basic Operating Principles

The cooling system, in spite of its compact size, handles a staggering amount of heat in order to protect the internal parts of the engine from the heat of combustion and friction. The cooling system of a modern car may remove about 6,000 BTU per minute, or considerably more heat than is required to comfortably warm a large home in extreme weather.

The coolant employed now is generally a mixture of water and ethylene glycol. Ethylene glycol is a chemical which, when mixed with water in the proper proportions, both lowers the freezing point and raises the boiling point of the solution. Most commercial antifreezes also contain additives designed to inhibit corrosion and foaming in the system.

The water pump is the heart of the cooling system. This is usually driven off the pulley on the front of the engine crankshaft by V belts. Its bearings are usually sealed ball bearing units located in the long snout of the front pump housing. The pump's impeller is a vaned wheel which fits the inside of the water pump housing with a very close clearance. Water trapped between the vanes is forced to rotate with the impeller around the inside of the water pump housing. The resultant centrifugal force raises the pressure in the pump discharge, causing water to flow through the pump.

The coolant is discharged into the front of the engine block and circulates in the water jackets around the cylinders. It then makes its way upward through ports in the block, head gasket, and head to the water passages around the combustion chambers. It leaves the engine through the front of the block, passing into the thermostat housing which, in V8 engines, is a part of the intake manifold. Here, the water flow splits, part of it returning directly to the water pump inlet through an external bypass hose or internal bypass passage, and part of it passing through the upper radiator hose.

The radiator is a heat exchanger consisting of a large number of thin water tubes fed through upper and lower or right and left side header tanks. Thin metal fins are soldered to the outside surfaces of the water tubes to increase the area of the hot metal surfaces available for transmission of heat to the air. A fan, usually driven off the water pump shaft, aids circulation of air through the radiator, especially at low speeds. Some fans have a thermostatically operated fluid drive clutch to adjust the fan speed to temperature conditions and engine speed.

A heater core, similar in construction to the radiator, receives coolant flow from the lower portion of the thermostat housing where coolant flows at all times. The heater hoses con-

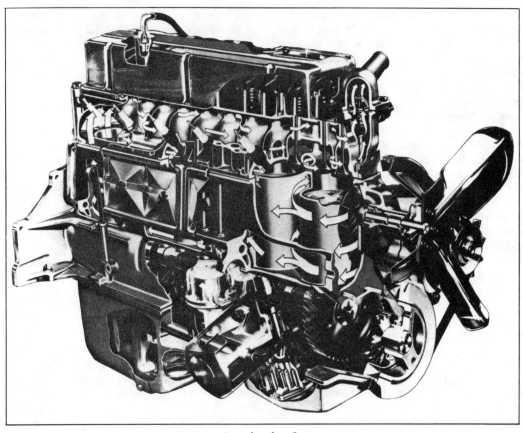

Typical coolant flow

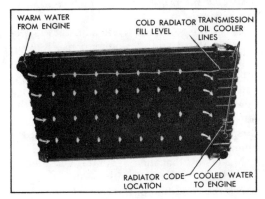

Typical cross-flow radiator

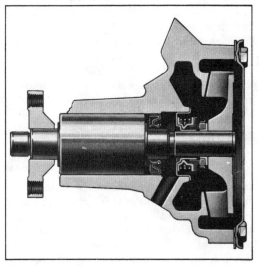

Cutaway view of a water pump

duct the water to the core and return it to the inlet side of the water pump. The heater core is usually in a heater air duct located in the dash panel.

A pressure cap seals the radiator against coolant leakage through the action of a sprung poppet valve whose rubber sealing ring bears against a surface inside the filler neck. The cap allows the escape of coolant when the system pressure reaches a predetermined level, usually about 15 psi, thus protecting the radia- tor, hoses, and other system components from excessive pressure. The cap also incorporates a vacuum relief valve which opens only during cooling of the system (when the engine is off) to prevent the formation of vacuum within the system.

The system adjusts its cooling capacity to the weather conditions, vehicle speed, and engine load through the action of a thermostat. The thermostat consists of a poppet or hinged flap type of valve actuated by pressure from a fluid-filled bellows or wax pellet. The valve remains tightly closed below the rated opening temperature, forcing all the coolant discharged from the water pump to return directly to the water pump inlet. This practically eliminates loss of heat from the engine during warm-up, while protecting the system from the formation of steam at hot spots. The bypass inlet is situated near the heat-sensing portion of the thermostat so the thermostat will receive a continuous indication of the water temperature, even when none of the fluid is passing through it.

When coolant temperature reaches the specified level (usually 180–195°), the thermostat will begin opening. The valve will be opened gradually as coolant temperatures rise, and will reach a wide-open position about 25° above the opening temperature. The radiator is slightly larger than required during most operating conditions. Thus, the thermostat is usually at least part-way closed, providing a precise control of engine temperature. One exception is when the engine is idled or turned off immediately after a hard run. The cooling system's capacity to throw off heat is vastly decreased under these conditions but the great amount of heat stored up in the heavy metal of the engine block continues to warm the coolant. It is normal for the engine temperature to rise substantially under these conditions. As long as water is not discharged from the pressure cap, there is nothing wrong with the system.

RUST AND SCALE

Rust and scale cause engine cooling problems in two different ways. First, they restrict the flow of coolant which decreases the flow through the entire system. Second, they build up a layer of insulating material on all the surfaces of the system. This not only reduces the capacity of the system to throw off heat but also keeps the coolant from picking up heat in the normal manner from hot engine parts even when the coolant is running at near normal temperatures.

Rust and scale are a result of chemical reactions between the metals in the cooling system and the minute amounts of air and exhaust gases that always enter the system through the water pump shaft seal and the head gasket and the block and head. Rust and scale cause what is perhaps the most common problem in poorly maintained systems, and can cause severe overheating even when there are no leaks in the system and the engine is in good mechanical condition.

COOLING SYSTEM TROUBLESHOOTING

A. Inspect the System

Check the fan for bent, cracked, or broken blades and replace it as necessary. A thermostatic fan may be checked as follows:

1. Allow the engine to cool until the engine compartment is well below 150° F.

2. Cover the radiator, leaving sufficient room for circulation so air will flow through the core and fan in the normal direction.

3. Measure the temperature of the fan air discharge with a 200° F thermometer. There should be a sudden increase in noise produced by the fan between 150 and 190° F. Otherwise the unit is faulty and should be replaced.

Check the belts that drive the water pump for cracks and glazing, and replace as necessary.

NOTE: *Replace paired belts with a set, even if one looks serviceable. Use the proper size. Do not pry the belt on. Tighten to specifications.*

Check the belt tension and adjust it to specifications if a strand tensioning gauge is available. If not, adjust the belt so that tension exists on it at all times, and heavy thumb pressure will permit it to flex about ½ in. Tighten a new belt just a bit more snugly to allow for the tension that will be lost as the belt adapts to the pulley grooves during the first few miles of operation.

Make sure that the engine has had time to cool down, and remove the radiator cap to check the condition of the coolant.

NOTE: *Unless the engine is cold, use a heavy rag to do this. Turn the cap very slowly, pausing to allow pressure to escape.*

The coolant level should be 1–2 in. below the filler neck if the engine is warm, and about 3 in. if it is cold. If the coolant level is low, start the engine and allow it to idle while adding a 50 percent antifreeze, 50 percent water solution to the radiator.

Check the condition of the coolant. It should be clear. If there is evidence of rust and scale and the coolant is dull brown or rusty red, flush the system because clogging and poor heat transfer are probably contributing to the problem.

Check the seal in the radiator cap for cracks or torn sections. Replace it if the seal is cracked, torn or hangs out over the edges of the metal backing.

Check the radiator and hoses, especially the hose connections, for rust marks that would indicate leakage. Tighten clamps or replace hoses and clamps as necessary.

In order to conserve weight and space, most modern cooling systems are carefully sized to provide just the capacity required under normal operating conditions. If the vehicle is being used to pull a trailer that weighs more than one ton, overheating problems are probably due to the load. Installation of a trailer towing package will probably cure the problem. If the vehicle has an aftermarket air conditioner, overheating is probably due to the extra resistance to air flow, engine load, and heat produced by the unit. Install a heavy-duty radiator and fan. Finally, if your vehicle overheats during prolonged idling with the air conditioning running and the automatic transmission in gear, a change in operating habits may cure the problem. The transmission should be shifted to neutral during such idling. The heat generated in the transmission under idling conditions is passed on to a transmission oil cooler located in the radiator. Under extreme conditions, the idle speed should be increased with the throttle and the air conditioning should be turned off. Overheating should not be considered a problem unless the vehicle has trouble cooling itself under normal road operating conditions.

Allow the engine to cool until it is well below normal operating temperature. Start the engine and operate it at fast idle. The radiator should remain fairly cool for a few minutes and then suddenly turn warm. Coolant should flow through the entire radiator and both hoses, making them warm to the touch. Scattered cool spots in the radiator mean clogging. Failure of the coolant to circulate through the lower hose may mean a faulty water pump or thermostat, or severe clogging. Slow warm-up of the engine and circulation of only moderately warm water through the radiator immediately after starting means a bad thermostat that might be causing overheating.

Accelerate the engine to check to see if the radiator's lower hose collapses at higher speeds. If it does, replace it. Listen to the water pump. A loud grinding noise usually indicates worn bearings and contact between the impeller blades and water pump housing because of the improper bearing clearances. Replace a noisy pump.

Road-test the vehicle, watching the temperature gauge or light, and stopping frequently to check for coolant loss from the overflow tube.

If the gauge or light indicates overheating, and water is expelled through the overflow tube, follow through with the rest of the checks in the suggested order. If the gauge indicates overheating but there is no evidence of coolant loss, see B. If the radiator cap checks out, go on to G. If the only problem is expulsion of coolant through the overflow, with no other signs of overheating, see B. If the radiator cap checks out, go to subsection E. If the only problem is slow warm-up, replace thermostat.

Adjust the ignition timing to specifications. Improper timing can result in overheating by reducing the efficiency of the engine.

B. Check the Radiator Pressure Cap with a Pressure Tester

A special tester with an air pump is available for this purpose. It is the only way to adequately test a pressure cap. Check the pressure rating of the cap (which is usually stamped on the top), wet the rubber seal, and install the cap onto the tester. Pump up the pressure tester until air bleeds out from under the seal. Note the pressure. It should be within one pound of the rating on the cap. Replace the cap if pressure is released at either too high or too low a pressure; a cap which retains excess pressure can damage the system and can also make removal of the cap dangerous.

C. Use a Radiator Pressure Tester to Test the System's Ability to Hold Pressure

Pressurize the system up to the rating of the cap. Carefully watch the pressure gauge for several minutes to see if there is a loss of pressure. If there is no pressure loss, go on to E. If pressure is lost, idle the engine and watch the gauge carefully for fluctuations. Be sure to release pressure if otherwise, remove the spark plug leads one by one to determine which cylinders are leaking. The leaking cylinder(s) will produce less fluctuation in the needle when the spark leads are removed. If obvious differences between cylinders are not noted in this test, perform a compression test as described in the previous section. Leaky

Pressure testing a radiator cap.

cylinders must be repaired by removing the cylinder head(s) affected and replacing the head gasket.

D. Check Further for Leaks, Keeping the System Pressurized

Keep the pressure in the system to within a pound or two of the full rating. This will cause leaks to show up that only exist under full operating pressure. Check the following parts of the system very carefully: hoses, radiator (especially at soldered joints between header tanks and water tubes), water pump (especially at the shaft seal), thermostat housing, heater core (check the floor in the passenger compartment for a light film of antifreeze), drain cocks and plugs, core plugs in block, and heater water valves (especially around valve stems). Replace any defective parts.

E. Check Strength of Antifreeze Solution

Regardless of the climate, a modern, high-pressure system should be protected down to 0° F because ethylene-glycol antifreeze in solution with water increases the boiling point. Even with all other cooling system components in perfect condition, a weak antifreeze solution could result in boiling of coolant under difficult operating conditions.

Make the test using a special hydrometer calibrated to show the freezing point of an ethylene-glycol and water solution. Pull the solution in and out of the hydrometer several times to make sure that any residue from the last test is removed and to bring the thermometer in the hydrometer to the temperature of the solution as quickly as possible. If the unit does not have a thermometer and is not equipped with a temperature conversion chart, a sample of coolant will have to be

brought to the temperature at which the unit is calibrated to obtain an accurate reading.

The test must either be performed at the specified temperature or corrected with a conversion chart because a change in temperature will affect the reading by changing the density of the sample. If there is not adequate protection, consult an antifreeze chart, drain the coolant, and replace it with the correct antifreeze solution. Be sure to retest the new solution to ensure adequate protection.

F. Remove the Thermostat and Test It for Proper Operation

Secure a new thermostat housing gasket before proceeding with this test, as disassembly of the housing usually ruins the old gasket. Drain coolant from the radiator down below the level of the thermostat housing. Remove the thermostat and notice whether or not the wax pellet or bellows was turned downward, toward the block. A thermostat that is upside down will respond improperly to temperature changes.

Suspend the thermostat in a pan full of water, keeping it well above the bottom so that heat will not be conducted directly to the sensing element from the bottom of the pan. Place the pan on a stove and heat it while measuring the water temperature with a 250° thermometer. The thermostat should open with 5° of its rated opening temperature (consult the owner's manual for the rating), and open fully about 25° above this temperature. (These conditions cannot be created for a 195° thermostat, but a check of opening temperature and freedom of operation can be made.) After proper opening and freedom of operation have been checked, allow the solution to

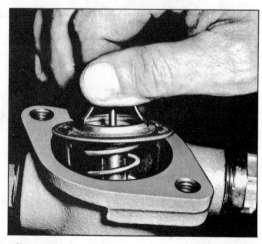

Thermostat removal

cool and make sure that the thermostat closes properly.

Replace the thermostat, if necessary. In reassembly, make sure that the wax pellet or bellows is downward (toward the main portion of the block). Clean the surfaces between the upper nad lower portions of the housing and replace the gasket.

If problems continue, remove the external bypass hose, if one is used, and inspect it for clogging or swelling. Replace it if it does not permit free passage of coolant.

G. Check Wiring-to-Temperature Light or Gauge. Replace Parts as Necessary

Sometimes temperature gauges or lights will indicate overheating when there is no loss of coolant, or will fail to show overheating when coolant is lost. Failure to indicate overheating even when coolant is being lost through the overflow tube can occur because of a bad radiator cap or weak antifreeze solution. A bad sensor can cause the light or gauge to show overheating even when no problem exists.

A preliminary check of the wiring should be made in either case. Check the connection at the sensor, which is usually located in the cylinder head, to make sure it is clean and tight. Check the wiring for frayed insulation and grounds, and replace or repair it as necessary. Check the other dash gauges for normal function and, if they function normally, proceed with the checks below. If the other gauges do not work properly, there is an electrical system problem which should be rectified before blaming the cooling system gauge.

If the system pushes water out through the overflow tube, check the antifreeze solution as in subsection E. and correct a weak solution. Check the radiator pressure cap. A weak cap could cause coolant to escape even when the engine is not overheating. A cap that traps too much pressure can allow the engine to overheat without loss of coolant.

If the problem is not corrected, replace the sensor in the block. This is by far the most common source of trouble. If this does not rectify the problem, see the section on dash gauges and indicators.

Air Cooling Systems

Air cooling systems are generally trouble-free. A few problems can occur, however. If an air-cooled engine operates sluggishly after a short period of driving in warm weather, make the following checks:

A. Check the belt for glazing and cracks. If evidence of slippage exists, remove the belt to check the fan for free rotation and then replace the belt, tightening it to specifications to ensure adequate cooling.

B. Check all ducting for loose or missing screws or bent parts which might cause cracks and leaks: Check the spark plugs' rubber seals and heater hoses and clamps, and replace any parts which do not seal properly.

C. Check the ignition timing and, if applicable, the adjustment of the valves; poor tuning can cause high operating temperatures. Make sure the engine is using the right viscosity of motor oil.

D. If problems persist, check compression and check the oil pressure relief valve for proper spring tension and free plunger operation. Make repairs as necessary.

E. If the problem is still not solved, it may be necessary to remove the ducting and clean the entire engine of accumulated dirt. An oil cooler that is clogged internally can also cause overheating problems because of the importance of the oil as a coolant in an air-cooled engine. If there is evidence of sludge in the engine, it should be removed and cleaned. Check the operation and mounting of the thermostat. The thermostat should be wide open when the engine is idling after a hard run. The operation of the cooling flaps may be checked by disconnecting the bellows from the housing, and moving it back and forth to each of the extremes of the travel of the mechanism. Make sure that the mounting bracket is positioned so the bellows can fully open the cooling flaps.

Chapter 10

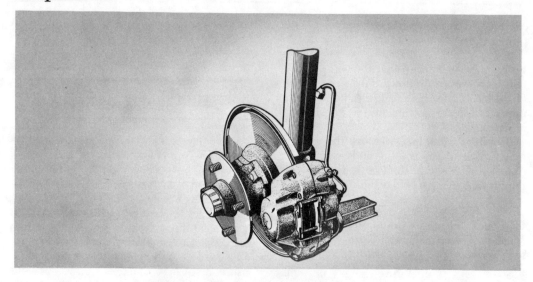

Brake Systems

Hydraulic System

BASIC OPERATING PRINCIPLES

Hydraulic systems are used to actuate the brakes of all modern automobiles. The system transports the power required to force the frictional surfaces of the braking system together from the pedal to the individual brake units at each wheel. A hydraulic system is used for two reasons. First, fluid under pressure can be carried to all parts of an automobile by small hoses—some of which are flexible—without taking up a significant amount of room or posing routing problems. Second, a great mechanical advantage can be given to the brake pedal end of the system, and the foot pressure required to actuate the brakes can be reduced by making the surface area of the master cylinder pistons smaller than that of any of the pistons in the wheel cylinders or calipers.

The master cylinder consists of a fluid reservoir and either a single or double cylinder and piston assembly. Double type master cylinders are designed to separate the front and rear braking systems hydraulically in case of a leak.

Steel lines carry the brake fluid to a point on the vehicle's frame near each of the vehicle's wheels. The fluid is then carried to the slave cylinders by flexible tubes in order to allow for suspension and steering movements.

In drum brake systems, the slave cylinders are called wheel cylinders. Each wheel cylinder contains two pistons, one at either end, which push outward in opposite directions. In disc brake systems, the slave cylinders are part of the calipers. One or four cylinders are used to force the brake pads against the disc, but all cylinders contain one piston only. All slave cylinder pistons employ some type of seal, usually made of rubber, to minimize the leakage of fluid around the piston. A rubber dust boot seals the outer end of the cylinder against dust and dirt. The boot fits around the outer end of the piston on disc brake calipers, and around the brake actuating rod on wheel cylinders.

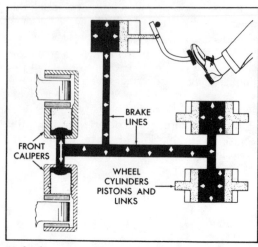

Hydraulic system schematic

The hydraulic system operates as follows: When at rest, the entire system, from the piston(s) in the master cylinder to those in the wheel cylinders or calipers, is full of brake fluid. Upon application of the brake pedal, fluid trapped in front of the master cylinder piston(s) is forced through the lines to the slave cylinders. Here, it forces the pistons outward, in the case of drum brakes, and inward toward the disc, in the case of disc brakes. The motion of the pistons is opposed by return springs mounted outside the cylinders in drum brakes, and by internal springs or spring seals, in disc brakes.

Upon release of the brake pedal, a spring located inside the master cylinder immediately returns the master cylinder piston(s) to the normal position. The pistons contain check valves and the master cylinder has compensating ports drilled in it. These are uncovered as the pistons reach their normal position. The piston check valves allow fluid to flow toward the wheel cylinders or calipers as the pistons withdraw. Then, as the return springs force the brake pads or shoes into the released position, the excess fluid returns to the master cylinder fluid reservoir through the compensating ports. It is during the time the pedal is in the released position that any fluid that has leaked out of the system will be replaced through the compensating ports.

Dual circuit master cylinders employ two pistons, located one behind the other, in the same cylinder. The primary piston is actuated directly by mechanical linkage from the brake pedal. The secondary piston is actuated by fluid trapped between the two pistons. If a leak develops in front of the secondary piston, it moves forward until it bottoms against the front of the master cylinder, and the fluid trapped between the pistons will operate the rear brakes. If the rear brakes develop a leak, the primary piston will move forward until direct contact with the secondary piston takes place, and it will force the secondary piston to actuate the front brakes. In either case, the brake pedal moves farther when the brakes are applied, and less braking power is available.

All dual-circuit systems use a distributor switch to warn the driver when only half of the brake system is operational. This switch is located in a valve body which is mounted on the firewall or the frame below the master cylinder. A hydraulic piston receives pressure from both circuits, each circuit's pressure being applied to one end of the piston. When the pressures are in balance, the piston remains stationary. When one circuit has a leak, however, the greater pressure in that circuit during application of the brakes will push the piston to one side, closing the distributor switch and activating the brake warning light.

In disc brake systems, this valve body also

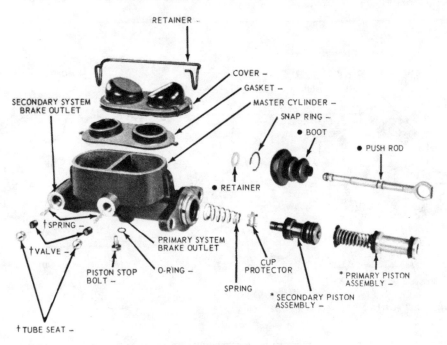

Master cylinder disassembled

Typical combination valve

contains a metering valve and, in some cases, a proportioning valve. The metering valve keeps pressure from traveling to the disc brakes on the front wheels until the brake shoes on the rear wheels have contacted the drums, ensuring that the front brakes will never be used alone. The proportioning valve throttles the pressure to the rear brakes so as to avoid rear wheel lock-up during very hard braking.

These valves may be tested by removing the lines to the front and rear brake systems and installing special brake pressure testing gauges. Front and rear system pressures are then compared as the pedal is gradually depressed. Specifications vary with the manufacturer and design of the brake system.

Brake system warning lights may be tested by depressing the brake pedal and holding it while opening one of the wheel cylinder

bleeder screws. If this does not cause the light to go on, substitute a new lamp, make continuity checks, and, finally, replace the switch as necessary.

The hydraulic system may be checked for leaks by applying pressure to the pedal gradually and steadily. If the pedal sinks very slowly to the floor, the system has a leak. This is not to be confused with a springy or spongy feel due to the compression of air within the lines. If the system leaks, there will be a gradual change in the position of the pedal with a constant pressure.

Check for leaks along all lines and at wheel cylinders. If no external leaks are apparent, the problem is inside the master cylinder.

Hydraulic System Troubleshooting Chart

Low Pedal

1. Brake fluid level low (If fluid is low, check all lines and wheel cylinders for leaks, and repair as necessary.)

2. Air in system (This will be accompanied by a spongy feel at the pedal, and by a low fluid level. Check as above.)

3. Master cylinder primary cup damaged, or cylinder bore worn or corroded

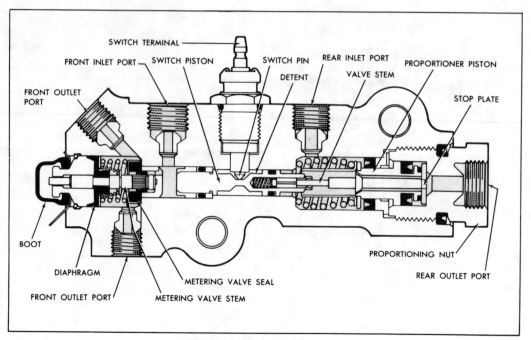

Cross-section of a combination valve

4. Use of improper fluid (Fluid boils from the heat and the resulting gas compresses during pedal application.)

SPONGY PEDAL

1. Air trapped in system (This may include the master cylinder. Check for leaks as described above.)
2. Use of improper fluid
3. Clogged compensating port in master cylinder (This may be checked for by watching for motion of fluid in master cylinder fluid reservoir during early part of brake pedal stroke. If no fluid motion, the port is clogged.)
4. Hoses soft (Expanding under pressure.)

ONE WHEEL DRAGS

1. Wheel cylinder piston cups swollen
2. Clogged line

ALL BRAKES DRAG

1. Clogged compensating port in master cylinder
2. Mineral oil in system

HIGH PEDAL PRESSURE REQUIRED

1. Corroded wheel cylinder
2. Clogged line
3. Clogged compensating port in master cylinder

Disc Brakes

BASIC OPERATING PRINCIPLES

Instead of the traditional expanding brakes that press outward against a circular drum, disc brake systems utilize a cast iron disc with brake pads positioned on either side of it. Braking effect is achieved in a manner similar to the way you would squeeze a spinning phonograph record between your fingers. The disc (rotor) is a one-piece casting with cooling fins between the two braking surfaces. This enables air to circulate between the braking surfaces making them less sensitive to heat buildup and more resistant to fade. Dirt and water do not affect braking action since contaminants are thrown off by the centrifugal action of the rotor or scraped off by the pads. Also, the equal clamping action of the two brake pads tends to ensure uniform, straight-line stops. All disc brakes are inherently self-adjusting.

MINIMUM THICKNESS MARKING

Disc brake and caliper assembly

There are three general types of disc brake:
1) A fixed caliper, four-piston type.
2) A floating caliper, single piston type.
3) A sliding caliper, single piston type.
The fixed caliper design uses two pistons mounted on either side of the rotor (in each side of the caliper). The caliper is mounted rigidly and does not move.

The sliding and floating designs are quite similar. In fact, these two types are often lumped together. In both designs, the pad on the inside of the rotor is moved into contact with the rotor by hydraulic force. The caliper, which is not held in a fixed position, moves slightly, bringing the outside pad into contact with the rotor. There are various methods of attaching floating calipers. Some pivot at the bottom or top, and some slide on mounting bolts. In any event, the end result is the same.

Drum Brakes

BASIC OPERATING PRINCIPLES

Drum brakes employ two brake shoes mounted on a stationary backing plate. These shoes are positioned inside a circular cast iron drum which rotates with the wheel assembly. The shoes are held in place by springs; this allows them to slide toward the drums (when they are applied) while keeping the linings and drums in alignment. The shoes are actuated by a wheel cylinder which is mounted at the top of the backing plate. When the

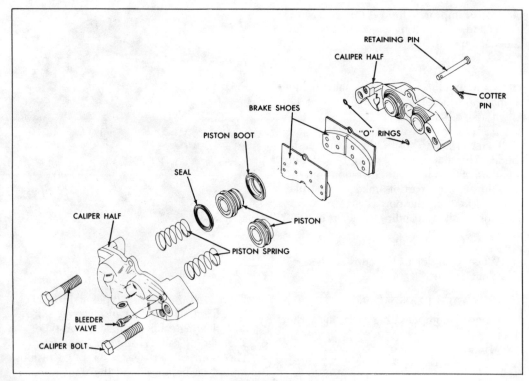

Four piston caliper assembly

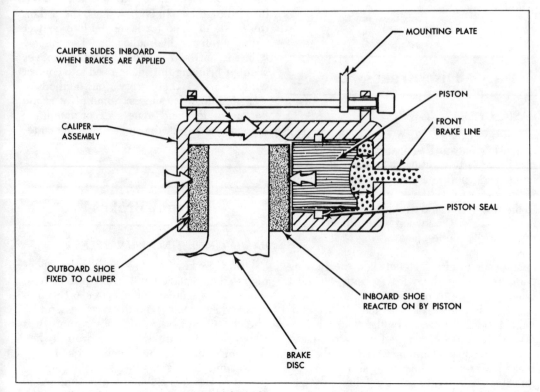

Sliding caliper operation

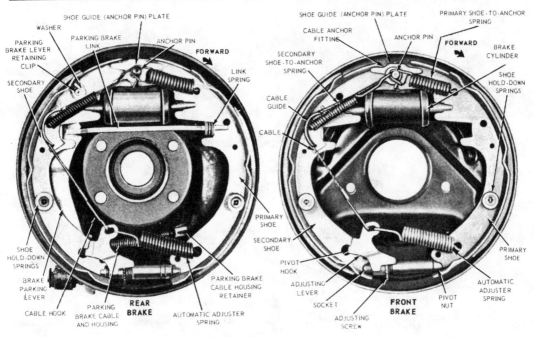

Drum brake assemblies

brakes are applied, hydraulic pressure forces the wheel cylinder's two actuating links outward. Since these links bear directly against the top of the brake shoes, the tops of the shoes are then forced outward against the inner side of the drum. This action forces the bottoms of the two shoes to contact the brake drum by rotating the entire assembly slightly (known as servo action). When pressure within the wheel cylinder is relaxed, return springs pull the shoes back away from the drum.

Most modern drum brakes are designed to self-adjust themselves during application when the vehicle is moving in reverse. This motion causes both shoes to rotate very slightly with the drum, rocking an adjusting

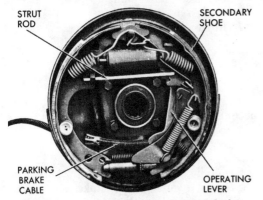

Typical rear brake assembly showing parking brake assembly

lever, thereby causing rotation of the adjusting screw by means of a star wheel.

Power Brake Boosters

Power brakes operate just as standard brake systems except in the actuation of the master cylinder pistons. A vacuum diaphragm is located on the front of the master cylinder and assists the driver in applying the brakes, reducing both the effort and travel he must put into moving the brake pedal.

The vacuum diaphragm housing is connected to the intake manifold by a vacuum hose. A check valve is placed at the point where the hose enters the diaphragm housing, so that during periods of low manifold vacuum brake assist vacuum will not be lost.

Depressing the brake pedal closes off the vacuum source and allows atmospheric pressure to enter on one side of the diaphragm. This causes the master cylinder pistons to move and apply the brakes. When the brake pedal is released, vacuum is applied to both sides of the diaphragm, and return springs return the diaphragm and master cylinder pistons to the released position. If the vacuum fails, the brake pedal rod will butt against the end of the master cylinder actuating rod, and

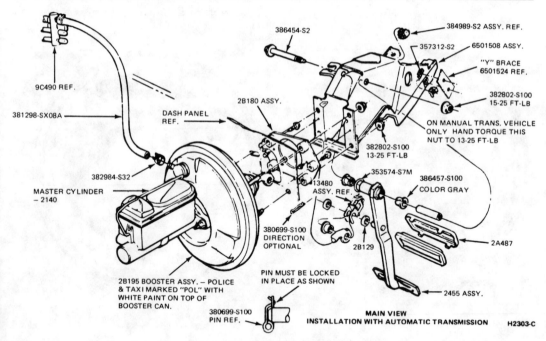

9C490 REF.

381298-SX08A

DASH PANEL
REF.

386454-S2

384989-S2 ASSY. REF.

357312-S2   6501508 ASSY.

"Y" BRACE
6501524 REF.

382802-S100
15-25 FT-LB

ON MANUAL TRANS. VEHICLE
ONLY HAND TORQUE THIS
NUT TO 13-25 FT-LB

2B180 ASSY.

382984-S32

MASTER CYLINDER
— 2140

382802-S100
13-25 FT-LB

13480
ASSY. REF.

353574-S7M

386457-S100
COLOR GRAY

380699-S100
DIRECTION
OPTIONAL

2B129

2A487

2B195 BOOSTER ASSY. — POLICE
& TAXI MARKED "POL" WITH
WHITE PAINT ON TOP OF
BOOSTER CAN.

PIN MUST BE LOCKED
IN PLACE AS SHOWN

2455 ASSY.

380699-S100
PIN REF.

MAIN VIEW
INSTALLATION WITH AUTOMATIC TRANSMISSION   H2303-C

Typical vacuum booster installation

direct mechanical application will occur as the pedal is depressed.

The hydraulic and mechanical problems that apply to conventional brake systems also apply to power brakes, and should be checked for if the tests and chart below do not reveal the problem.

Test for a system vacuum leak as described below:

1. Operate the engine at idle with the transmission in Neutral without touching the brake pedal for at least one minute.

2. Turn off the engine, and wait one minute.

3. Test for the presence of assist vacuum by depressing the brake pedal and releasing it several times. Light application will produce less and less pedal travel, if vacuum was present. If there is no vacuum, air is leaking into the system somewhere.

Test for system operation as follows:

1. Pump the brake pedal (with engine off) until the supply vacuum is entirely gone.

2. Put a light, steady pressure on the pedal.

3. Start the engine, and operate it at idle with the transmission in Neutral. If the system is operating, the brake pedal should fall toward the floor if constant pressure is maintained on the pedal.

Power brake systems may be tested for hydraulic leaks just as ordinary systems are tested, except that the engine should be idling with the transmission in Neutral throughout the test.

Power Brake Booster Troubleshooting Chart

HARD PEDAL

1. Faulty vacuum check valve
2. Vacuum hose kinked, collapsed, plugged, leaky, or improperly connected
3. Internal leak in unit
4. Damaged vacuum cylinder
5. Damaged valve plunger
6. Broken or faulty springs
7. Broken plunger stem

GRABBING BRAKES

1. Damaged vacuum cylinder
2. Faulty vacuum check valve
3. Vacuum hose leaky or improperly connected
4. Broken plunger stem

PEDAL GOES TO FLOOR

Generally, when this problem occurs, it is not caused by the power brake booster. In rare cases, a broken plunger stem may be at fault.

Disc Brake Performance Diagnosis

The Condition	The Possible Cause	The Corrective Action
Noise—Groan—Brake noise emanating when slowly releasing brakes (creep-groan).	(a) Not detrimental to function of disc brakes—no corrective action required. (Indicate to operator this noise may be eliminated by slightly increasing or decreasing brake pedal efforts.)	
Rattle—Brake noise or rattle emanating at low speeds on rough roads, (front wheels only).	(a) Shoe anti-rattle spring missing or not properly positioned.	(a) Install new anti-rattle spring or position properly.
	(b) Excessive clearance between shoe and caliper.	(b) Install new shoe and lining assemblies.
Scraping	(a) Mounting bolts too long.	(a) Install mounting bolts of correct length.
	(b) Loose wheel bearings.	(b) Readjust wheel bearings to correct specifications.
Front Brakes Heat Up During Driving and Fail to Release	(a) Operator riding brake pedal.	(a) Instruct owner how to drive with disc brakes.
	(b) Stop light switch improperly adjusted.	(b) Adjust stop light to allow full return of pedal.
	(c) Sticking pedal linkage.	(c) Free up sticking pedal linkage.
	(d) Frozen or seized piston.	(d) Disassemble caliper and free up piston.
	(e) Residual pressure valve in master cylinder.	(e) Remove valve.
	(f) Power brake malfunction.	(f) Replace.
Leaky Wheel Cylinder	(a) Damaged or worn caliper piston seal.	(a) Disassembly caliper and install new seat.
	(b) Scores or corrosion on surface of cylinder bore.	(b) Disassemble caliper and hone cylinder bore. Install new seal.
Grabbing or Uneven Brake Action	(a) Causes listed under "Pull."	(a) Corrections listed under "Pull."
	(b) Power brake malfunction.	(b) Replace.
Brake Pedal Can Be Depressed Without Braking Effect	(a) Air in hydraulic system or improper bleeding procedure.	(a) Bleed system.
	(b) Leak past primary cup in master cylinder.	(b) Recondition master cylinder.
	(c) Leak in system.	(c) Check for leaks and repair as required.
	(d) Rear brakes out of adjustment.	(d) Adjust rear brakes.
	(e) Bleeder scew open.	(e) Close bleeder screw and bleed entire system.
Excessive Pedal Travel	(a) Air, leak, or insufficient fluid in system or caliper.	(a) Check system for leaks and bleed.
	(b) Warped or excessively tapered shoe and lining assembly.	(b) Install new shoes and linings.
	(c) Excessive disc runout.	(c) Check disc for runout with dial indicator. Install new or refinished disc.

Disc Brake Performance Diagnosis (cont.)

The Condition	The Possible Cause	The Corrective Action
Excessive Pedal Travel	(d) Rear brake adjustment required.	(d) Check and adjust rear brakes.
	(e) Loose wheel bearing adjustment.	(e) Readjust wheel bearing to specified torque.
	(f) Damaged caliper piston seal.	(f) Install new piston seal.
	(g) Improper brake fluid (boil).	(g) Drain and install correct fluid.
	(h) Power brake malfunction.	(h) Replace.
Brake Roughness or Chatter (Pedal Pumping)	(a) Excessive thickness variation of braking disc.	(a) Check disc for thickness variation using a micrometer.
	(b) Excessive lateral runout of braking disc.	(b) Check disc for lateral runout with dial indicator. Install new or refinished disc.
	(c) Rear brake drums out-of-round.	(c) Reface rear drums and check for out-of-round.
	(d) Excessive front bearing clearance.	(d) Readjust wheel bearings to specified torque.
Excessive Pedal Effort	(a) Brake fluid, oil or grease on linings.	(a) Install new shoe linings as required.
	(b) Incorrect lining.	(b) Remove lining and install correct lining.
	(c) Frozen or seized pistons.	(c) Disassemble caliper and free up pistons.
	(d) Power brake malfunction.	(d) Replace.
Pull	(a) Brake fluid, oil or grease on linings.	(a) Install new shoe and linings.
	(b) Unmatched linings.	(b) Install correct lining.
	(c) Distorted brake shoes.	(c) Install new brake shoes.
	(d) Frozen or seized pistons.	(d) Disassemble caliper and free up pistons.
	(e) Incorrect tire pressure.	(e) Inflate tires to recommended pressures.
	(f) Front end out of alignment.	(f) Align front end and check.
	(g) Broken rear spring.	(g) Install new rear spring.
	(h) Rear brake pistons sticking.	(h) Free up rear brake pistons.
	(i) Restricted hose or line.	(i) Check hoses and lines and correct as necessary.
	(j) Caliper not in proper alignment to braking disc.	(j) Remove caliper and reinstall. Check alignment.

Drum Brake Performance Diagnosis

The Condition	The Possible Cause	The Corrective Action
Pedal Goes to Floor	(a) Fluid low in reservoir.	(a) Fill and bleed master cylinder.
	(b) Air in hydraulic brake system.	(b) Fill and bleed hydraulic brake system.
	(c) Improperly adjusted brake.	(c) Repair or replace self-adjuster as required.

Drum Brake Performance Diagnosis (cont.)

The Condition	The Possible Cause	The Corrective Action
Pedal Goes to Floor	(d) Leaking wheel cylinders.	(d) Recondition or replace wheel cylinder and replace both brake shoes.
	(e) Loose or broken brake lines.	(e) Tighten all brake fittings or replace brake line.
	(f) Leaking or worn master cylinder.	(f) Recondition or replace master cylinder and bleed hydraulic system.
	(g) Excessively worn brake lining.	(g) Reline and adjust brakes.
Spongy Brake Pedal	(a) Air in hydraulic system.	(a) Fill master cylinder and bleed hydraulic system.
	(b) Improper brake fluid (low boiling point).	(b) Drain, flush and refill with brake fluid.
	(c) Excessively worn or cracked brake drums.	(c) Replace all faulty brake drums.
	(d) Broken pedal pivot bushing.	(d) Replace nylon pivot bushing.
Brakes Pulling	(a) Contaminated lining.	(a) Replace contaminated brake lining.
	(b) Front end out of alignment.	(b) Align front end.
	(c) Incorrect brake adjustment.	(c) Adjust brakes and check fluid.
	(d) Unmatched brake lining.	(d) Match primary, secondary with same type of lining on all wheels.
	(e) Brake drums out of round.	(e) Grind or replace brake drums.
	(f) Brake shoes distorted.	(f) Replace faulty brake shoes.
	(g) Restricted brake hose or line.	(g) Replace plugged hose or brake line.
	(h) Broken rear spring.	(h) Replace broken spring.
Squealing Brakes	(a) Glazed brake lining.	(a) Cam grind or replace brake lining.
	(b) Saturated brake lining.	(b) Replace saturated lining.
	(c) Weak or broken brake shoe retaining spring.	(c) Replace retaining spring.
	(d) Broken or weak brake shoe return spring.	(d) Replace return spring.
	(e) Incorrect brake lining.	(e) Install matched brake lining.
	(f) Distorted brake shoes.	(f) Replace brake shoes.
	(g) Bent support plate.	(g) Replace support plate.
	(h) Dust in brakes or scored brake drums.	(h) Blow out brake assembly with compressed air and grind brake drums.
Chirping Brakes	(a) Out of round drum or eccentric axle flange pilot.	(a) Repair as necessary, and lubricate support plate contact areas (6 places).

Drum Brake Performance Diagnosis (cont.)

The Condition	The Possible Cause	The Corrective Action
Dragging Brakes	(a) Incorrect wheel or parking brake adjustment.	(a) Adjust brake and check fluid.
	(b) Parking brakes engaged.	(b) Release parking brakes.
	(c) Weak or broken brake shoe return spring.	(c) Replace brake shoe return spring.
	(d) Brake pedal binding.	(d) Free up and lubricate brake pedal and linkage.
	(e) Master cylinder cup sticking.	(e) Recondition master cylinder.
	(f) Obstructed master cylinder relief port.	(f) Use compressed air and blow out relief port.
	(g) Saturated brake lining.	(g) Replace brake lining.
	(h) Bent or out of round brake drum.	(h) Grind or replace faulty brake drum.
Hard Pedal	(a) Brake booster inoperative.	(a) Replace brake booster.
	(b) Incorrect brake lining.	(b) Install matched brake lining.
	(c) Restricted brake line or hose.	(c) Clean out or replace brake line or hose.
	(d) Frozen brake pedal linkage.	(d) Free up and lubricate brake linkage.
Wheel Locks	(a) Contaminated brake lining.	(a) Reline both front or rear of all four brakes.
	(b) Loose or torn brake lining.	(b) Replace brake lining.
	(c) Wheel cylinder cups sticking.	(c) Recondition or replace wheel cylinder.
	(d) Incorrect wheel bearing adjustment.	(d) Clean, pack and adjust wheel bearings.
Brakes Fade (High Speed)	(a) Incorrect lining.	(a) Replace lining.
	(b) Overheated brake drums.	(b) Inspect for dragging brakes.
	(c) Incorrect brake fluid (low boiling temperature).	(c) Drain, flush, refill and bleed hydraulic brake system.
	(d) Saturated brake lining.	(d) Reline both front or rear or all four brakes.
Pedal Pulsates	(a) Bent or out of round brake drum.	(a) Grind or replace brake drums.
Brake Chatter and Shoe Knock	(a) Out of round brake drum.	(a) Grind or replace brake drums.
	(b) Loose support plate.	(b) Tighten support plate bolts to proper specifications.
	(c) Bent support plate.	(c) Replace support plate.
	(d) Distorted brake shoes.	(d) Replace brake shoes.
	(e) Machine grooves in contact face of brake drum. (Shoe Knock).	(e) Grind or replace brake drum.
	(f) Contaminated brake lining.	(f) Replace either front or rear or all four linings.

Drum Brake Performance Diagnosis (cont.)

The Condition	The Possible Cause	The Corrective Action
Brakes Do Not Self Adjust	(a) Adjuster screw frozen in thread.	(a) Clean and free-up all thread areas.
	(b) Adjuster screw corroded at thrust washer.	(b) Clean threads and replace thrust washer if necessary.
	(c) Adjuster lever does not engage star wheel.	(c) Repair, free up or replace adjusters as required.
	(d) Adjuster installed on wrong wheel.	(d) Install correct adjuster parts.

Parking Brake Adjustment

Parking brakes generally do not require adjustment if the automatic adjusters are working properly. If adjustment is required, proceed as follows:

1. Put the vehicle on a lift so neither rear wheel is touching the ground.

2. Engage the parking brake about halfway.

3. Loosen the locknut on the equalizer yoke, located under the ear, and then turn the adjusting nut just until drag can be felt on both rear wheels.

4. Release the brake and check for free rotation of the rear wheels.

On systems where a floor-mounted hand-lever is used, the adjustment is usually contained under the rubber boot which covers the base of the lever. Tighten each of the adjusting nuts on these systems until an equal, slight torque is required to turn each rear drum.

Brake Bleeding

There are two ways to bleed brakes; pressure bleeding and manual bleeding. Pressure bleeding requires the use of an air tank and is not generally used except in shops. Manual bleeding requires an assistant, but no exotic or expensive tools. The procedure given here is for manual bleeding.

1. Make sure the master cylinder is filled with brake fluid. Keep the master cylinder filled during this entire procedure. Do not use used brake fluid to refill the master cylinder.

2. Jack up the car to allow access to the bleeder valves. On drum brake systems, they are located on the top of the backing plate. On disc brakes, they are located on the caliper. Be careful when loosening these bleeders, since it's quite easy to break them off or round off the flats. Penetrating oil is advised, along with a lot of patience if they are stubborn.

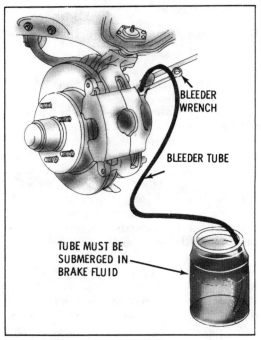

BLEEDER WRENCH

BLEEDER TUBE

TUBE MUST BE SUBMERGED IN BRAKE FLUID

Brake bleeding

3. When bleeding an entire system, always start at the right rear wheel since it is farthest from the master cylinder. The second brake to be done is obviously the left rear, then the right front, and finally the left front.

4. Attach a tube to the bleeder valve and submerge the other end in a jar that has been partially filled with *clean* brake fluid. This is done to check for air bubbles and to make sure no air gets back in the system.

5. Have someone pump the brake pedal slowly several times and then open the bleeder valve. Repeat this until the fluid coming out has no air bubbles.

6. Tighten the valve while steady pressure is being applied to the pedal.

7. Repeat this procedure for the other wheels.

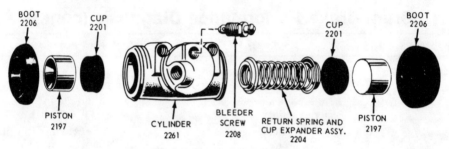

Exploded view of a wheel cylinder

8. Throw away the fluid in the jar because it is full of microscopic air bubbles, then refill the master cylinder.

Drum Brake Adjustment

1. Raise the car and support it with safety stands.

2. Remove the rubber plug from the adjusting slot on the backing plate.

3. Insert a brake adjusting spoon into the slot and engage the lowest possible tooth on the starwheel. Move the end of the brake spoon downward to move the starwheel upward and expand the adjusting screw. Repeat this operation until the brakes lock the wheel.

4. Insert a small screwdriver or piece of firm wire (coat-hanger wire) into the adjusting slot and push the automatic adjuster lever out and free of the starwheel on the adjusting screw.

5. Holding the adjusting lever out of the way, engage the topmost tooth possible on the starwheel with a brake adjusting spoon. Move the end of the adjusting spoon upward to move the adjusting screw starwheel downward and contract the adjusting screw. Back off the adjusting screw starwheel until the wheel spins freely with a minimum of drag.

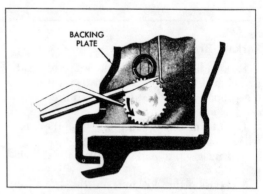

Brake adjustment procedure

Keep track of the number of turns the starwheel is backed off.

6. Repeat this operation for the other side. When backing off the brakes on the other side, the adjusting lever must be backed off the same number of turns to prevent side-to-side brake pull.

7. Repeat this operation on the other set of brakes (front or rear).

8. When all 4 brakes are adjusted, make several stops, while backing the car, to equalize all of the wheels.

9. Road-test the car.

Appendix

General Conversion Table

Multiply by	To convert	To	
2.54	Inches	Centimeters	.3937
30.48	Feet	Centimeters	.0328
.914	Yards	Meters	1.094
1.609	Miles	Kilometers	.621
.645	Square inches	Square cm.	.155
.836	Square yards	Square meters	1.196
16.39	Cubic inches	Cubic cm.	.061
28.3	Cubic feet	Liters	.0353
.4536	Pounds	Kilograms	2.2045
4.226	Gallons	Liters	.264
.068	Lbs./sq. in. (psi)	Atmospheres	14.7
.138	Foot pounds	Kg. m.	7.23
1.014	H.P. (DIN)	H.P. (SAE)	.9861
———	To obtain	From	Multiply by

Note: 1 cm. equals 10 mm.; 1 mm. equals .0394".

Conversion—Common Fractions to Decimals and Millimeters

INCHES			INCHES			INCHES		
Common Fractions	Decimal Fractions	Millimeters (approx.)	Common Fractions	Decimal Fractions	Millimeters (approx.)	Common Fractions	Decimal Fractions	Millimeters (approx.)
1/128	.008	0.20	11/32	.344	8.73	43/64	.672	17.07
1/64	.016	0.40	23/64	.359	9.13	11/16	.688	17.46
1/32	.031	0.79	3/8	.375	9.53	45/64	.703	17.86
3/64	.047	1.19	25/64	.391	9.92	23/32	.719	18.26
1/16	.063	1.59	13/32	.406	10.32	47/64	.734	18.65
5/64	.078	1.98	27/64	.422	10.72	3/4	.750	19.05
3/32	.094	2.38	7/16	.438	11.11	49/64	.766	19.45
7/64	.109	2.78	29/64	.453	11.51	25/32	.781	19.84
1/8	.125	3.18	15/32	.469	11.91	51/64	.797	20.24
9/64	.141	3.57	31/64	.484	12.30	13/16	.813	20.64
5/32	.156	3.97	1/2	.500	12.70	53/64	.828	21.03
11/64	.172	4.37	33/64	.516	13.10	27/32	.844	21.43
3/16	.188	4.76	17/32	.531	13.49	55/64	.859	21.83
13/64	.203	5.16	35/64	.547	13.89	7/8	.875	22.23
7/32	.219	5.56	9/16	.563	14.29	57/64	.891	22.62
15/64	.234	5.95	37/64	.578	14.68	29/32	.906	23.02
1/4	.250	6.35	19/32	.594	15.08	59/64	.922	23.42
17/64	.266	6.75	39/64	.609	15.48	15/16	.938	23.81
9/32	.281	7.14	5/8	.625	15.88	61/64	.953	24.21
19/64	.297	7.54	41/64	.641	16.27	31/32	.969	24.61
5/16	.313	7.94	21/32	.656	16.67	63/64	.984	25.00
21/64	.328	8.33						

Conversion—Millimeters to Decimal Inches

mm	inches	mm	inches	mm	inches	mm	inches	mm	inches
1	.039 370	31	1.220 470	61	2.401 570	91	3.582 670	210	8.267 700
2	.078 740	32	1.259 840	62	2.440 940	92	3.622 040	220	8.661 400
3	.118 110	33	1.299 210	63	2.480 310	93	3.661 410	230	9.055 100
4	.157 480	34	1.338 580	64	2.519 680	94	3.700 780	240	9.448 800
5	.196 850	35	1.377 949	65	2.559 050	95	3.740 150	250	9.842 500
6	.236 220	36	1.417 319	66	2.598 420	96	3.779 520	260	10.236 200
7	.275 590	37	1.456 689	67	2.637 790	97	3.818 890	270	10.629 900
8	.314 960	38	1.496 050	68	2.677 160	98	3.858 260	280	11.032 600
9	.354 330	39	1.535 430	69	2.716 530	99	3.897 630	290	11.417 300
10	.393 700	40	1.574 800	70	2.755 900	100	3.937 000	300	11.811 000
11	.433 070	41	1.614 170	71	2.795 270	105	4.133 848	310	12.204 700
12	.472 440	42	1.653 540	72	2.834 640	110	4.330 700	320	12.598 400
13	.511 810	43	1.692 910	73	2.874 010	115	4.527 550	330	12.992 100
14	.551 180	44	1.732 280	74	2.913 380	120	4.724 400	340	13.385 800
15	.590 550	45	1.771 650	75	2.952 750	125	4.921 250	350	13.779 500
16	.629 920	46	1.811 020	76	2.992 120	130	5.118 100	360	14.173 200
17	.669 290	47	1.850 390	77	3.031 490	135	5.314 950	370	14.566 900
18	.708 660	48	1.889 760	78	3.070 860	140	5.511 800	380	14.960 600
19	.748 030	49	1.929 130	79	3.110 230	145	5.708 650	390	15.354 300
20	.787 400	50	1.968 500	80	3.149 600	150	5.905 500	400	15.748 000
21	.826 770	51	2.007 870	81	3.188 970	155	6.102 350	500	19.685 000
22	.866 140	52	2.047 240	82	3.228 340	160	6.299 200	600	23.622 000
23	.905 510	53	2.086 610	83	3.267 710	165	6.496 050	700	27.559 000
24	.944 880	54	2.125 980	84	3.307 080	170	6.692 900	800	31.496 000
25	.984 250	55	2.165 350	85	3.346 450	175	6.889 750	900	35.433 000
26	1.023 620	56	2.204 720	86	3.385 820	180	7.086 600	1000	39.370 000
27	1.062 990	57	2.244 090	87	3.425 190	185	7.283 450	2000	78.740 000
28	1.102 360	58	2.283 460	88	3.464 560	190	7.480 300	3000	118.110 000
29	1.141 730	59	2.322 830	89	3.503 903	195	7.677 150	4000	157.480 000
30	1.181 100	60	2.362 200	90	3.543 300	200	7.874 000	5000	196.850 000

To change decimal millimeters to decimal inches, position the decimal point where desired on either side of the millimeter measurement shown and reset the inches decimal by the same number of digits in the same direction. For example, to convert 0.001 mm into decimal inches, reset the decimal behind the 1 mm (shown on the chart) to 0.001; change the decimal inch equivalent (0.039″ shown) to 0.000039″.

Tap Drill Sizes

National Fine or S.A.E.		
Screw & Tap Size	Threads Per Inch	Use Drill Number
No. 5	44	37
No. 6	40	33
No. 8	36	29
No. 10	32	21
No. 12	28	15
1/4	28	3
5/16	24	1
3/8	24	Q
7/16	20	W
1/2	20	29/64
9/16	18	33/64
5/8	18	37/64
3/4	16	11/16
7/8	14	13/16
1 1/8	12	1 3/64
1 1/4	12	1 11/64
1 1/2	12	1 27/64

National Coarse or U.S.S.		
Screw & Tap Size	Threads Per Inch	Use Drill Number
No. 5	40	39
No. 6	32	36
No. 8	32	29
No. 10	24	25
No. 12	24	17
1/4	20	8
5/16	18	F
3/8	16	5/16
7/16	14	U
1/2	13	27/64
9/16	12	31/64
5/8	11	17/32
3/4	10	21/32
7/8	9	49/64
1	8	7/8
1 1/8	7	63/64
1 1/4	7	1 7/64
1 1/2	6	1 11/32

Decimal Equivalent Size of the Number Drills

Drill No.	Decimal Equivalent	Drill No.	Decimal Equivalent	Drill No.	Decimal Equivalent
80	.0135	53	.0595	26	.1470
79	.0145	52	.0635	25	.1495
78	.0160	51	.0670	24	.1520
77	.0180	50	.0700	23	.1540
76	.0200	49	.0730	22	.1570
75	.0210	48	.0760	21	.1590
74	.0225	47	.0785	20	.1610
73	.0240	46	.0810	19	.1660
72	.0250	45	.0820	18	.1695
71	.0260	44	.0860	17	.1730
70	.0280	43	.0890	16	.1770
69	.0292	42	.0935	15	.1800
68	.0310	41	.0960	14	.1820
67	.0320	40	.0980	13	.1850
66	.0330	39	.0995	12	.1890
65	.0350	38	.1015	11	.1910
64	.0360	37	.1040	10	.1935
63	.0370	36	.1065	9	.1960
62	.0380	35	.1100	8	.1990
61	.0390	34	.1110	7	.2010
60	.0400	33	.1130	6	.2040
59	.0410	32	.1160	5	.2055
58	.0420	31	.1200	4	.2090
57	.0430	30	.1285	3	.2130
56	.0465	29	.1360	2	.2210
55	.0520	28	.1405	1	.2280
54	.0550	27	.1440		

Decimal Equivalent Size of the Letter Drills

Letter Drill	Decimal Equivalent	Letter Drill	Decimal Equivalent	Letter Drill	Decimal Equivalent
A	.234	J	.277	S	.348
B	.238	K	.281	T	.358
C	.242	L	.290	U	.368
D	.246	M	.295	V	.377
E	.250	N	.302	W	.386
F	.257	O	.316	X	.397
G	.261	P	.323	Y	.404
H	.266	Q	.332	Z	.413
I	.272	R	.339		

ANTI-FREEZE CHART

Temperatures Shown in Degrees Fahrenheit
+32 is Freezing

Cooling System Capacity Quarts	Quarts of ETHYLENE GLYCOL Needed for Protection to Temperatures Shown Below													
	1	2	3	4	5	6	7	8	9	10	11	12	13	14
10	+24°	+16°	+ 4°	−12°	−34°	−62°								
11	+25	+18	+ 8	− 6	−23	−47								
12	+26	+19	+10	0	−15	−34	−57°							
13	+27	+21	+13	+ 3	− 9	−25	−45							
14			+15	+ 6	− 5	−18	−34							
15			+16	+ 8	0	−12	−26							
16			+17	+10	+ 2	− 8	−19	−34	−52°					
17			+18	+12	+ 5	− 4	−14	−27	−42					
18			+19	+14	+ 7	0	−10	−21	−34	−50°				
19			+20	+15	+ 9	+ 2	− 7	−16	−28	−42				
20				+16	+10	+ 4	− 3	−12	−22	−34	−48°			
21				+17	+12	+ 6	0	− 9	−17	−28	−41			
22				+18	+13	+ 8	+ 2	− 6	−14	−23	−34	−47°		
23				+19	+14	+ 9	+ 4	− 3	−10	−19	−29	−40		
24				+19	+15	+10	+ 5	0	− 8	−15	−23	−34	−46°	
25				+20	+16	+12	+ 7	+ 1	− 5	−12	−20	−29	−40	−50°
26					+17	+13	+ 8	+ 3	− 3	− 9	−16	−25	−34	−44
27					+18	+14	+ 9	+ 5	− 1	− 7	−13	−21	−29	−39
28					+18	+15	+10	+ 6	+ 1	− 5	−11	−18	−25	−34
29					+19	+16	+12	+ 7	+ 2	− 3	− 8	−15	−22	−29
30					+20	+17	+13	+ 8	+ 4	− 1	− 6	−12	−18	−25

For capacities over 30 quarts divide true capacity by 3. Find quarts Anti-Freeze for the ⅓ and multiply by 3 for quarts to add.

For capacities under 10 quarts multiply true capacity by 3. Find quarts Anti-Freeze for the tripled volume and divide by 3 for quarts to add.

To Increase the Freezing Protection of Anti-Freeze Solutions Already Installed

Cooling System Capacity Quarts	Number of Quarts of ETHYLENE GLYCOL Anti-Freeze Required to Increase Protection													
	From +20°F. to					From +10°F. to					From 0°F. to			
	0°	−10°	−20°	−30°	−40°	0°	−10°	−20°	−30°	−40°	−10°	−20°	−30°	−40°
10	1¾	2¼	3	3½	3¾	¾	1½	2¼	2¾	3¼	¾	1½	2	2½
12	2	2¾	3½	4	4½	1	1¾	2½	3¼	3¾	1	1¾	2½	3¼
14	2¼	3¼	4	4¾	5½	1¼	2	3	3¾	4½	1	2	3	3½
16	2½	3½	4½	5¼	6	1¼	2½	3½	4¼	5¼	1¼	2¼	3¼	4
18	3	4	5	6	7	1½	2¾	4	5	5¾	1½	2½	3¾	4¾
20	3¼	4½	5¾	6¾	7½	1¾	3	4¼	5½	6½	1½	2¾	4¼	5¼
22	3½	5	6¼	7¼	8¼	1¾	3¼	4¾	6	7¼	1¾	3¼	4½	5½
24	4	5½	7	8	9	2	3½	5	6½	7½	1¾	3½	5	6
26	4¼	6	7½	8¾	10	2	4	5½	7	8¼	2	3¾	5½	6¾
28	4½	6¼	8	9½	10½	2¼	4¼	6	7½	9	2	4	5¾	7¼
30	5	6¾	8½	10	11½	2½	4½	6½	8	9½	2¼	4¼	6¼	7¾

Test radiator solution with proper hydrometer. Determine from the table the number of quarts of solution to be drawn off from a full cooling system and replace with undiluted anti-freeze, to give the desired increased protection. For example, to increase protection of a 22-quart cooling system containing Ethylene Glycol (permanent type) anti-freeze, from +20°F. to −20°F. will require the replacement of 6¼ quarts of solution with undiluted anti-freeze.

790496

790496